Creating and Managing a Sustainable Sporting Future

Creating and Managing a Sustainable Sporting Future contributes to a critical understanding of the challenges key stakeholders across the globe encounter as they seek to manage periods of transition brought about by policy change relating to the provision of sport and physical activity.

The book uncovers the global challenges in terms of managing the re-orientation of stakeholder activities and organisational strategies, in response to the aspirations for a wider range of outcomes through sport-based interventions and establishment of partnerships with non-sport sectors. It illuminates the increasingly erratic trajectory of sport development service providers, as the environment within which sport organisations operate changes – through for example, climate change, demographic shifts, changing features of local economies and alterations to the structures of local government and governance – and the responses of sport organisations to these new realities differ greatly depending on location, institutional structures and leadership. The chapters highlight the changing social, economic, environmental and policy contexts within which sports organisations operate, and explain the subsequent need for new approaches to partnership working, physical activity re-scoping and integrated education programming.

Showing that the international mandate of creating active lifestyles and subsequent re-orientation of stakeholders towards physical activity cannot only contribute to redefining sport but also in identifying novel ways for building a sustainable sports sector, *Creating and Managing a Sustainable Sporting Future* is ideal for sports scholars, and particularly those working on Sport Policy and Sustainable Sport Development.

This book was originally published as a special issue of *Managing Sport and Leisure*.

Vassilios Ziakas studies cross-sectoral policy issues among sport, tourism, leisure and events at the regional, national and international levels with an emphasis on strategic planning, community development and sustainability aimed at enabling optimal programme design, delivery and leveraging. He is the author of *Event Portfolio Planning and Management* (2014) and co-edited the *Routledge Handbook of Popular Culture and Tourism* (2018).

Aaron Beacom has researched and published in the areas of sport in international development and disability/Paralympic sporting cultures. His editing experience includes co-editing *Sport and International Development* (with Roger Levermore, 2009 and 2012) and the *Palgrave Handbook of Paralympic Studies* (with Ian Brittain, 2017).

Creating and Managing a Sustainable Sporting Future

Issues, Pathways and Opportunities

Edited by
Vassilios Ziakas and Aaron Beacom

LONDON AND NEW YORK

First published 2020
by Routledge
2 Park Square, Milton Park, Abingdon, Oxon, OX14 4RN

and by Routledge
52 Vanderbilt Avenue, New York, NY 10017

Routledge is an imprint of the Taylor & Francis Group, an informa business

First issued in paperback 2021

Editorial, Chapters 1–4, 6–10 © 2020 Taylor & Francis
Chapter 5 © 2018 David Ekholm and Magnus Dahlstedt. Originally published as Open Access.

With the exception of Chapter 5, no part of this book may be reprinted or reproduced or utilised in any form or by any electronic, mechanical, or other means, now known or hereafter invented, including photocopying and recording, or in any information storage or retrieval system, without permission in writing from the publishers. For details on the rights for Chapter 5, please see the chapter's Open Access footnote.

Trademark notice: Product or corporate names may be trademarks or registered trademarks, and are used only for identification and explanation without intent to infringe.

British Library Cataloguing-in-Publication Data
A catalogue record for this book is available from the British Library

ISBN13: 978-0-367-36926-2 (hbk)
ISBN13: 978-1-03-208959-1 (pbk)

Typeset in Myriad Pro
by codeMantra

Publisher's Note
The publisher accepts responsibility for any inconsistencies that may have arisen during the conversion of this book from journal articles to book chapters, namely the inclusion of journal terminology.

Disclaimer
Every effort has been made to contact copyright holders for their permission to reprint material in this book. The publishers would be grateful to hear from any copyright holder who is not here acknowledged and will undertake to rectify any errors or omissions in future editions of this book.

Contents

Citation Information vii
Notes on Contributors ix

Editorial: Re-thinking sport and physical activity: management responses to policy change 1
Vassilios Ziakas and Aaron Beacom

1 Whose job is it anyway? Public–private partnerships in youth sport 7
  Eric Legg, Gareth J. Jones and Misha White

2 Watching the pennies and the people – how volunteer-led sport facilities have transformed services for local communities 23
  Lindsay Findlay-King, Geoff Nichols, Deborah Forbes and Gordon Macfadyen

3 Playing the climate game: climate change impacts, resilience and adaptation in the climate-dependent sport sector 39
  Greg William Dingle and Bob Stewart

4 Understanding the growth in outdoor recreation participation: an opportunity for sport development in the United Kingdom 61
  C. Mackintosh, G. Griggs and R. Tate

5 Rationalities of goodwill: on the promotion of philanthropy through sports-based interventions in Sweden 82
  David Ekholm and Magnus Dahlstedt

6 Developing workreadiness; a Glasgow housing association sports-based intervention 96
  Catherine Mary Walker

7 Sport development in challenging times: leverage of sport events for legacy in disadvantaged communities 115
  Barbara Bell and John Daniels

8 Inspiring a generation: an examination of stakeholder relations in the context of London 2012 Olympics and Paralympics educational programmes 137
Verity Postlethwaite, Geoffery Z. Kohe and Gyozo Molnar

9 Understanding the management challenges associated with the implementation of the physically active teaching and learning (PATL) pedagogy: a case study of three Isle of Wight primary schools 154
Oscar Mwaanga, Henry Dorling, Samantha Prince and Matthew Fleet

10 Environmental sustainability and sport management education: bridging the gaps 168
Jeffrey Graham, Sylvia Trendafilova and Vassilios Ziakas

Index 181

Citation Information

The chapters in this book were originally published in *Managing Sport and Leisure*, volume 23, issues 4–6 (November 2018). When citing this material, please use the original page numbering for each article, as follows:

Editorial
Re-thinking sport and physical activity: management responses to policy change
Vassilios Ziakas and Aaron Beacom
Managing Sport and Leisure, volume 23, issues 4–6 (November 2018) pp. 255–260

Chapter 1
Whose job is it anyway? Public–private partnerships in youth sport
Eric Legg, Gareth J. Jones and Misha White
Managing Sport and Leisure, volume 23, issues 4–6 (November 2018) pp. 261–276

Chapter 2
Watching the pennies and the people – how volunteer-led sport facilities have transformed services for local communities
Lindsay Findlay-King, Geoff Nichols, Deborah Forbes and Gordon Macfadyen
Managing Sport and Leisure, volume 23, issues 4–6 (November 2018) pp. 277–292

Chapter 3
Playing the climate game: climate change impacts, resilience and adaptation in the climate-dependent sport sector
Greg William Dingle and Bob Stewart
Managing Sport and Leisure, volume 23, issues 4–6 (November 2018) pp. 293–314

Chapter 4
Understanding the growth in outdoor recreation participation: an opportunity for sport development in the United Kingdom
C. Mackintosh, G. Griggs and R. Tate
Managing Sport and Leisure, volume 23, issues 4–6 (November 2018) pp. 315–335

Chapter 5
Rationalities of goodwill: on the promotion of philanthropy through sports-based interventions in Sweden
David Ekholm and Magnus Dahlstedt
Managing Sport and Leisure, volume 23, issues 4–6 (November 2018) pp. 336–349

Chapter 6
Developing workreadiness; a Glasgow housing association sports-based intervention
Catherine Mary Walker
Managing Sport and Leisure, volume 23, issues 4–6 (November 2018) pp. 350–368

Chapter 7
Sport development in challenging times: leverage of sport events for legacy in disadvantaged communities
Barbara Bell and John Daniels
Managing Sport and Leisure, volume 23, issues 4–6 (November 2018) pp. 369–390

Chapter 8
Inspiring a generation: an examination of stakeholder relations in the context of London 2012 Olympics and Paralympics educational programmes
Verity Postlethwaite, Geoffery Z. Kohe and Gyozo Molnar
Managing Sport and Leisure, volume 23, issues 4–6 (November 2018) pp. 391–407

Chapter 9
Understanding the management challenges associated with the implementation of the physically active teaching and learning (PATL) pedagogy: a case study of three Isle of Wight primary schools
Oscar Mwaanga, Henry Dorling, Samantha Prince and Matthew Fleet
Managing Sport and Leisure, volume 23, issues 4–6 (November 2018) pp. 408–421

Chapter 10
Environmental sustainability and sport management education: bridging the gaps
Jeffrey Graham, Sylvia Trendafilova and Vassilios Ziakas
Managing Sport and Leisure, volume 23, issues 4–6 (November 2018) pp. 422–433

For any permission-related enquiries please visit:
http://www.tandfonline.com/page/help/permissions

Notes on Contributors

Aaron Beacom is a Senior Lecturer in the School of Sport, Health and Wellbeing at Plymouth Marjon University, UK.

Barbara Bell is a Senior Lecturer in Sport Development in the Department of Exercise and Sport Sciences at Manchester Metropolitan University, UK.

Magnus Dahlstedt is a Professor in the Department of Social and Welfare Studies (ISV) at Linköping University, Sweden.

John Daniels is the Department Lead for Internationalisation: Manchester City Football Club Community Football Coaching in the Department of Exercise and Sport Sciences at Manchester Metropolitan University, UK.

Greg William Dingle is a Lecturer in Sport Management in the Department of Management Sport and Tourism in the College of Arts, Social Sciences and Commerce at La Trobe University, Melbourne, Australia.

Henry Dorling is a Senior Lecturer of Sport, Education & Development in the School of Sport, Health and Social Science at Southampton Solent University, UK.

David Ekholm is a Postdoctoral Researcher in the Department for Studies of Social Change and Culture (ISAK) at Linköping University, Sweden.

Lindsay Findlay-King is a Principal Lecturer/Teaching Fellow in the Department of Sport, Exercise and Rehabilitation at Northumbria University, Newcastle upon Tyne, UK.

Matthew Fleet is a Senior Lecturer in Sport, Education & Development in the School of Sport, Health and Social Science at Southampton Solent University, UK.

Deborah Forbes is a Lecturer in Marketing at Newcastle University Business School at Newcastle University, UK.

Jeffrey Graham is an Assistant Professor in Sport Management in the Department of Kinesiology, Recreation, and Sport Management at the University of Tennessee, Knoxville, USA.

G. Griggs is the Head of Academics at the University College of Football Burnley (UCFB), UK.

Gareth J. Jones is an Assistant Professor in the School of Sport, Tourism and Hospitality Management at Temple University, Philadelphia, USA.

NOTES ON CONTRIBUTORS

Geoffery Z. Kohe is a Lecturer in the School of Sport and Exercise Sciences at the University of Kent, UK.

Eric Legg is an Assistant Professor in the School of Community Resources & Development at Arizona State University, USA.

Gordon Macfadyen is a Senior Lecturer in the Department of Sport, Exercise and Rehabilitation at Northumbria University, Newcastle upon Tyne, UK.

C. Mackintosh is a Senior Lecturer at Manchester Metropolitan University Business School, UK.

Gyozo Molnar is a Principal Lecturer in Sport Studies in the School of Sport and Exercise Science at the University of Worcester, UK.

Oscar Mwaanga is an Associate Professor of Sport, Education & Development in the School of Sport, Health and Social Science at Southampton Solent University, UK.

Geoff Nichols is a Senior Lecturer in Sport and Leisure Management at Sheffield University Management School at the University of Sheffield, UK.

Verity Postlethwaite is a PhD Research Student in the School of Sport and Exercise Science at the University of Worcester, UK.

Samantha Prince is an Impact Analyst at Crisis, UK. She was previously a Lecturer in Sport Management in the Faculty of Management at Bournemouth University, UK.

Bob Stewart is an Associate Professor in Leisure Studies in the College of Sport & Exercise Science at Victoria University, Melbourne, Australia.

R. Tate is affiliated with the Sport and Recreation Alliance (SRA), UK.

Sylvia Trendafilova is an Associate Professor in Sport Management in the Department of Kinesiology, Recreation, and Sport Management at the University of Tennessee, Knoxville, USA.

Catherine Mary Walker is a Senior Lecturer in Sport Development in the Faculty of Education, Health and Community at Liverpool John Moores University, UK.

Misha White is a Foundation Associate at the Bob and Renee Parsons Foundation, USA. She was affiliated with the School of Community Resources & Development at Arizona State University, USA.

Vassilios Ziakas is an Associate Professor in the School of Sport, Health and Wellbeing at Plymouth Marjon University, UK.

EDITORIAL

Re-thinking sport and physical activity: management responses to policy change

Vassilios Ziakas and Aaron Beacom

Purpose and scope

This special issue contributes to a critical understanding of the challenges key stakeholders across the globe encounter as they seek to manage periods of transition brought about by public policy change relating to the provision of sport and physical activity. Such challenges have, for example, characterised work across the UK where policy change and subsequent strategic responses have been predicated on an alternative vision for the development of an active nation through engagement with broader physical culture. This engagement typically requires established stakeholders across sports sector to operate as part of a new configuration of actors where partnerships are encouraged with a range of public, private and third sector organisations. In the UK the government's sport strategy *A sporting future; A new strategy for an active nation* (2015), which has promoted concerns for wellbeing, is reflected variously in physical activity, community development, public health, education and environmental agendas.

Seeking a wider range of outcomes through sport-based interventions and establishment of partnerships with non-sport sectors is characteristic of policy aspirations internationally (e.g. Grix & Carmichael, 2012; Kumar et al., 2018; Lyras & Welty-Peachey, 2011; Mansfield, 2016; Skinner, Zakus, & Cowell, 2008; Trendafilova, Ziakas, & Sparvero, 2017; Weed, 2016; Weed et al., 2015; Ziakas, 2015). This special issue, triggered by the thematic problematics emerging from the UK Sport Development Network (UKSDN) 2017 conference, seeks to uncover the global challenges in terms of managing the re-orientation of stakeholder activities and organisational strategies in response to re-alignments of sport policy. The resulting collection of papers in the special issue constitutes a balanced synthesis of contributions from those present at the conference and from academics and practitioners who form part of the wider global sport and leisure management research community.

Issues, challenges and trajectories

Sport and physical activity have become increasingly prominent in contemporary political debate and policy development (Bloyce & Smith, 2009; Houlihan & Lindsey, 2013; King, 2014). Most commentators suggest that in the UK a ratcheting up of such engagement took place as part of the New Labour administrations (1997–2010) attempts to address a range of social, educational, health and community challenges through sport, whilst the interventionist tenets were carried through into the Coalition government of David Cameron and beyond. At the same time, the principles of sport-based interventions associated with individual and community development initiatives, are reflected internationally, for example, through the relatively recent Sport-for-Development and Peace movement; whose principles are explored and critiqued by a series of commentators (Coalter, 2007; Darnell, 2012; Levermore & Beacom, 2012). Perhaps the greatest challenge in this process is the evaluation of the efficacy of sport and physical activity-based interventions in delivering anticipated outcomes. This has led to a growing body of literature which addresses emerging evaluative frameworks and questions the capacity of sport-for-development to achieve many of the claims made for it (Coalter, 2013; Schulenkorf & Adair, 2014). The potential for such narratives to penetrate the policy domain, given the outcomes-based nature of policy making is worthy of consideration when attempting to map the future trajectory of sport and related policy areas.

The example of the UK Government's most recent public sport policy document (*Sporting Future*) is illustrative of signaling a fundamental shift in the approach to engaging more physically active lifestyles. It envisaged such engagement as predicated on forging partnerships outside the traditional sporting community as a means of promoting behavioural change amongst those alienated by the mainstream sporting culture. As in any policy shift, the management of funding streams has become a key tool in the pursuit of these new priorities. In response to this shift toward physical activity broadly defined, the role of local coordinators and providers has become pivotal for sport and physical activity provision and delivery. To respond to the changing political environment, local sport organisations must re-imagine their mission and recalibrate their objectives. This special issue is concerned in part, with a better understanding that ongoing process. From this perspective, we can examine the responses of sport organisations to the waxing and waning influence of key strategic partners and the emerging dichotomy between "sporting" and "physical" cultures. This line of inquiry can suggest approaches to the management of these tensions and pinpoint subsequent research priorities required to better understand the emerging physical activity landscape worldwide.

Strategies for increasing sport participation exemplify the conventional dichotomy between sport narrowly defined as organised/structured, and physical activity broadly defined as unstructured/recreational encompassing different forms of physical expression. The divide is clear within an institutional landscape, which promotes a disconnect between the delivery of sport and physical activity and subsequently constrains the development of integrated approaches. The fragmentation of organisational actors along with the constant change of local sport and physical activity priorities, restrain the development of stable collaborations between agencies involved in sport and physical activity (Lindsey, 2009). In the case of the UK, the activities of multiple stakeholders operating locally against the backdrop of a rapidly changing policy and funding environment, generates additional complexity with attendant management issues. For example, the management of sport services by Local Authorities faces challenges around accountability, equity, service quality and sustainability (King, 2014). At the same time, the role of regional sport coordinators and providers is construed in a number of contrasting ways by partner agencies, creating the potential for misunderstanding over the shifting priorities for sports development (Mackintosh, 2011). This creates concerns about the effectiveness of the Government's physical activity and sport participation strategy at the local level (Grix & Phillpots, 2011); concerns that are brought into sharp focus at a time of rapid change and thus challenge the sustainability of sport and physical activity provision strategies. At the same time, from a global perspective, the economic downturn and the imposition of austerity measures in different countries limit available funding for sport organisations (Giannoulakis, Papadimitriou, Alexandris, & Brgoch, 2017; Parnell, May, Widdop, Cope, & Bailey, 2018).

The reduction in funding and the imperative to enhance capacity to secure funds from alternative sources has created increasing pressures on non-profit sport development organisations already experiencing a number of operational and strategic challenges (Berry & Manoli, 2018). As a result, these organisations have to institute re-structuring towards a more entrepreneurial model in order to align with the new realities and serve their sport-for-development, educational, wellbeing, public health, economic or environmental purpose. This raises questions about the position of non-profit sport development organisations within the sector and the extent of their operational reach. It is at such times of transition that the more unpredictable future policy priorities become, that the more transient policy networks appear as individual stakeholders responding to rapid policy changes through strategic re-positioning. At the same time, the environment within which sport organisations operate is itself changing – through, for example, climate change, demographic shifts, changing features of local economies and alterations to the structures of local government and governance. The responses of sport organisations to these new realities will differ greatly depending on location, institutional structures and leadership. There is a need therefore to illuminate the increasingly erratic trajectory of sport development service providers.

Overview of contributions

The special issue contributions highlight the changing social, economic, environmental and policy contexts within which sports organisations operate and seek to understand the need for new approaches to partnership working, physical activity re-scoping and integrated education programming in response to these changes. The first article by Legg, Jones and White examines Public–Private Partnerships (PPPs) in United States Youth Sport. They argue that as youth sport programmes are delivered by public recreation agencies in the United States, the current political environment creates increased pressure to either increase fees or "contract out" to private providers to compensate for budget reductions. This study contributes to understanding PPPs as an essential driver to the sustainability of youth sport by analysing the perceptions of PPPs that involve public recreation agencies and private youth sport providers. In a similar vein, the need to attain economic sustainability for the management of public sport facilities is raised in the second article by Findlay-King, Nichols, Forbes and Macfadyen who examine how volunteer-led sport facilities have transformed services for local communities in England. The paper explains how the transfer of public sport facilities to management led by volunteer groups (for example in the form of local Trusts) has increased the responsiveness of services to local needs; whilst at the same time reducing running costs. This also promotes volunteer effort by changing the public perception of the facility to an asset created by the community, rather than just as a public service consumed by it.

The third article by Dingle and Stewart expands the focus on the relationship between sport and the environment by investigating the implications of climate change for major sport stadia in Australia and their subsequent organisational responses. The study demonstrates that the primacy of commercial and operational imperatives determine organisational responses ahead of government climate policy. Given that different public policy and regulatory responses to climate change apply across the globe, this article brings to the fore the need to further understand how sport managers interpret climate risks to inform management processes and effective adaptive responses. The pragmatic connection of sport to the natural environment is not only apparent in the context of facility management but is also evidenced in the domain of outdoor recreation. Mackintosh, Griggs and Tate in the next article look at the growth in importance and scale of the outdoor recreation sector in the United Kingdom. They establish a five component model to help understand the growth in this sub-sector of the wider sport and physical activity industry. From determining the factors that are underpinning the growing importance of the sector, the authors go on to draw implications for policy and practice in sport policy and development in the UK and beyond. In addition, they identify potential future research directions for those working in outdoor recreation and physical activity spaces and places.

The intersections of sport and social sustainability are brought to the fore in the next two articles. These examine the potential of sport to enable social change, given that community organisations are increasingly employing sport-based programmes to foster social as well as individual development. Ekholm and Dahlstedt provide a critical analysis of philanthropy and the promotion of sport-based interventions in Sweden. They examine two midnight football projects located in two mid-sized Swedish cities that aim to promote social inclusion. Their study explores how supportive community actors conceptualise their charitable contributions that enable opportunities for under-privileged youth to participate in sports. They find that these interventions are guided by certain notions of the good society and of the good citizen. The article concludes that the involvement of community actors provides a site for realising particular visions of social change. Along the same lines, Walker focuses on a sport-based project delivered by a Housing Association in Glasgow. The programme uses rugby to promote personal development and employability for unemployed individuals, incorporating behaviour change processes to help participants move into potential employment. The research demonstrates that participants perceived an increased sense of belonging demonstrated by increased autonomy, relatedness and the development of competencies necessary for future employment opportunities. The paper identifies that the provision of these key skills provides a key step towards work-readiness, benefitting both the individuals and the Housing Association community investment activities; extending their role as social landlords.

The potential of sport to enable social change is also predicated in the leveraging of sport events for positive legacy outcomes by the next two articles. First, Bell and Daniels focus on legacy following the 2016 BMX World SuperCross event held in Manchester at the National Cycling Centre. This article considers the impacts on people, processes and practice, or "soft legacy", through the realistic evaluation of two BMX projects established around the hosting of the BMX World Cup event. Using a realistic evaluation framework the impact of attempts to leverage social and sport development outcomes in particularly challenging circumstances and communities are highlighted. This paper has implications for those planning event-based sport development interventions that are used as part of an attempt to engage hard-pressed communities. Second, Postlethwaite, Kohe and Molnar highlight some additional challenges for event-based sport interventions in the context of London 2012 Olympic and Paralympic legacy planning. They explore how London's 2012 educational legacy programmes, such as the Get Set programme, affected relations between stakeholders in the Olympic and Paralympic movement, and those in the UK sport and education sectors. They explain that discourses emerging around the purpose of the educational programmes and London 2012 were a missed opportunity. The findings also highlight the tension between competitive sport-based and values-based education discourse. Furthermore, tension was created from the fragmented accountability between the local organising committee and the representatives of the host city. The authors argue that stakeholders should be encouraged to reflect on potential fragmented accountability and the purpose of sport-based educational programmes.

The final two papers examine the role of education to achieve sustainable sport development. Mwaanga, Dorling, Prince and Fleet focus on the management challenges associated with the implementation of the Physical Activity Teaching and Learning (PATL) pedagogy. The authors study the case of three schools on the Isle of Wight (UK) that have adopted PATL as part of a holistic island-wide intervention aimed at increasing pupils educational attainment, health and wellbeing. This has entailed a shift for some UK schools towards promoting a physical activity culture that complements traditional PE and school sports provision. Findings support PATL pedagogies as a holistic and joined-up policy response to this challenge. However, they also highlight the need for critical conversations in order to unravel and unlock collaborative solutions when discussing physical activity in schools.

The last article by Graham, Trendafilova and Ziakas explores how the gaps between environmental sustainability and sport management education can be bridged. Their study conducted an audit of environmental sustainability courses offered in sport management programmes in North American higher education institutions; this was complemented by a series of expert panel interviews regarding the benefits, drawbacks and challenges of including sustainability in sport management curricula. Findings reveal that there are significant barriers to adopting environmental sustainability in sport as a stand-alone course and module. The paper suggests ways to overcome barriers and integrate environmental and sport management education.

Present tensions, future avenues

The special issue sheds light on evolving responses to the management of sport and leisure at a time of changing policy priorities. The international mandate of creating active lifestyles requires the exploration of the policy trajectory, appropriate mode of governance and local service delivery models. As the papers in this special issue illustrate, the fluid nature of the contemporary sport policy domain means that its boundaries are increasingly difficult to define. Public policy areas of transport, environment, education, health, social, community and economic development all provide links to the sport and physical activity agendas. To maximise the potential of sport and physical activity discourses to penetrate these extant policy areas, stakeholders are increasingly required to operate as boundary spanners, that is to identify areas of common concern and effectively manage relationships as organisational entrepreneurs. At the same time, conceptually, there is a need to address the dichotomy between sport and physical activity, perhaps synthesised as physical culture. This involves the re-constitution of regional sport strategies centred on physical activity while re-thinking roles, responsibilities, parameters and partnership-building as shaped by the funding imperative and the subsequent partnership responses to the new sport-physical activity environment. Within complex sport policy environments, we need to find innovative means to better connect national sport-physical activity participation policies with local network entities and non-sporting sectors. On the whole, a new reality is manifesting itself in search for new skill sets and competencies. In response, sport organisations need to become more externally facing; establishing links and networks with non-sport sectors to develop strategic intelligence that traverses long-established insularities, and promoting adaptation to changing conditions. Such a process cannot only contribute to re-defining sport but also in identifying novel ways for building and managing a sustainable sporting future.

Disclosure statement

No potential conflict of interest was reported by the authors.

ORCID

Vassilios Ziakas http://orcid.org/0000-0002-1501-7863

References

Berry, R., & Manoli, A. E. (2018). Alternative revenue streams for centrally funded sport governing bodies. *International Journal of Sport Policy and Politics*, 10(3), 429–450.
Bloyce, D., & Smith, A. (2009). *Sport policy and development: An introduction*. London: Routledge.
Coalter, F. (2007). *A wider social role for sport: Who's keeping score?* London: Routledge.
Coalter, F. (2013). *Sport for development: What game are we playing?* London: Routledge.
Darnell, S. (2012). *Sport for development and peace: A critical sociology*. London: Routledge.
Giannoulakis, C., Papadimitriou, D., Alexandris, K., & Brgoch, S. (2017). Impact of austerity measures on National Sport Federations: Evidence from Greece. *European Sport Management Quarterly*, 17 (1), 75–97.
Grix, J., & Carmichael, F. (2012). Why do governments invest in elite sport? A polemic. *International Journal of Sport Policy and Politics*, 4(1), 73–90.
Grix, J., & Phillpots, L. (2011). Revisiting the 'governance narrative': 'Asymmetrical network governance' and the deviant case of the sports policy sector. *Public Policy and Administration*, 26(1), 3–19.
Houlihan, B., & Lindsey, I. (2013). *Sport policy in Britain*. London: Routledge.
King, N. (2014). Local authority sport services under the UK coalition government: Retention, revision or curtailment? *International Journal of Sport Policy and Politics*, 6(3), 349–369.
Kumar, H., Manoli, A. E., Hodgkinson, I. R., & Downward, P. (2018). Sport participation: From policy, through facilities, to users' health, well-being, and social capital. *Sport Management Review*, 21(5), 549–562.
Levermore, R., & Beacom, A. (eds.). (2012). *Sport and international development*. Basingstoke: Palgrave.
Lindsey, I. (2009). Collaboration in local sport services in England: Issues emerging from case studies of two local authority areas. *International Journal of Sport Policy and Politics*, 1(1), 71–88.
Lyras, A., & Welty-Peachey, J. (2011). Integrating sport-for-development theory and praxis. *Sport Management Review*, 14(4), 311–326.
Mackintosh, C. (2011). An analysis of County Sports Partnerships in England: The fragility, challenges and complexity of partnership working in sports development. *International Journal of Sport Policy and Politics*, 3(1), 45–64.
Mansfield, L. (2016). Resourcefulness, reciprocity and reflexivity: The three Rs of partnership in sport for public health research. *International Journal of Sport Policy and Politics*, 8(4), 713–729.
Parnell, D., May, A., Widdop, P., Cope, E., & Bailey, R. (2018). Management strategies of non-profit community sport facilities in an era of austerity. *European Sport Management Quarterly*, in Press. doi:10.1080/16184742.2018.1523944
Schulenkorf, N., & Adair, D. (eds.). (2014). *Global sport for development: Critical perspectives*. Basingstoke: Palgrave.
Skinner, J., Zakus, D. H., & Cowell, J. (2008). Development through sport: Building social capital in disadvantaged communities. *Sport Management Review*, 11(3), 253–275.
Sporting Future: A New Strategy for an Active Nation. (2015). Retrieved from https://www.gov.uk/government/publications/sporting-future-a-new-strategy-for-an-active-nation
Trendafilova, S., Ziakas, V., & Sparvero, E. (2017). Linking corporate social responsibility in sport with community development: An added source of community value. *Sport in Society*, 20(7), 938–956.
Weed, M. (2016). Should we privilege sport for health? The comparative effectiveness of UK government investment in sport as a public health intervention. *International Journal of Sport Policy and Politics*, 8 (4), 559–576.
Weed, M., Coren, E., Fiore, J., Wellard, I., Chatziefstathiou, D., Mansfield, L., & Dowse, S. (2015). The Olympic Games and raising sport participation: A systematic review of evidence and an interrogation of policy for a demonstration effect. *European Sport Management Quarterly*, 15 (2), 195–226.
Ziakas, V. (2015). For the benefit of all? Developing a critical perspective in mega-event leverage. *Leisure Studies*, 34(6), 689–702.

Whose job is it anyway? Public–private partnerships in youth sport

Eric Legg, Gareth J. Jones and Misha White

ABSTRACT
In the United States, youth sport programs delivered by public recreation agencies face increased pressure to either increase fees or "contract out" to private providers to compensate for budget reductions. Understanding these private–public partnerships (PPPs) is essential to the sustainability of youth sport. This study contributes to that objective by analyzing the perceptions of PPPs involving public recreation agencies and private youth sport providers. Using a qualitative interpretive approach, data were collected through semi-structured interviews with 22 administrators in youth sport programs, including 12 from public recreation departments and 10 from outside organizations. Thematic analysis was utilized to uncover the perceptions of both sides of these PPPs. Guided by principal-agency and stewardship theory, results are organized across three partnership phases: (1) initiation, (2) management; and (3) outcomes to help inform best practices and identify barriers to effective collaboration.

Introduction

Parks and recreation administrators must frequently navigate shifts in the social, economic, and political climate. In the United States (US), one of the most dramatic shifts came in the 1980s when models of New Public Management (NPM) introduced private sector policies and practices into public management (More, 2005). Under growing pressure from increased privatization, commercial practices such as fee-based programing (Jung & Bae, 2011) and corporate sponsorships (Pitas, Mowen, Liechty, & Trauntvein, 2015) filtered into the operation of public recreation departments. In particular, contracting out, or public–private partnerships (PPPs), became a popular strategy for reducing service costs and promoting efficiency by creating competition, economies of scale, and stakeholder choice (Hefetz & Warner, 2012; Pitas et al., 2015).

This trend is especially evident in youth sport, as PPPs have become a hallmark of the US youth sport system. Similar to other public service managers, recreation administrators must often decide between supporting direct in-house programing or contracting out to external providers. In the US there has been a trend towards the latter, as national adult-organized leagues and associations (e.g. Pop Warner Football, Little League Baseball) have become key providers of youth sport services. In addition, local travel teams and community sport clubs, many of which are designated as nonprofits, have grown dramatically (Coakley,

2010). These organizations are capable of managing all aspects of the youth sport delivery process (e.g. administration, scheduling, coaches, officials), yet often rely on publicly managed facilities to operate their programs. As a result, many PPPs have formed from the need to coalesce complementary resources.

However, there has been far less consideration of the values undergirding these partnering decisions. Youth sports delivered by public recreation departments typically reflect their institutional values including health, wellness, and community development (Bedimo-Rung, Mowen, & Cohen, 2005). Yet this differs from the broader American sport culture, which has historically revolved around elite sport systems (Jayanthi, Pinkham, Dugas, Patrick, & LaBella, 2013). Evidence of this culture is seen at the youth level, as some youth sport providers have capitalized on a $15 billion youth sport market (Gregory, 2017) by prioritizing elite player pathways and competitions. Chalip and Hutchinson (2017) suggest these programs have professionalized youth sport, "with increasing emphasis on early childhood specialization and intensified competition, despite evidence that so doing can discourage participation ... " (p. 31). As the prevalence and scale of youth sport PPPs continue to grow, it is important to understand the role of sport values in the formation, management, and evaluation of partnerships.

This study contributes to that objective by analyzing the perceptions of PPPs from the perspective of public recreation departments and external youth sport providers. Semi-structured interviews were conducted with 22 key informants, and data analysis focuses on how/if sport values influenced the formation, management, and evaluation of PPPs. A principal-agency framework is utilized to guide analysis (Caers et al., 2006), focusing specifically on formative aspects of the principal–agent relationship, control and collaboration, and perceived outcomes.

Literature review

Public–Private partnerships (PPPs)

PPPs have become a hallmark of public service delivery. Driven by a belief in the efficiency of free markets, PPPs have been utilized to contract out public services in order to improve efficiency, meet the needs of increasingly diverse stakeholders, and reduce the transaction costs often associated with bureaucratic government structures (Hefetz & Warner, 2012). The rationale for integrating businesslike tactics into public sector operations is derived from assumptions regarding public choice (Osborne & Gaebler, 1992). When services are decentralized and delivered through a larger number of external providers, stakeholders have more options to meet their needs. Likewise, to remain competitive in the marketplace, external providers are motivated to efficiently deliver high-quality services (Osborne & Gaebler, 1992). PPPs ostensibly capitalize on these mutually beneficial market forces by redirecting funds from unilateral government programs to multiple private parties who provide services under the oversight of public managers (Connolly, 2017).

Growing interest in PPPs has contributed to a rather broad spectrum of definitions (Weihe, 2008). In many cases, this ambiguity has been strategic, as Linder (1999) describes how proponents of privatized systems have utilized a grammar of multiple meanings to gloss underlying strategies and purposes. Indeed, expressions such as "contracting out" and "privatization" tend to carry negative connotations that are rarely conducive to generating public support (Hodge & Greve, 2007). Conversely, discussing the same strategies in terms of "alternative delivery systems" or "partnerships" is more likely to sway public discourse in positive directions (Savas, 2000).

In addition to discursive variations, the exact components of PPPs have also been loosely characterized, with PPPs often referred to as a form of governance, public policy delivery tool, and institutional arrangement between public and private sector entities (Hodge, Greve, & Boardman, 2010). Yet regardless of function, PPPs share commonalities related to their organization and purpose (Hodge & Greve, 2007; Van Ham & Koppenjan, 2001). First, most PPPs are established because they purportedly benefit the public and private sector (Vaillancourt Rosenau, 2000). Second, PPPs entail some form of risk sharing, as public and private entities are both accountable for the risks associated with their joint service production. Finally, PPPs represent long-term collaborations between partners and should be distinguished from more informal agreements (Hodge & Greve, 2007).

PPPs in youth sport

Traditionally, many recreational youth sport programs in the US were delivered public recreation departments who managed facilities and organized all aspects of programing (Crompton, 1998). Like other public services, recreation departments have detailed protocols for programming, facility use, and management, coupled with extensive documentation and multiple layers of oversight. Although these elements are essential to ensuring the transparency of publicly funded programs, some argue they introduce unnecessary red tape that creates inefficiencies in terms of time and money. Ongoing frustration with the perceived bureaucracy of unilateral government-led systems led to widespread public sector reform in the 1980s, known as NPM (Haque, 2007).

The NPM movement was characterized by the infusion of the private sector and market-based tactics into various spheres of public management (Haque, 2007). This trend was especially evident in youth sports. Facing budget reductions and resource constraints, recreation administrators outsourced many youth sport programs to a variety of non- and for-profit providers (King, 2014). This ongoing process has created a complex web of multi-sector partners who, despite being connected through PPPs, have surprisingly little strategic coordination (Bowers, Chalip, & Green, 2011; Jones, Edwards, Bocarro, Bunds, & Smith, 2017).

Interestingly, there has been little attention paid to the values undergirding these partnering decisions, a trend which is evident in broader recreation research as well (Stone, Gagnon, Witesman, & Garst, 2016). Although the previous research indicates youth sport PPPs are most effective when there is strong value alignment between partners (Cousens, Barnes, Stevens, Mallen, & Bradish, 2006; Harris & Houlihan, 2014; Misener & Doherty, 2013), it is currently unclear how/if these values are considered during the formative stages of PPPs. Moreover, since many recreation departments have limited capacity to manage multiple partnerships (Frisby, Thibault, & Kikulis, 2004), strategies for monitoring youth sport PPPs can become lost in the complex web of delivery networks. Understanding the role of sport values in the formation and management of youth sport PPPs is key to maximizing their effectiveness (Babiak, 2009; Parent & Harvey, 2009).

Theoretical framework

The principal–agent framework provides a useful lens for analyzing this aspect of youth sport PPPs. Principal–agent relationships occur when one entity (the principal) engages one or more other entities (the agents) to perform a service on their behalf (Jensen & Meckling, 1976). These entities can represent relationships between individuals (e.g. employer-worker) or organizations involved in partnerships (De Palma, Leruth, & Prunier, 2012). In the context of the current study, public recreation departments represent the principal, and contracted external youth sport providers represent the agents. Two predominant theories have been utilized to understand the formation, management, and effectiveness of principal–agent relations: agency theory and stewardship theory.

Agency theory assumes principals and agents partner on the basis of utility maximization (Van Puyvelde, Caers, Du Bois, & Jegers, 2012). This implies a transactional relationship in which principals and agents are primarily concerned with extracting the maximum yield from their partnership (Caers et al., 2006). Based on economic theories of organizational behavior, agents engage in self-interested action that is not always in line with the interests of the principal, leading to conflicts when goals become misaligned (Caers et al., 2006). Thus, control is an important element of partnerships that is captured in the concept of agency costs, defined by Jensen and Meckling (1976) as the culmination of bonding costs (i.e. costs incurred ensuring agent alignment), monitoring costs (i.e. costs incurred constraining deviant agents), and residual losses (i.e. losses incurred by agent divergence). To minimize agency costs, principals control agents through strict monitoring and performance incentives (Tosi, Brownlee, Silva, & Katz, 2003). Monitoring is achieved by building information models to track agent behavior (Dickinson & Villeval, 2008), while incentives are utilized to encourage alignment and promote shared interest in the performance of the principal (Van Puyvelde et al., 2012).

Conversely, stewardship theory highlights the importance of goal alignment between principals and agents (Gazley & Brudney, 2007), and posits that efficiency is maximized when agents identify with the values of the principal (Van Puyvelde et al., 2012). This places an emphasis on collaboration more than control, as agents are viewed as stewards that connect with the principal and internalize their mission and goals (Sundaramurthy & Lewis, 2003). According to Davis, Schoorman, and Donaldson (1997), the behavior of stewards "is ordered such that pro-organizational, collectivistic behaviors have higher utility than individualistic, self-serving behaviors" (p. 24). This limits the need for monitoring and incentives, as stewards are driven by intrinsic rather extrinsic forms of motivation. Moreover, stewardship theory assumes that even when conflicts between principals and agents exist, agents are still motivated to act within the interests of the principals. In these instances, agents realize that cooperation is more valuable than defection, since acting within the interests of principals will ultimately generate greater utility for *both* parties (Davis et al., 1997).

Caers et al. (2006) suggest principal–agent relations are best understood on a stewardship-agency axis. Previous research provides examples of successful principal–agent relations that exist along this continuum, as both agency- and stewardship-based PPPs have proven effective at tackling common problems, disseminating risk, and sharing resources in certain instances. However, Gazley and Brudney (2007) suggest PPPs can also be problematic, stating "governments using public-private partnerships may experience a loss of control, threats to authority, or greater difficulty in holding private organizations accountable to public standards" (p. 380). This highlights the importance of considering stewardship and agency perspectives when forming, managing, and evaluating partnerships.

In particular, critiques regarding the values undergirding PPPs have become increasingly salient (Gawthorp, 1998). Despite the public choice rationale often espoused by advocates of PPPs, empirical evidence of their effectiveness remains mixed (Roehrich, Lewis, & George, 2014). Although they can improve efficiency in certain instances, PPPs are rarely lauded for their attunement to public values (Rhodes, 1996). As Hefetz and Warner (2012) indicate, "new research has challenged privatization, especially outsourcing public services, as efficiency oriented rather than service-quality oriented, and missing the importance of citizen and government engagement in the democratic process" (p. 291). Interestingly, although values have become an increasingly salient factor in PPP policy discussions, empirical analyses of such dimensions has been slow to follow suit in the public administration (see Bovaird, 2010) or leisure, sport, and recreation literatures (see Stone et al., 2016). Analyzing this dimension within the context of youth sport appears especially relevant considering the growing importance of PPPs in delivering both recreational and competitive youth sport.

Methods

The purpose of this study was to understand how specific people interpret and make meaning of their lived experiences, so a descriptive qualitative methodology was considered appropriate (Merriam, 2009). In particular, a critical realist approach was adopted to understand individual's lived experiences and the social contextual features that influenced that reality (Willig, 1999). The following sections provide a detailed overview of the participants, data generation, and data analysis.

Participants

Participants (*n* = 22) from both municipal organizations and private youth sport organizations were selected using a combination of purposive and snowball sampling. Potential participants who met predetermined criteria were initially contacted and asked if they would be willing to participate. Criteria included that the participant worked for a municipality and had direct contact with community sport organizations (CSOs) that were offering youth sport programs within the municipal geographic boundaries. For example, participants included sport municipal sport programmers, and schedulers as well as CSO league administrators. These participants were then asked to provide a list of contacts of CSOs that provided programing within the municipality, and a member of the research team then reached out to those contacts to recruit participants from CSOs.

Two broad geographic locations were chosen for targeted recruiting. One area – a metropolitan region in the Eastern United States – was deemed information rich and thus specifically selected for this study. Information-rich cases represent cases from which one can learn a great deal about the primary issue of the research (Patton, 2002). In this case, the municipality has been recognized for its PPPs, including receiving awards and presenting at professional conferences related to best practices in PPPs. Half of the sample was recruited from this area. The second half of the sample was selected to provide both geographic balance (organizations in the Southwest United States) and to provide views from areas that may not be as developed in their PPPs.

The final sample included 22 participants, 12 from municipalities, and 10 from CSOs. Fourteen participants identified as male and eight identified as female. The age of participants ranged from 30 to 64 with an average age of 44, and a median age of 33. Participants' experience in their current position ranged from under a year to 27 years, with a mean of 5.75 years of experience, and a median of 3 years of experience. There were no significant differences between participants from municipalities and private organizations in either age or years of experience. Participant confidentiality was protected through the use of pseudonyms throughout the analysis.

Data generation

To meet the purposes of this study, semi-structured interviews were conducted with study participants. The combination of a general structure and the flexibility of this approach were appropriate for this study as it allowed participants to provide the researcher with deeper knowledge about the topic of interest than a structured interview (Sparks & Smith, 2014). The interview guide prompted participants to discuss the relationships they had with their counterparts (e.g. with the municipality if the interviewee was from a CSO), including the goals of the relationship and what made it effective or ineffective. Probing and follow-up questions sought to clarify and elicit additional insight. Interviews averaged approximately 30 min each and resulted in 217 pages of transcribed data.

Data analysis

Since our analysis was driven by the principal–agent framework, a deductive theoretical thematic analysis approach was taken (Braun & Clarke, 2006). Three theoretically salient coding categories were established to represent partnership formation, management, and effectiveness. Within formation, coding focused specifically on the sub-categories of utility maximization and goal alignment. Within management, coding focused specifically on the sub-categories of collaboration and control. Finally, coding related to partnership effectiveness focused specifically on whether or not PPPs contributed to utility maximization or goal achievement. A realist approach was taken to interpret and code the experiences, meanings and reality of participants within these categories (Braun & Clarke, 2006).

All coding was completed in QSR Nvivo 10. Multiple techniques were used to enhance the confirmability and trustworthiness of our findings. Specifically, to enhance the confirmability of analysis, both researchers worked through the transcripts line-by-line to code the data independently (Lincoln & Guba, 1985). These codes were then shared and discussed by the researchers to clarify any discrepancies. To enhance the credibility of themes, the researchers strived to provide verbatim quotations that represented multiple voices and provided thick descriptions of participants lived experiences (Tracy, 2010). Moreover, the trustworthiness of findings was enhanced through data triangulation, as the sampling approach allowed for multiple perspectives to enrich the depth and clarity of analysis (Denzin, 2008).

Results

Formation

Coding within this category focused on the degree to which utility maximization and goal alignment influenced youth sport PPP formation.

Utility maximization

The primary impetus for PPP formation was utility maximization, which for external providers related mostly to field and facility access. Many youth sport organizations do not own their own facilities, and securing appropriate space is often highlighted as a key organizational challenge (Doherty, Misener, & Cuskelly, 2014; Jones, Edwards, Bocarro, Bunds, & Smith, 2018; Misener & Doherty, 2009). This was evident in the data, as respondents from external agencies indicated that acquiring space was the primary reason for PPPs. For example, Warren stated, "there's certain things we don't have, like tennis courts and buildings to do registration and promotional stuff. Our benefit to the county is that we provide a specific service, and they provide the infrastructure." This was also reflected in responses from parks and recreation directors, with Charlie indicating, "we hold the ruby slippers, the facility space, that's what they need … none of these groups own any county property, so the county is the liaison for them assigning field space."

In addition, respondents noted the perceived resource efficiencies associated with PPPs. On the parks and recreation side, Carey explained, "we lost [our coordinators] and it fell on two part-time staff to run these leagues, so we saw a major decline in just the coordination piece of it, and thought it would be best [to outsource]." Similarly, Marie mentioned how PPPs helped her parks and recreation department recoup some of their operating budget, stating, "if we were running the programs ourselves we wouldn't be paying ourselves back for the fields." Additionally, Frank, a parks and recreation employee, added, "... it saves manpower, it kind of helps us with our budget because we are not purchasing any of the equipment or paying for the staff to be out there."

Several respondents also indicated that since external providers do not have the same regulations as parks and recreation departments, they were able to manage certain aspects of the service delivery process more efficiently. Martin, a nonprofit administrator, explained, "governments [can] fall over themselves, they trip over their own rules and regulations." Similarly, James explained how his nonprofit organization began assuming certain field maintenance duties from the county because they "can do some things with certain efficiencies [that] is a little bit different than [the county]." Ellen, a parks and recreation coordinator, acknowledged some of these potential inefficiencies when describing how the municipality negotiates with external sponsors, stating, "the moment money exchanges then it [becomes] a whole tracking, auditing ... everything." Moreover, since most external partners only provided one sport, they felt there were additional efficiencies gained through specialization. For example, Warren noted, "[Parks and Rec] don't have to do registration *and* be the coach ... they bring in a company that knows how to do it," and Steve mentioned, "... they're dealing with everything that relates to parks and recreation of a major city like ours ... whereas we concentrate exclusively on baseball."

Goal alignment

Though utility maximization was the primary motivator for PPPs, organizations also attempted to address goal alignment between partners. All parks and recreation departments had some form of tiered or "preferred partner" system that allowed them to distinguish outsourced partners. For example, Carey mentioned, "with our [affiliate] agreement, [it] is very hands on, the scope of work is included in the packet here with the agreement." Charlie, a parks and recreation supervisor, described a similar approach, stating, "most of ours are the traditional sports organizations that we partner with, we have agreements in place with these groups that lay out their expectations for the staff and for the organization ... we have MOU's in place with them."

However, the criteria of these contractual agreements typically revolved around functional and legal aspects of the organization, not sport values. For example, Ron described how his department also designated certain programs as "affiliates," which gave them priority on facilities and discounts on permit fees, yet this designation was based on the size of the organization and their tenure within the county. Brendan also explained how the fee structure for certain facilities depended on the tenure of the organization, stating, "community organizations that have been established over the years with our city or recreation department, they have a fee structure in place ... whereas new organizations that haven't worked out agreements and contracts and all that stuff [pay a separate fee]." Other common stipulations included the number of local residents served and documentation of required background checks and clearances. In addition, several parks and recreation directors indicated they preferred to partner with nonprofit providers since their goals were not commercially focused, with Frank mentioning, "we would rather let the [nonprofits] run their programs on our fields first because they're not a commercial business."

One exception was described by Ellen, who explained how her parks and recreation department implemented a formalized designation for programs who aligned with their values:

> [We] have what are called community youth groups (CYGs) ... They go through the application process and if they meet certain criteria

then they get to be a CYG with us and we allocate field space for them ... If they don't meet criteria they just rent facilities from us. There are a lot of clubs that don't meet criteria ... big youth tournaments want to come in and all that but they don't get the discount or qualify as the CYG where they get discounts, they are just a general user.

Ellen described that the main impetus for creating a stricter policy was "the direction of club sports," and specifically mentioned how some organizations "started as 501(c)3's and [had] the right cause, but after they realized how lucrative youth sports can be they changed." Restructuring and formalizing the PPP process to include more than just the "nuts and bolts" was noted as a priority for several recreation administrators. As Carey stated, "we're looking at [restructuring] cooperative agreements, putting standards in place [rather] than just signing an agreement because of need."

Management

Coding within this category focused on the level of collaboration and control related to PPP monitoring.

Collaboration

Data indicate the level of collaboration within PPPs is varied. For example, Martin, a CSO administrator, described, "the travel basketball relationship with the county is really good right now, and I think it's partially because both sides are completely invested." Similarly, Warren explained how his for-profit program worked with parks and recreation to design and market a sport program, stating, "the nice part is it's a collaborative process ... each side is kind of working from their area of expertise ... we'll draft the schedule [and] the municipality will have input into what facilities we use." On the parks and recreation side, Ron described how some external partners have helped co-manage certain facilities, and mentioned how "they have taken on an ownership role adopting fields, working with our people to identify what we can do ... so I think that is when we really collaborate a lot."

However, the degree of collaboration was not always high. For example, James, a nonprofit administrator, indicated, "there are affiliated sport organizations that run X,Y,Z and the county doesn't do anything other than schedule it or provide the fields." Similarly, when talking about non-CYG programs from the parks and recreation perspective, Ellen described partnerships as "basically a field rental relationship," and added "those organizations are run on their own." Other parks and recreation respondents indicated the level of collaboration depended on the partner, with Carey stating, "the relationship with them varies, anywhere from just solely renting our fields, to kind of being a little more hands on and marketing as well." Similarly, Ron added, "there are some folks who get things through the funnel of contact and things get lost in translation."

Although the lack of collaboration was partly attributed to a lack of goal alignment during the formative stages of the partnerships, there were also environmental and structural issues that were highlighted as impediments to collaboration. For example, Paul explained, "we are nonprofits ... but at the same time we all compete in the same space. A kid that signs up for us ... to [another team] it's [not only] a kid, it's a financial piece that leaves as well." Ellen, a parks and recreation supervisor, also noted the competition between external providers, stating, "its competitive for them [and] I wish we could change that mentality to where you can coexist, you can compete and coexist." Deficiencies in organizational capacity on *both* sides of the PPPs also made collaboration much more difficult. For example, Richard indicated his relationship with parks and recreation was "very strong" because a "point person" was established to handle communication. Yet most departments could not afford to devote one full time equivalent to partnership coordination, and external groups also struggled to provide a consistent "point person."

Looking forward, James stated his hope from the nonprofit provider perspective, "youth sport groups are figuring out that because of the challenges it really is helpful to band together and provide a common voice rather than having these individual forays into conversations with [the county]." Both sides also noted the potential value in formalizing this process through "coalitions" or "roundtables," which would allow them to hash out differences and streamline communication. For example, Paul, a nonprofit administrator, mentioned, "I think having some sort of organized entity where all of these groups can come together in a centralized forum would provide a lot of value."

Control

A necessary component of PPPs is the nature of control. Most PPPs revolved around field allocations, and the diversity of external providers made this an extremely difficult process to control. Several respondents from parks and recreation agencies described these challenges. As Ron indicated, "you only have so much pie to separate out ... so it's trying to figure out how can we do something for everybody but not make people feel disproportioned or unequal." Frank also highlighted the additional factor of time, stating, "there may be enough fields but there's not enough time, or hours between 5 and 8pm with lights that everyone wants." To combat these issues, Marjorie described how her department is in the process of developing a more formalized field allocation policy, and described the current climate as "a free-for-all." Similarly, Ron detailed how his department was shifting to a more formalized approach, explaining, "we have a field allocation policy that was approved by the parks and recreation commission so it becomes a little bit more of a document with some teeth ... you [have] to do it through policy."

Even after field allocations were made, monitoring conduct and programing was extremely difficult. These challenges were compounded by the sheer number of PPPs. For example, Ellen indicated her department currently partners with "dozens and dozens of private clubs," and Ron added that "different organizations want different things." In attempt to control programs, explicit language was often included in the partnership contracts. For example, Charlie described, "we have [MOUs] in place with these groups that lay out their expectations for the staff," and Frank mentioned, "when we get the parents we have a code of conduct that we make our parents sign, and if a parent gets out of hand we remind them of [that]." Yet the degree to which agent conduct was monitored throughout the program year varied dramatically, and Ron juxtaposed the challenge of managing multiple partners with the more streamlined model for in-house programing:

> You have full control of all the aspects, so how the teams are assembled, who's coaching the teams, when they're going to practice, where they're going to practice, their game schedules ... we can simply handle that all in house with our scheduling units. We don't deal with registration for the affiliates, so if [parents] are unhappy with their team placement we don't really know about it, we can't really control it ...

By contracting out services, parks and recreation departments also lost the ability to control agents through compensation. For example, Charlie indicated how in-house, staff-led programs ran much smoother because "this is what they do, they get paid for this, [whereas] a lot of these partner programs are volunteers and they don't get paid." Similarly, Ron mentioned, "when [employees] are being paid to handle something ... it streamlines and becomes more efficient, with volunteers it can become cumbersome at times [because] they've got a lot of folks who seem to feel like they are involved [for different reasons]." Steve, a nonprofit administrator, acknowledged that since his program was mostly volunteer-based, it was difficult to ensure accountability, stating, "I can't fire anybody, I can't yell at them either [because] if I chew somebody's butt tonight, they quit, [they] don't want to do it anymore."

Outcomes

Coding within this category focused on the perceived effectiveness of PPPs, focusing primarily on the efficiency of partnerships, along with their level of public service.

Utility maximization

Data indicated several examples of how PPPs contributed to resource efficiencies. For example, Warren mentioned how his for-profit organization improved resource efficiency, "There's one program we started out in the town, they didn't have a program so those [facilities] were sitting idle ... and we've turned those [facilities] into revenue generators for the municipality." Similarly, Richard mentioned that outsourcing helped the parks and recreation department "save a little money on the budget." Stephanie also explained how the autonomy of external providers was beneficial, stating,

> they have more independence, they can do things that we couldn't as a county, like their travel program is getting alignments with the [the local professional team] and some other leagues that would be hard for us as a county entity to do.

Another efficiency associated with PPPs was the overall scaleability of youth sport programs. By utilizing PPPs, parks and recreation managers felt they were able to deliver more youth sport opportunities than what would be possible operating entirely in-house. For example, Stephanie described how outsourcing helped the parks and recreation department handle large programs such as soccer, stating, "you can't make us big enough to run the soccer program ... so I think overall the [outsourcing] stuff works really well." Similarly, Marjorie mentioned, "there's definitely a need for other organizations, I mean, we can't do it all, so I feel like they definitely provide a benefit." Paul also mentioned scalability as one of the primary benefits that outside organizations such as his brought to PPPs, stating, "the cost of running a program for 35 kids, per kid, is substantially higher than running a program where we have 1,000 kids a year, [so] I can scale a lot of things and negotiate better."

However, there were instances of PPPs creating inefficiencies, especially when larger external partners were involved. For example, Frank used one story to explain how a PPP actually led to significant agency costs:

> [A tournament director] rented the facilities for girl's fast pitch softball, he didn't have to pay the overhead that comes along with the fields. He shows up to the fields, he beats the hell out of my fields, I charge him $20/$25 bucks an hour for the fields. At the end of the day he walks away with *a lot* of money in his pocket. He doesn't have to repair the turf, doesn't have to repair the kitchen areas, he doesn't have to buy the toilet paper, doesn't have to clean and empty the trash, doesn't have to water the grass, doesn't have to pay the electric bill.

These agency costs were noted on the external provider side as well. In fact, Steve, a nonprofit administer, mentioned he didn't want to own his own facility because of the overhead costs, stating, "that just means I have that much more to maintain [and] clean, and that much more to fix when the kids scribble graffiti on the backstop. And at least I don't have to do that [now]."

Data also indicated undermanaged PPPs became operationally inefficient as well, with Ron stating, "it does not [always] feel like it's coordinated [when] we have to respond to all those people," and Charlie adding, "by having our staff do it ... it [would] just create more efficiency." Ellen also mentioned how turnover among external providers compounded managerial inefficiencies, stating, "there is a lot of turnover [so] we are reinventing the wheel with them because you're re-teaching people and it's constantly new people with new attitudes and philosophies." In addition, the convoluted structure of the current system also made it difficult to monitor agents, which in some cases led to self-interested action. For example, Jim, a nonprofit administrator, explained how certain teams overbook space in case they need to cancel or reschedule, and suggested that county's need to "follow up on what they've assigned." Ellen from parks and recreation echoed similar sentiments and explained how some organizations "ask for all this space and don't use it, so we'll show up and nobody's there." Charlie actually mentioned that one county found they were "over-allocated by 1,000 hours" due to external providers purposively overbooking space, which not only leads to service-level inefficiencies but also diverges from the needs of the principal.

Goal achievement

PPPs are ultimately expected to result in a public service to the communities being served, and part of the potential value of PPPs is ensuring those goals are met Richard, a nonprofit administrator, indicated this service was providing different "levels" for participants who enjoyed sports, stating, "I think it's nice that [the parks and recreation department] kind of helps us run the programs for kids that want to play at a different level than house. I think we have a common goal." Ron, a parks and recreation manager, agreed, stating, "there is some benefit to being a part of an organization where you have the chance to go out and compete at the national, regional type level," but also mentioned that by running programs directly the parks and recreation department can "ensure that the goals of recreation are being met."

However, there were also legitimate concerns raised by stakeholders on both sides. For example, some of the criteria for preferred partners and affiliates seemed to unwittingly crowd out certain programs. Jim explained how the residency criteria were difficult for his nonprofit program because they were located on the border of two municipalities, stating, "we are genuinely close to the border ... we cross jurisdictions, [but] no one can think outside the box in terms of their rules, and so basically we fail on both sides." Marie, a parks and recreation supervisor, also described how criteria related to organizational size made it difficult to balance smaller partners, stating, "over the years it has become a situation where these few groups take a lot of space and then if there is a new sport or another sport or a different organization that wants to get in, they can't." Ellen from parks and recreation expressed similar concerns regarding whether or not the current system is sending the wrong message, stating, "[the programs are] numbers driven because the more numbers you have the more field space you're allocated, and they want to be bigger [and] will do anything to build their numbers up."

In addition, several conflicts were raised related to the monetization of facilities and programs on both sides. On the parks and recreation side, administrators have had difficulty balancing how they generate revenue from facilities while also recognizing their role as public spaces. For example, Marjorie mentioned that some residents were upset that the county monetized the field rental process, stating, "I have rentals saying, 'why don't we get space, we [are] all residents ... we're giving you revenue', which is true." On the external provider side, Warren mentioned, "we're finding a lot of people offering lessons in the same places that we teach, and they have no contracts ... so it's something we just have to keep an eye on because it's not fair." Richard, a nonprofit administrator, also recognized this problem, stating, "it makes it tough on parks and recreation when organizations tell coaches [to] just show up and use the city park [because] 'you're a taxpayer [so technically] those fields are for the general public'."

Discussion and implications

As participation in youth sport programs continues to grow, a better understanding of the formation, management, and evaluation of PPPs is essential to ensuring the sustainability of youth sport systems. This study contributes to that objective and the overall focus of this special issue by exploring PPPs through a principal–agent framework that accounts for the perspectives of both public and private providers. Findings indicate the primary impetus behind youth sport PPPs is utility maximization, yet potential efficiencies are not always realized due to a lack of goal alignment and limited resources.

Stewardship theory highlights the importance of goal alignment to PPPs. Though our findings suggest a broad level of goal alignment between partners was established (i.e. – the goal of delivering youth sports), this was secondary to the potential for utility maximization. According to stewardship theory, organizations that invest in confirming goal alignment can rely on collaborative management structures more than control (Sundaramurthy & Lewis, 2003), which is especially salient for parks and recreation administrators who typically have limited resources and cannot afford the agency costs associated with control-based strategies (e.g. monitoring, incentives). If goals are aligned, controlling mechanisms are not as necessary since both parties are working cooperatively toward a common purpose.

Previous research has emphasized establishing goal alignment during formative partnership stages (Weihe, 2008), and many parks and recreation administrators alluded to MOUs that set these expectations up front. However, results indicate the degree to which partners collaborated past this initial phase varied considerably. Since many PPPs were based on facility allocations, partners often operated independently after agreements were signed. With limited collaboration or oversight from the principal (i.e. parks and recreation), some agents engaged in self-interested action that contradicted established goals. In addition, several parks and recreation administrators alluded to external providers whose values and mission evolved over time and deviated from those established in MOUs. Theoretically, these findings extend the literature by highlighting the importance of ensuring goal alignment *throughout* successive partnership stages, not just formation. To ensure this alignment, parks and recreation administrators can implement collective management structures that guide program delivery (collaboration), or regulate agent behavior through increased monitoring and incentives (control). From a stewardship-agency perspective, it is important to consider that the exact strategy employed may vary along this axis and should be tailored to specific partners, contexts, and populations. Ideally, this will not only improve the efficacy of PPPs but also enhance the experiences of participants and families through increased coordination and consistency.

Of course, given the multitude of PPPs, ensuring goal alignment across a large number of agents can be difficult. Previous research shows youth sport organizations in the US often function independently of each other, with little strategic coordination (Jones et al., 2017). Findings indicate this climate creates complex systems that are difficult to manage, and both parks and recreation administrators and external providers expressed a desire to improve communication. One possible solution would be to enlist a third-party broker to improve collaboration among agents in the external provider network (Jones et al., 2017). Though this approach risks an added layer of bureaucracy, it also has the potential of simplifying an overly complex network by redirecting communication through to a single entity. This entity could also ensure affiliated providers have aligned goals and values, and would provide additional mechanisms for control and oversight.

The importance of sufficient resources was another key finding with theoretical and practical implications. Previous research indicates recreation departments are currently stretched to capacity, which limits their ability to manage partnerships (Frisby et al., 2004). Though stewardship theory emphasizes the importance of collaboration (Gazley & Brudney, 2007), and agency theory highlights control (Van Puyvelde et al., 2012), both approaches are predicated on adequate resources. While PPPs are often positioned as useful strategies to acquire resources and maximize efficiencies, they require substantial resources to operate effectively. Our findings indicate that the potential effectiveness of PPPs was constrained due to limited resources from both principals and agents. Specifically, a lack of resources led to inefficiencies in structures (e.g. bureaucracy and staff turnover, inconsistent partnership agreements), inadequate control (e.g. overbooked field space), and divergent goals (e.g. revenue generation vs. service delivery). These findings are consistent with previous research highlighting the importance of adequate resources for partnership management (Misener & Doherty, 2013).

Finally, it is important to consider these findings in light of public values that underpin the justification for PPPs (Rhodes, 1996). One of the purported benefits of PPPs is their contribution to public values through increased efficiency and higher quality services (Vaillancourt Rosenau, 2000). Our findings suggest this contribution is an unfinished product. Many PPPs arose organically in response to resource-based needs, yet optimal structures for managing a growing system of partnerships was not considered. As the number of external youth sport provider continues to increase (Coakley, 2010), the importance of critically evaluating youth sport systems becomes paramount. For parks and recreation departments, it is critical to ensure youth sport programs that supplement or replace in-house programming reflect values of public service, health, wellness, and community development (Bedimo-Rung et al., 2005). Although many community-based external providers provide fantastic opportunities to reinforce these values, it must be recognized that a growing number of youth sport programs are organized around commercialization and competition (Coakley, 2010). These organizations have a legitimate place in the overall *system* of youth sport, yet they should not be considered substitutes for recreational programs that are more aligned with public values.

In addition, findings suggest a more critical and comprehensive review of the efficiencies created by PPPs is needed. Previous critiques suggest that while PPPs do not always provide adequate opportunities for public engagement, they can enhance public value through service efficiencies (Hefetz & Warner, 2012; Rhodes, 1996). However, parks and recreation administrators outlined significant overhead costs and externalities incurred as a direct result of PPPs. In addition, some administrators described how managing field allocations, schedules, and communication channels for multiple partners actually created inefficiencies from a managerial and logistical standpoint. When considering the potential value added by PPPs, it is important to also consider the full breadth of these potential costs before engaging in partnerships.

Conclusion

In the US sport context, PPPs represent an essential delivery mechanism for youth sport programs. Thus, the sustainability of youth sport programs rests on understanding how these partnerships work. This study contributes to that objective through the use of a stewardship-agency framework to discuss the formation, management, and outcomes of PPPs. In so doing, we provide theoretical and practical insights that can help improve PPPs and enhance public values. Future research may wish to provide an in-depth analysis of the current goals of both public and private providers, as well as examinations of best practices to determine their effectiveness. Furthermore, as this research focused on two specific geographic areas, so findings may not necessarily generalize to different community contexts. Although we have sought to include areas that both represented best practices and geographic variety, additional research may wish to explore the efficacy of PPPs in different contexts.

Disclosure statement

No potential conflict of interest was reported by the authors.

References

Babiak, K. M. (2009). Criteria of effectiveness in multiple cross-sectoral interorganizational relationships. *Evaluation and Program Planning, 32*(1), 1–12.

Bedimo-Rung, A. L., Mowen, A. J., & Cohen, D. A. (2005). The significance of parks to physical activity and public health. *American Journal of Preventive Medicine, 28*(2), 159–168.

Bovaird, T. (2010). A brief intellectual history of the public-private partnership movement. In G. A. Hodge, C. Greve, & A. E. Boardman (Eds.), *International handbook on public-private partnerships* (pp. 43–67). Northampton, MA: Edward Elgar.

Bowers, M. T., Chalip, L., & Green, B. C. (2011). Beyond the façade: Youth sport development in the United States and the illusion of synergy. In B. Houlihan & M. Green (Eds.), *Routledge handbook of sport development* (pp. 173–183). Abingdon: Routledge.

Braun, V., & Clarke, V. (2006). Using thematic analysis in psychology. *Qualitative Research in Psychology, 3*(2), 77–101.

Caers, R., Du Bois, C., Jegers, M., De Gieter, S., Schepers, C., & Pepermans, R. (2006). Principal-agent relationships on the stewardship-agency axis. *Nonprofit Management & Leadership Quarterly, 36*(3), 389–415.

Chalip, L., & Hutchinson, R. (2017). Reinventing youth sport: Formative findings from a state-level action research project. *Sport in Society, 20*(1), 30–46.

Coakley, J. (2010). The "logic" of specialization: Using children for adult purposes. *Journal of Physical Education, Recreation & Dance, 81*(8), 16–25.

Connolly, J. M. (2017). The impact of local politics on the principal-agent relationship between council and manager in municipal government. *Journal of Public Administration Research and Theory, 27*(2), 253–268.

Cousens, L., Barnes, M., Stevens, J., Mallen, C., & Bradish, C. (2006). "Who's your partner? Who's your ally?" exploring the characteristics of public, private, and voluntary recreation linkages. *Journal of Park and Recreation Administration, 24*(1), 32–55.

Crompton, J. L. (1998). Forces underlying the emergence of privatization in parks and recreation. *Journal of Park and Recreation Administration, 16*(2), 88–101.

Davis, J. H., Schoorman, D., & Donaldson, L. (1997). Toward a stewardship theory of management. *Academy of Management Review, 22*(1), 20–47.

Denzin, N. K. (2008). The new paradigm dialogs and qualitative inquiry. *International Journal of Qualitative Studies in Education, 21*, 315–325.

De Palma, A., Leruth, L., & Prunier, G. (2012). Towards a principal-agent based typology of risks in public-private partnerships. *Reflets et Perspectives de la Vie Economique, 51*(2), 57–73.

Dickinson, D., & Villeval, M. (2008). Does monitoring decrease work effort? The complementarity between agency and crowding-out theories. *Games and Economic Behavior, 63*(1), 56–76.

Doherty, A., Misener, K., & Cuskelly, G. (2014). Toward a multidimensional framework of capacity in community sport clubs. *Nonprofit and Voluntary Sector Quarterly, 43*(2), 124S–142S.

Frisby, W., Thibault, L., & Kikulis, L. (2004). The organizational dynamics of under-managed partnerships in leisure service departments. *Leisure Studies, 23*, 109–126.

Gawthorp, L. C. (1998). *Public service and democracy: Ethical imperatives for the 21st century*. New York, NY: Chatham House.

Gazley, B., & Brudney, J. L. (2007). The purpose (and perils) of government-nonprofit partnership. *Nonprofit and Voluntary Sector Quarterly, 36*(3), 389–415.

Gregory, S. (2017). How kids sports' became a $15 billion industry. *Time*. Retrieved from http://time.com/4913687/how-kids-sports-became-15-billion-industry/

Haque, M. S. (2007). Revisiting the new public management. *Public Administration Review, 67*(1), 179–182.

Harris, S., & Houlihan, B. (2014). Delivery networks and community sport in England. *International Journal of Public Sector Management, 27*(2), 113–127.

Hefetz, A., & Warner, M. E. (2012). Contracting or public delivery? The importance of service, market, and management characteristics. *Journal*

of *Public Administration Research and Theory*, 22, 289–317.
Hodge, G. A., & Greve, C. (2007). Public-private partnerships: An international performance review. *Public Administration Review*, 67(3), 545–558.
Hodge, G. A., Greve, C., & Boardman, A. E. (2010). Introduction: The PPP phenomenon and its evaluation. In G. A. Hodge, C. Greve, & A. E. Boardman (Eds.), *International handbook on public-private partnerships* (pp. 3–16). Northampton, MA: Edward Elgar.
Jayanthi, N., Pinkham, C., Dugas, L., Patrick, B., & LaBella, C. (2013). Sports specialization in young athletes: Evidence-based recommendations. *Sports Health: A Multidisciplinary Approach*, 5(3), 251–257.
Jensen, M. C., & Meckling, W. H. (1976). Theory of the firm: Managerial behavior, agency costs and ownership structure. *Journal of Financial Economics*, 3(4), 305–360.
Jones, G. J., Edwards, M. B., Bocarro, J. N., Bunds, K. S., & Smith, J. W. (2017). Collaborative advantages: The role of inter-organizational partnerships for youth sport non-profit organizations. *Journal of Sport Management*, 31(2), 148–160.
Jones, G. J., Edwards, M. B., Bocarro, J. N., Bunds, K. S., & Smith, J. W. (2018). A structural perspective of cross-sector partnerships involving youth sport nonprofit organizations. *European Sport Management Quarterly*, 18(2), 133–155.
Jung, C., & Bae, S. (2011). Changing revenue and expenditure structure and the reliance on user charges and fees in American counties, 1972–2002. *The American Review of Public Administration*, 41(1), 92–110.
King, N. (2014). Making the case for sport and recreation services: The utility of social return on investment (SROI) analysis. *International Journal of Public Sector Management*, 27(2), 152–164.
Lincoln, Y. S., & Guba, E. G. (1985). *Naturalistic inquiry*. Newbury Park: Sage.
Linder, S. (1999). Coming to terms with the public-private partnership: A grammar of multiple meanings. *American Behavioral Scientist*, 43(1), 35–51.
Merriam, S. B. (2009). *Qualitative research: A guide to design and implementation*. San Francisco, CA: Jossey-Bass.
Misener, K., & Doherty, A. (2009). A case study of organizational capacity in nonprofit community sport. *Journal of Sport Management*, 23(4), 457–482.
Misener, K., & Doherty, A. (2013). Understanding capacity through the processes and outcomes of interorganizational relationships in non-profit community sport organizations. *Sport Management Review*, 16, 135–147.
More, T. A. (2005). Public to private: Five concepts of park management and their consequences. *The George Wright Forum*, 22(2), 12–20.
Osborne, D. E., & Gaebler, T. (1992). *Reinventing government: How the entrepreneurial spirit is transforming the public sector*. Reading, MA: Addison-Wesley.
Parent, M. M., & Harvey, J. (2009). Towards a management model for sport and physical activity community-based partnerships. *European Sport Management Quarterly*, 9(1), 23–45.
Patton, M. Q. (2002). *Qualitative research & evaluation methods*. London: Sage.
Pitas, N. A., Mowen, A. J., Liechty, T., & Trauntvein, N. (2015). "Proceed with caution": public perceptions regarding corporate sponsorship of park and recreation services. *Journal of Park and Recreation Administration*, 33(4), 1–15.
Rhodes, R. A. W. (1996). The new governance: Governing without government. *Political Studies*, 44(4), 652–667.
Roehrich, J. K., Lewis, M. A., & George, G. (2014). Are public-private partnerships a healthy option? A systematic literature review. *Social Science & Medicine*, 113, 110–119.
Savas, E. S. (2000). *Privatization and public-private partnerships*. New York, NY: Chatham House.
Sparks, A., & Smith, B. (2014). *Qualitative research methods in sport, exercise, and health: From process to product*. London: Routledge.
Stone, G. A., Gagnon, R. J., Witesman, E., & Garst, B. A. (2016). Values and decision-making: Introducing the public servant values questionnaire to recreation administrators. *Journal of Unconventional Parks, Tourism & Recreation Research*, 6(1), 13–20.
Sundaramurthy, C., & Lewis, M. (2003). Control and collaboration: Paradoxes of governance. *Academy of Management Review*, 28(3), 397–415.
Tosi, H. L., Brownlee, A. L., Silva, P., & Katz, J. P. (2003). An empirical exploration of decision-making under agency controls and stewardship structure. *Journal of Management Studies*, 40, 2053–2071.
Tracy, S. J. (2010). Qualitative quality: Eight "big-tent" criteria for excellent qualitative research. *Qualitative Inquiry*, 16(10), 837–851.
Vaillancourt Rosenau, P. (2000). *Public-private policy partnerships*. Cambridge, MA: MIT Press.
Van Ham, H., & Koppenjan, J. (2001). Building public-private partnerships: Assessing and managing risks in port development. *Public Management Review*, 3(4), 593–616.
Van Puyvelde, S., Caers, R., Du Bois, C., & Jegers, M. (2012). The governance of nonprofit organizations:

Integrating agency theory with stakeholder and stewardship theories. *Nonprofit and Voluntary Sector Quarterly, 41*(3), 431–451.

Weihe, G. (2008). Public-private partnerships and public-private value trade-offs. *Public Money and Management, 28*(3), 153–158.

Willig, C. (1999). Beyond appearances: A critical realist approach to social constructionism. In D. J. Nightingale & J. Cromby (Eds.), *Social constructionist psychology: A critical analysis of theory and practice* (pp. 37–51). Philadelphia: Open University Press.

Watching the pennies and the people – how volunteer-led sport facilities have transformed services for local communities

Lindsay Findlay-King, Geoff Nichols, Deborah Forbes and Gordon Macfadyen

ABSTRACT

Rationale/purpose: This paper shows how the transfer of public sport facilities to management led by volunteers has increased the responsiveness of services to local needs; while at the same time reducing running costs. It provides a contrast to previous research on transfer to large leisure trusts.

Design/methodology/approach: It draws on interviews with key personnel at eight sport facilities transferred to small volunteer-led community groups.

Findings: Running costs have been cut because of the greater attention to detail and flexibility of volunteer-managed services. The service has become more sensitive and flexible to the needs of the local community because volunteers are their own marketing information system, rooted in that community. The positive outcomes are driven by needs to attain economic sustainability and to renew volunteer effort by changing the public perception of the facility to an asset created by the community, rather than just as a public service consumed by it.

Practical implications: The paper shows the progressive potential of the small trusts in meeting local leisure needs, making a case to support this type of sport facility delivery.

Research contribution: These small leisure trusts retain advantages of the large leisure trusts, established in the 1990s, but with further advantages derived from local production.

Introduction

In recent years, the UK media have frequently reported on the vulnerability of local government sport centre provision. Sport centres have closed, whilst some centres have transferred to delivery by large trusts and some have been taken over by the local community (Conn, 2015; Sheffield, 2018). Year on year there has been a decline in sport centre numbers (Mintel, 2018). There is no clear record of how many of the closing sport centres are owned by local authorities, but the CLOA (2015) report on the reduction in funding to sport. At the same time, the outsourcing of sport facility management by local authorities has grown (King, 2014) and most recently, the proportion of leisure centres and swimming pools managed by local authorities has declined from 25% in 2014 to 18% in 2018, whilst the number of facilities operated by Trusts has increased by 22% in the same period (Mintel, 2018). Thirty-five per cent of the UK's leisure centres and swimming pools are now managed by Trusts and as a group, they are the largest operator in the sector (Mintel, 2018).

As context, the management of public sports facilities in the UK has changed significantly since the 1990s. The process of Compulsory Competitive Tendering (CCT) allowed costs to be allocated to public leisure provision (Nichols, 1996). Combined with a more market-led ideology and a continued shift away from leisure being regarded as a right of citizenship, this led to more market-oriented leisure services (Nichols & Taylor, 1995). From the 1990s delivery of leisure services through trusts enabled significant cost savings through their eligibility for rate relief. A small number of private sector providers and trusts emerged from those able to bid for contracts within CCT (Nichols, 1995). These were prepared to take large local authority contracts. As the coalition government from 2010 cut local authority budgets, the provision of leisure, as a discretionary service, was vulnerable. This led to the closure of some facilities and a consolidation of the oligopoly of trusts, who offered local government a way of maintaining provision through transferring facility management, while reducing public expenditure. Whilst the original leisure trusts had started out as small trusts, these quickly grew as they had taken on multiple leisure facilities and, or provision across multiple local authority areas (Mintel, 2018). Trust delivery of leisure facilities in the UK is dominated by these large trusts. However, there has always been some involvement of local small volunteer-led groups since the first trust takeovers of sport centres from local authority provision. More recently in the current decade, this type of delivery by small community groups appears to have increased (King, 2014). This was facilitated by the Localism Act (2012) and reflected a policy of reducing the central state and devolving power and responsibility to voluntary groups (King, 2014) through promoting a 'Big Society', which could be regarded as a variety of associative democracy (Nichols, Forbes, Findlay-King, & Macfadyen, 2015). King (2014) also reported an expectation by local authorities that the role of the voluntary and community sport sector would increase in sport facility and service management. The impact of these small, volunteer led, leisure trusts are therefore the focus of this study. They are different to the large trusts, which emerged from the 1990s in several respects. In the large trusts, the trustees are volunteers; although often seconded from other organisations. The process of transfer from local authority management was led by paid employees of the local authority and the facilities continue to be managed and operated by paid staff. In the small volunteer-led trusts, volunteers planned and executed the transfers to trust status themselves. This was often done relatively quickly to avert closure of the facility. Volunteers take roles of governance and delivery after transfer (Findlay-King, Nicholls, Forbes, & Macfadyen, 2018).

Therefore, as the volunteers are embedded in the community, the facility serves; does this enable it to be more sensitive to the leisure needs of local people? Further, does the more "hands-on" role of local volunteers enable a tighter control of costs through an attention to detail? Thus, the focus of this paper is on the possible advantages of delivery of leisure services by local volunteers, in contrast to large leisure trusts, in the areas of cost reduction, enterprise and innovation. We also consider why these changes have taken place. By doing this, we aim to contribute academically to the literature on trust-led sport services and public service management. Additionally, we offer some practical insight for small volunteer groups and local authorities as to whether small trust management is advantageous.

Drivers to and benefits of sport facility provision by voluntary leisure trusts

Third sector delivery of public services

Research into the role that the third sector can have in the delivery of public services/facilities is limited but there have been studies that have evidenced the positives of social entrepreneurship in delivering public services (Addicott, 2011; Hazenberg & Hall, 2016, for example). This has been of note in the leisure sector (Reid, 2003; Simmons, 2004, 2008) which we will discuss shortly, but also in health and community work (Farmer & Kilpatrick, 2009; Hall, Alcock, & Millar, 2012). Third-way delivery has often been uncritically sold as the saviour of public services, as Dey and Steyaert observe (2010, p. 91) referring to the "double bottom line" of "doing good" (the social) and "doing well" (the economic). The literature referred to above in this area commonly refers to more efficient models of delivery, accompanied by better service for users, enabled by greater freedom and innovation.

Large leisure trusts

In leisure, previous research has focused on the transfer of sport facilities from the UK public sector to large leisure trusts. Simmons (2004, 2008) and Reid (2003) focused on the first wave of transfers in the 1990s. Simmons (2004, 2008) examined five leisure trusts through qualitative interviews with key stakeholders in the Trusts and their parent authorities and documentary analysis. Reid (2003) examined a large single trust, with 10 leisure facilities, similarly through qualitative interviews with key stakeholders at the Trust, leisure centres and the local authority.

Simmons (2004) identified the advantages of leisure trusts in five leisure trusts examined, as increased income, reduced expenditure and greater customer orientation and responsiveness, although service improvements were minor and likely to be focused on extending service hours. Greater financial flexibility, savings and ability to apply for external funding and increased usage led to improved financial performance. In some cases, this enabled facilities to be developed, cross subsidy of sports development work (if this had been transferred to the Trust) and concessionary pricing. He noted that involvement of service users and community representatives on the trust boards encouraged debate over service provision, but closeness to the community was little mentioned apart from this. The local authority had the strongest influence on how business was conducted. As the community were minimally involved in decision-making or shaping services, he argued that the public would not change their view of the facility from being consumers to being partners in provision.

In further work, Simmons (2008) considered how the five trusts had contributed to the Department of Trade and Industry's (2002) dimensions of measuring success in: enterprise, competitiveness, innovation and social inclusion. He observed a culture change in which trust management was able to be more flexible in resource allocation and responding to local needs. The approach entailed:

> clearer goal setting, proactive management to these goals, attempts to remove 'red tape', increased use of performance-related incentives, greater attention to organisational communication strategies, and improvements in the quality and usage of information management systems. (Simmons, 2004, p. 167)

However, Simmons (2008) found that financial viability was reliant on business rate relief and VAT savings. Although Trusts were in a position to raise external finance to refurbish facilities, this fundraising was not always successful. The trusts all had different levels of engagement with user groups, so one could not generalise about the closeness of the relationship to the community they served. Overall, there was a sense that there was "more to do" to better involve community and users.

Similarly to Simmons, Reid's study of one Trust (2003) noted how the establishment of a large leisure trust was promoted by budget cuts, leading to an inability to subsidise running costs and capital investment. As the trust studied by Simmons, Reid's facilities were able to benefit from exemption from non-domestic rates (which the local authority had previously been obliged to pay to central government). A further similarity was that facility management had more autonomy, with "centre managers reporting that the board had transferred greater decision-making powers to them which, whilst placing them under additional pressure, also increased their job satisfaction" (p. 179). A culture of greater responsibility was evident, with managers "acutely aware of their budget ... and income patterns" (p. 180). However, autonomy was limited by financial reliance on local authority grants and requirements to use Council services (limiting the ability to achieve greater value). A contrast with Simonds's findings was that the facility did not have responsibility for sports development and community education, which led to a lack of co-ordination with this work. The Trust representatives claimed a "greater customer focus" (p. 180) and more sophisticated marketing, enabled by new IT systems.

Thus, both Simmonds and Reid found a synergy between greater managerial flexibility to become more customer focussed and improved financial performance; although the major financial advantage of trust status was relief from non-domestic rates. Both found a greater attention to costs, although cost reductions were still constrained in Reid's example by the link to the local authority. In both examples, the trusts' focus on leisure and a limited number of facilities; in contrast to an authority's responsibility for multiple facilities enabled a greater attention to details of costs and marketing. However, in neither case were local people directly involved in management. For example, in Reid's trust, the increased customer focus and service quality improvements resulted from the need to survive independently without the Council as a "safety-net" (Reid, 2003, p. 174) rather than resulting from the engagement of local volunteers in management. Thus for Reid, the Trust was not able to fully realise its potential as a "third way" of providing services. This is a contrast to the facilities in our study in which volunteers are involved in governance and delivery.

We can turn to public service management literature to explore this further. The drive to reduce costs, increase income, be enterprising and responsive to customers that Simmons (2004, 2008) and Reid (2003) both found, can be viewed as a reflection of what Hodgkinson (2013) in a study of public leisure services conceptualised as a "hybrid strategy" typology (p. 106). Hodgkinson presented the hybrid strategy as fit for purpose in the public leisure sector – seeking to add value, whilst keeping the cost base low enough to have low prices relative to competitors. Using a positivist approach to measure relationships between five strategic approaches in public leisure services and business and social outcomes, Hodgkinson (2013) claims that a strategy characterised as "hybrid" is the most successful in achieving both outcomes. This strategy was defined as one that "provide(s) a service that is superior to competitors, whilst simultaneously maintaining a tight control on costs for a lower cost-base relative to competitors" (p. 101). Leisure centre manages who indicated on a Likert scale that they had this type of strategy also tended to report strong business performance – measured by perceptions of "new customers, profitability, market share and marketing" (p. 99) and had a centre usage representative in demographic characteristics to a three-mile radius catchment. This leads Hodgkinson to conclude further, that "strategy content developed in a private sector context is relevant to the study of generic strategies in the public sector" (p. 105). This study is limited by the necessarily imprecise measurements of the independent measures of "strategy" and dependent measures of "performance" and one might question if the independent variable of "hybrid strategy" is actually independent of the outcomes it is claimed to predict. However, this supports the need for public leisure services to try to achieve both economic and social objectives, which Reid (2003) and Simmons (2004, 2008) previously examined in the large trusts; and the need to understand how they can do this. Further, while Hodgkinson's sample included 280 responses, it did not analyse by size of centre or identify those where local volunteers had a role in management so there is a place for research, to examine the small centres.

Small leisure trusts

Finally, there has been limited research specifically into the small trusts, which have emerged largely to save individual facilities from closure in response to budget cuts of local government since 2010 (Findlay-King et al., 2018). This has included the transfer of a local authority swimming pool in 1990 and its re-opening under community trust leadership (Fenwick and Gibbon, 2016); two studies of grass-roots-based takeover of sport facilities, a multi-sport facility which transferred from a large leisure trust in 2011 (Reid, 2016) and a football-focused facility which became a social enterprise in 2014 (Reid, 2017). In all cases, similarly to the large trusts, service improvements were identified and a change in management culture. Fenwick and Gibbon (2016) note an increase in trading income for the pool since transfer and a culture of enterprise developing alternative income streams. Likewise, Reid (2016) comments on entrepreneurial innovation and greater risk-taking evident within the multi-sport facility, including provision of alternative non-sport services, attraction of non-sport funding and partnership working used to develop usage in quiet day time periods. The facility developed sustainable niches in under-served segments of the local sporting market and used a key holder system for clubs to independently use the facility and operate without staff, at evenings and weekends. This latter development shows a process that:

… would be impossible within risk averse local government, where clubs are mere recipients of a space from those delivering a "job" there, customers become volunteers and were integrated within the sustainable business model. (Reid, 2016, p. 9)

With the football-focused facility, Reid (2017) notes that the success was down to the main entrepreneur's extensive time spent in the community, understanding local needs and developing ownership.

Thus, limited research into small leisure trusts notes some similar changes to the large trusts; reduced costs, increased income, a change in management culture including greater flexibility and greater responsiveness to customers. However, Reid's work hints at the benefits of close community engagement. The small leisure trusts in our study all manage one, or at the most, two facilities. They have been established at a time when the strain on local government budgets has become even greater to the extent that a transfer to volunteer-led groups has been proposed (often by the groups themselves) as the only alternative to closure and the loss of services. In contrast to the early leisure trusts examined by Simmons (2004, 2008) and Reid (2003), the trusts we focus on are comprised of local volunteers who have been motivated by a desire to contribute to their own community. They represent associative democracy (Nichols et al., 2015) in the sense that they represent people living in the immediate vicinity who have joined to provide their own facility and who take governance and delivery roles. This is different from the large leisure trusts who did not always draw trustees from the local community or where they did this was limited. Thus, we expect that while the small volunteer-led transfers do not have the same level of general management expertise of the earlier trusts, they may have greater sensitivity to the local community. Further, the greater involvement of volunteers in day-to-day decisions, as well as strategic management, means they can pay greater attention to costs and income.

Thus the research questions for this paper are:

(1) Have the Trust facilities been able to reduce costs (apart from by no longer having to pay non-domestic rates)?
(2) Have the facilities been able to be more enterprising and innovative in response to local community needs?
(3) Why have these changes taken place and what has brought them about?

Research approach

To address these questions, this paper draws from exploratory, inductive, qualitative research conducted to examine the issues arising with the asset transfer of public sport facilities in the UK from the local public sector. The full study examined a range of sport and library facilities which had asset transferred to voluntary groups from previous local authority management. For these we looked at the background of the organisation, the reason for transfer, the process of transfer, the involvement of stakeholders (e.g. local authority, volunteer groups), the role of volunteers before and after the transfer, the benefits and challenges of volunteer delivery and the long-term prospects and sustainability (Findlay-King et al., 2018). This paper was drawn from the study findings on management change, and its impact within the sport facilities.

After University ethical approval for the project, empirical data were gathered from in-depth semi-structured interviews with stakeholders in eight small volunteer-led leisure trusts. These were defined as small by their inception and continued operation as a community or sport club-based asset take over. They all operated one sport facility, except trust D which operated two facilities (one standard size sports centre and a small gym) and had operated an additional two small facilities in the past. The sport trusts were from the north of England due to researcher travel limitations. The trusts were selected to represent those, which operated asset transferred sport facilities, were community-led and had varying operational delivery models: by volunteers only, paid staff and volunteers and paid staff only. Both urban- and rural-based trusts were chosen, but it was not the intention to compare these.

An initial questionnaire to 2000 members of the Chartered Institute for the Management of Sport and Physical Activity, through their email bulletin, had served as a small scale, scoping exercise to show the extent of asset transfer in leisure services. This had a very limited response, too small to conduct any meaningful analysis, which led us to redesign the research to use qualitative methods, as more suitable for meeting our research objectives. However, from this survey, an initial four respondents who were willing to talk about their experiences of sport centre asset transfer were identified. This was followed by a UK ESRC sponsored Festival of Social Science event, in 2014 to discuss Asset Transfer, through this a further four case studies were identified. Interviews were conducted with volunteers who had led the transfer process, managers of transferred facilities and a manager of a community action organisation (CAO) (Table 1 shows the sample).

A semi-structured interview schedule was designed to explore several areas for the full study, including the areas relevant to this paper; the management change, service transformation, critical success factors and challenges. The limited responses from the CIMSPA survey, and more usefully, the ESRC seminar helped formulate the interview questions used. Open-ended headline questions on these areas and probing questions for examples were used. Interviews were in-depth and lasted on average 2 hours, additionally, interviewers spent time touring facilities with the interviewees. Interviews with sport trusts were conducted by three members of the research team, who all had experience of social research

Table 1. Facility overview.

Facility	Facility type	Context	Interviewee role
Sport Facility A	Swimming pool	Urban	Trustee (volunteer)
Sport Facility B	Single sport Academy	Rural	Director (volunteer)
Sport Facility C	Swimming pool and gym	Urban	Chief Executive (paid)
Sport Facility D	Swimming pool and gym	Urban	Trustee (volunteer)
Sport Facility E	Swimming pool	Urban	Manager (paid)
Sport Facility F	Swimming pool	Rural	Trustee(volunteer)
Sport Facility G	Swimming pool	Rural	Three interviewees: all trustees (volunteers – including CEO of Community Action Organisation)
Sport Facility H	Swimming pool	Rural	Facility Manager (paid)

interviewing to build rapport. The interviews were transcribed and case study summaries approved by the participants. Transcribed interviews were shared within the team and regular debriefs were held during the data collection process to ensure that interviews were similar in standard open-questions, probing and length.

The full set of transcripts from sport centres and libraries were analysed using open, axial and selective coding (Strauss & Corbin, 1990) by two of the authors. First-order themes were manually identified across the transcripts and then grouped into emerging second and higher order themes by the two authors independently. The two authors then met to discuss and reach consensus on the themes. From this, the key themes emerged, which included within the sport facilities: cost saving, income generation, programme change and culture change.

Results and discussion

We address research questions 1 and 2 in this section, in order to fully illustrate the changes. We then compare these changes with those achieved by the previous wave of large trusts. We then explore how these changes have come about, to answer research question 3.

The trusts ability to reduce costs?

Across staff in the facilities we looked at there was a strong focus on and impetus to reduce expenditure to ensure the facility was successful. This occurred in several ways. The facilities now had control over their costs and no longer needed to use local authority service providers. All reported that they closely monitored each cost item to manage or reduce where possible, some reporting that they did this on a weekly basis.

> ... every night I get in I've got to do the accounts because I don't like to get behind but it's good that you can see each day or ... week compared to the previous year ... if we are down a bit I need to make sure we can get that up or we've got to make savings and things .... (Facility B)

This would not have been possible under a local authority where costs are often recorded above the facility level. All of the organisations had reduced their utility costs by re-negotiation and some spoke of changing providers every couple of years for the best deal, this flexibility would not have been possible under the local authority.

One facility found that the authority had lighting excessively above the legally required level, so they were able to reduce this. This facility and others introduced energy management measures and significantly reduced costs.

> Basic stuff, turning motors off if we didn't need them, turning lights off ... literally staying on top of every little thing, pennies make pounds. (Facility E)

> ... the building didn't have any sensors in, so we put sensors in ... I mean kids are kids, they put a light on and left it on, so we

changed all of that to save us money. (Facility B)

Facility E spoke of needing to change the culture of staff in relation to cost attention, they were used to thinking that whilst the building was open they would have all electrical equipment working, instead of turning items off as described above.

They were also able to get reduced prices on services that the facility was previously required to use from the local authority. Facility maintenance and development costs were reduced by procuring materials and volunteer trades work, locally either free or at low cost. Volunteer groups worked to achieve either a full or a partial refurbishment after taking on the facilities. For example, Facility B used free end of line paint from a DIY chain, furniture from a charity and ceiling tiles from a shop being refurbished. The ability to save on trade services depended on local contacts, at one facility a trustee was a local builder and in another local electricians volunteered " … three years of free labour" (Facility B). In Facility H, they benefited from financial support in the form of free services and materials from:

> … a land owner … [who] donated the land and a substantial amount of materials, cash and expertise in terms of architects … joiners. (Facility H)

These benefits were possible because of the charitable status of the Trusts and would not have been available under local authority management.

Facilities spoke about key cost reduction coming from the utility, maintenance savings, but the most significant savings from reducing staff costs.

> … don't worry about a marketing budget of a couple of grand when you are spending £160,000 on staff, you save 2 or 3 percent of that, then that's a lot of money …. (Facility C)

All facilities used volunteers in some operational jobs. In many of the facilities, the staff team working under the local authority had been made redundant which saved the burden of the previous staff salaries, terms and conditions. In most facilities, using volunteers provided a considerable saving on salary costs and the new staff structure was streamlined, with most staff on the minimum wage. Some facilities operated with no paid staff in the initial years and only one or two after this. For example, Facility B stated " … the first year we ran absolutely 100% with volunteers because we didn't have the money to take staff on … " The volunteers across facilities were used for a wide variety of roles from reception, programme service and duty management roles, to "everything really maintenance wise … " (Facility H) and professional services. There were facilities that had only paid staff in some particular roles, for example, life guarding or duty management, but in some, there was a mixture of paid staff and volunteers in the same roles, for example, reception and management. Several facilities noted that replacing paid staff with volunteers represented significant cost savings:

> I think the sort of jobs that I've got people doing as volunteers tend to be more professional-type jobs which would cost us quite a lot of money to get done by somebody externally. (Facility F)

Different methods of volunteer recruitment and management were evident which worked effectively to ensure tasks were covered. Several facilities also talked about ensuring that members knew about volunteer involvement and that if staff had to be employed to cover volunteer duties, fees would rise, so they are compelled to also help.

In contrast to the local authority, the facilities also reported that they used paid staff in a different way, with an expectation that they are multi-skilled and work inter-changeably between roles, reducing costs required for multiple specialists. For example at Facility H – all staff including the manager, are expected to interchange between lifeguard, gym instructor, reception, swim teacher and pool technician roles. At Facility E "… we didn't have cleaners, we didn't have reception…" More was expected of the staff, than would have been the case under the local authority culture. There were multiple examples of facilities that previously had "dead time" where the facility was closed with staff in. Programmes were changed to ensure staff were used for all of their working hours:

> … they would have a school in for half an hour and then close for half an hour after that, they would have to have a cup of tea, it was just ridiculous. (Facility C)

> Before we took over, the pool was open from 7 am with the staff, but they didn't start until 8.15 or 8.30am… We opened at 7 am and we started at 7.15am letting people through the door, it wasn't an hour and a half of staffing before we had actually started the programme. (Facility E)

Being independent of the local authority meant that the Trusts had greater capacity to raise grant income and all had benefited from this and noted numerous grant support received. "One benefit of being a community asset is that we can apply for grants that the Council wasn't able to apply for" (Facility G). All facilities also spoke about fundraising organised by volunteers from the community, which became an important source of continued funding to offset costs. However, whilst the facilities had reduced costs and increased grant income, they were not cost neutral and did not envisage becoming so. One trustee spoke about the desire to become sustainable through income and other grants, and less reliant on the local authority, but thought that the demographic catchment market constrained them from achieving this.

> I know in some areas Trusts are cost neutral and they can even generate income to survive on their own but due to demographics and the nature of [location] I'm not sure we will ever be able to get to that point at the swimming pool and if the local community didn't want to put money into it, it… would have to close. (Facility D)

All the groups relied on local authority support in the form of a peppercorn rent, rate relief and in a few cases grants or donations from the authority. Some were concerned about the continuation of this support:

> … we've had no rates at all to pay. We've just gone through a review… so we're not sure whether they are going to ask for that 20% as from now (Facility B).

The facilities are vulnerable, as a major capital bill or loss of key volunteers may threaten their viability.

> … this year we're forecasting an £8,000 surplus and that's not a big surplus to forecast at all, so if the boiler breaks it can cost £10,000 to fix … if we lose a cylinder … we haven't got that kind of wriggle room in the budget this year, so there's more grey hairs …. (Facility A)

> You might have £100,000 in the bank but that doesn't go far if you have a failure of something …. (Facility H)

Overall, the cost savings were possible because of the charitable status and small size of these trusts, with the ability to be flexible and pay attention to detail, in contrast to under previous local authority control. As the Chief Executive of Facility C observed the local authority was struggling because of costs management:

> … some places you go they are fairly busy and I've thought, 'why are you closing that'? They're closing it because the costs are so ridiculous because they are paying staff far more than they should do for what they are doing and they are not open enough, so I've thought you can do that much slicker than that, but bureaucracy stops them …. (Facility C)

Enterprise and innovation in response to local community needs?

All facilities spoke about developing and investing in their facility, as soon they took over the management of it. The facilities had often been left in a poor state of repair by the local authority. Minimally in all facilities, there was a thorough clean up and repair completion. This was considered key to relaunching the facility under their management so that they were not perceived as the "same old". Pride was taken in a facility, with some describing how staff and volunteers treated it like their own home, keeping it well maintained, clean and tidy.

> ... everyone has ownership so it's almost their own home type thing, so if there's something spilt on the floor they won't just walk past it, they'll actually pick it up and clean it ... I think when you have staff who are employed it just becomes a job and it's almost well it's not mine so I cannot really be bothered about it. (Facility B)

Service provision was under close management, with an immediate re-assessment of space use and programming. All described how they were running existing services better. For example, the CE of Facility C swimming pool said that under the local authority formula, they had only been allowed to take 30 swimmers at one time, but by their own re-assessment, they were able to take 60, so provision expanded immediately. Many of the facility Directors talked about how services were now built around customer needs, not staff constraints. For example, at Facility C again, on taking on the facility, they had been told that there were 42 hours in a week of available swim space, but they managed to increase this to 82 in the first weeks (by opening earlier, having a consistent programme on weekends and bank holidays and operating back to back sessions). They commented on how timings had been driven by a focus on staff in the past, now they wanted to be open every day at the same times to avoid confusing the customer, creating a facility that was fully "open" and customer focused. This was similarly mentioned at Facility E "I just tried to formalise everything so we've got set days, set times, so people knew when we were open, what we were doing ... "

However, all realised that sport services were difficult to make profitable, particularly standalone swimming pools, so they developed new services, including non-sport ones, for example, Facility D offered cultural and community hub activities, Facility A ran circus skills for children, and a gardening group, Facility B hosted community events such as election counts and blood donation. For example, Facility A used the arts to bring in different community users:

> ... we got a big outdoor cinema screen ... in the swimming pool and we showed Finding Nemo and Jaws, so you could swim and watch films ... they showed Ghostbusters for Halloween ... we've got a group of mermaids that come in and do synchronised swimming demonstrations.

Some of this had to be creative change to fit with UK transfer of undertakings regulations, for example, a gym club that took on one leisure centre could not run the previous programme of "kick boxing, tumble tots, dance etc." but adapted all to a gym theme with gym fit, baby gym and gym dance. Participants talked about thinking creatively about how their facilities could be used.

> I think it has changed the community's perceptions about what a swimming pool could be or what a leisure centre could be or what it could be used for ... when X City Council had it, it was just the very minimum .... (Facility A)

Programme management focused on keeping existing customers and in particular ensuring that group "sport club" users, as consistent, frequent customers were satisfied, but also developing new markets.

Overall, the volunteer Directors reported greater customer orientation, with customer needs being understood better and a closer relationship with customers. The volunteers represented the community and there appeared to be great willingness to listen to customers. "I think communication now between the pool and the pool users is streets ahead of where it used to be" (Facility G). There was a sense that they could change to give the community what they want. Directors are embedded in (reside in the community) or linked to the community (Head Teacher, GP, retired local politicians). Volunteers, in operational roles as well as Directors with an expected strategic role, brought forward ideas from the community. The CEO of Facility C talked about how they further involve the public in annual strategy days:

> we take all of the Trustees and staff away … we take volunteers along … and we might even invite members of the public who we think might have an opinion and might be useful.

Staff contrasted this to where these services had previously been constrained. For example, at Facility B, baby gym was previously a taught session. The centre wanted it to be a structured education-led session but listened to the parents who wanted to come in and explore with their children. This is now facilitated with just with a staff member on hand for safety. Parents use it as a social setting to come and meet other parents. They also adjusted the start time to allow for parents dropping off older children at school.

The responses to customer needs were possible not only because of improved closeness to the local market, but because they now had the benefits of having control and flexibility to make adjustments, free and autonomous from local authority control.

> … essentially there are good things about running a relatively small organisation because you've got people on the Board that are from the community, the staff all live locally and they've got good links into the community so you can make decisions based on the local offering or what locals want and if you're a larger Local Authority or even a larger Leisure Trust or own operator you get told to roll out the corporate offers and those corporate offers might not necessarily be what the local community wants or needs but they do that everywhere. We have this ethos where if you're a small Trust like ours and you've got the ability to change things you are not under the demand of the Local Authority. (Facility D)

The Directors spoke of an enterprising culture, where the innovation we have discussed above was a result of greater idea creation from staff, volunteers and managers. This entrepreneurialism was driven by the freedom from corporate local authority shackles and political interference, and with a shorter chain of command, but also by the need to compete to survive. They were able to use finance flexibly and respond to trends quickly, as we saw above. This meant they could assess, with more sensitive appraisal of the local market, appropriate programmes and prices and make changes without bureaucratic delays.

> We looked at our pricing and we thought we can change things, the next day change the programme … you didn't have to put a report in to account for something, it was a bureaucracy of the local authority then which slowed everything down. (Facility C)

A sense of shared responsibility among the organisations was evident and some talked of feeling that the facility operated as a community or like a "family". Volunteers and paid staff, alike, felt responsible for the facility survival and success thereby encouraging change and innovation. Paid staff had an opportunity to be more involved in decision-making, in contrast to during local authority control. Managers talked of a culture change, where staff created programme ideas to fill low use times, contrasting to how in the past they were not concerned about customer levels.

> From day one the staff were always here and any activity we had done and think it's not been busy enough they would come and tell us that session was quiet. In the past staff would never go to the manager but all these staff have been involved in the development. The staff supply the ideas, they say we

should change that, we should change that because they work with the public all the time so have always been dead sensitive to what the public wanted. (Facility C)

There were also many examples of paid staff growing community engagement, using their own time to promote the facility, for example, leafleting door to door. In other examples, the whole organisation impetus to be successful led to enterprising solutions such as a:

> …facility's purpose-built swimming lessons database, designed by one of the volunteers. With its specificity to the pool's layout, teaching stations and procedures, it is far more fit-for-purpose than anything else on the market. (Facility H)

Whilst the management spoke of working directly with paid staff and volunteers and a sense of ownership from all, some felt that it was the involvement of volunteers, from the community, that led to a more committed organisation:

> …there is perhaps more of a feeling of connection with the pool with the volunteers (than perhaps with the paid staff who are doing it for a job) who have been there for the long haul as it were and consequentially perhaps a bit more dedicated to the task. (Facility F)

To an extent, the Manager drove this sense of shared ownership and responsibility and the Volunteer Directors stressed the need to get an entrepreneurial person in post, who understood the sport service delivery and had experience of recruiting and managing volunteers. Other aspects needed for the role e.g. technical operations could be learnt.

The innovative culture was coupled with a greater focus on a single or smaller number of facilities, rather than several sport centres or a mix of leisure, arts and tourism services, meaning that they could focus all efforts into making one space well used. However, whilst there was an impetus to increase income and reduce costs, a few facilities noted that they could be become a victim of their own success, as they saw local authority support reduced where it was judged not to be needed. One Director in negotiation with their local authority over purchase of the facility equipment said:

> [The local authority] came back to us with "you've got a massive surplus, so you're being greedy now, you can afford that". (Facility A)

Comparison of small sport trusts, to the previous wave of large trusts

The facilities we have examined show that there are benefits to small-scale community trust management. They have become more competitive by reducing costs, but they are still sustained by local authority financial support and without this, it is unlikely that they would be viable. Innovation and enterprise is evident, with an improved facility, range of programmes and customer orientation.

In comparison to the first wave of leisure trusts (Simmons, 2004, 2008 and Reid, 2003) responsibility for, and efforts in, cost-cutting are evident in both sets of trusts. However, the small trusts we examined were acutely aware of the responsibility across all staff. As smaller entities, they were able to scrutinise costs in more detail and change quickly. They could also change suppliers, unlike the previous Trusts constrained to using some services because of the local authority. They used volunteers in operational roles to a greater or lesser degree and therefore made considerable savings on staff salaries. Our Trusts were able to save money more effectively but were still as reliant on local authority financial support. All trusts were eligible for grant funding, but the smaller trusts appeared to be utilising this more than what Simmons and Reid observed in the larger trusts. However, the smaller trusts were more vulnerable to the impact of capital cost change. Overall the smaller trusts appeared to be more competitive on cost reduction, but as reliant on local authority financial support.

The response to local community needs was enterprising and innovative. Similar to the observations on the larger trusts, the smaller ones had a change to an entrepreneurial culture, with quicker decision-making and empowerment of staff; however, notably these included active involvement of volunteers at operational levels as well. Programmes and facilities had improved and whilst the investment in equipment or facility development would have been less extensive than in the larger trusts, there was a sense that this was changing to what the community wanted, resulting in improved income. Simmons (2004) noted that service improvements had been relatively minor in the large trusts, with this likely to be focused on extending service hours, likewise our facilities extended service hours, but they changed far more with regard to the facility and programmes. The examples given in the trusts we looked at appeared to suggest a careful consideration of customer feedback and interest – with bespoke programming. Simmons and Reid had spoken about staff feeling responsible for the success of their facility, in our cases, whilst staff responsibility improved, with multiple volunteers involved in the facility, the Trustees talked about how volunteers treated the facility as carefully as if it was their own home. As we noted from the small number of previous studies on small leisure trusts, our cases have similarly increased trading income and developed alternative income streams (Fenwick and Gibbon, 2016). However, like Reid (2016) found in small trusts, the changes in some programming were more diverse and involved greater risk-taking than previously. The alternative non-sport programmes and partners were outside of the usual area of a sports centre.

Looking at the management strategy in public services, the facilities appear to typify the hybrid strategy that Hodgkinson (2013) identified as particularly fit for purpose for public leisure provision. There was a drive to innovate and provide an enhanced programme offer superior to competitors, and, necessarily at a relative lower cost-base. The closeness to the customer is necessary to add customer value and to establish where costs can be saved without affecting valued service (p. 107). This is possible as they have the freedom to make these enhancements and savings.

Why have these changes taken place and what has brought them about?

Overall, there are benefits from small community management of facilities, but why have these changes taken place? The smaller size of the new trusts means that greater attention can be placed on the management of every cost and offers a greater flexibility for changing services quickly in response to local demand, improving their sustainability. The role of volunteers in all aspects of governance and delivery, as associative democracy, characterise a different enterprise where the community is close thereby offering a greater sensitivity to understanding their needs. Simmons (2004) noted that the public were not partners in the previous wave of large trusts, the models we looked at were closer to this, with the community inside the management model as partners in governance and delivery. This is the closer community engagement that Reid (2016) had also observed in a small leisure trust. Whilst Hodgkinson (2013) did not distinguish size of centres or identify those that had volunteers in management roles, it appears that the smaller, volunteer-led facilities we looked at are particularly adept at operating a "hybrid strategy" due to their ability to control costs and make responsive decisions on costs and community programme needs.

The small enterprises also had a different relationship with the local authority than the previous wave of trusts. Where an authority had leased several facilities to a trust they held an influence and the Trustees talked about challenges of authorities that wanted accountability and had concerns about democratic deficit (Simmons, 2008). With the small single facility trusts, whilst they were financially reliant on the authority, there was a little mention of constraining authority influence on decision-making, more over in some cases, there was a criticism of a lack of attention and interest from the authority. There was still a benefit from a positive relationship with the authority for advice, but the main contact was a financial one. This meant that the small trusts had greater freedom. Whilst the small size and far greater role of volunteers' characteristic of these enterprises brings benefits, this in turn means that they are more vulnerable. A major capital bill or loss of key volunteers may threaten their existence. The politics of these enterprises can also reveal problems, similar to those raised by Reid (2017) – long hours and stress for volunteers, vulnerability of previous local authority facility staff who may be made redundant or continue on different or detrimental terms and conditions, for example, Facility E casualised all of its staff onto zero-hour contracts.

The driver to the initial asset transfer is important to consider. The trusts we examined have come about because of local authority budget cuts. This has led to greater involvement by the community in the delivery of services. This appears to be a reaction to cost-cutting, rather than an ideologically led change. Participants did talk about thinking that they could run a facility better than the local authority and meet community needs. However, any vision of a different way of doing things came after the need to act to save a facility, as local authorities announced closure or transfer plans.

Conclusion

We can draw from this research the following. Firstly academically, we can conclude that the small leisure trusts we examined retain the advantages of the first wave of large leisure trusts of the 1990s (Reid, 2003; Simmons, 2004, 2008), but with further advantages because they are produced for the community by the community. The use of volunteers from the community as trustees and in operational roles brings the trust closer to the community to understand and respond to needs. Volunteers in operational roles lead to a significant saving. Meanwhile, the trusts are enterprising, think carefully and creatively about space use to maximise income and minimise costs. They have a different relationship with the local authority to the previous Trusts, where the authority appears to be less of an influencer on business conduct, but still a key source of financial support. However, this, in turn, is a disadvantage, bringing vulnerability, reliant as they are on local authority peppercorn rent and rate relief. In contrast to the larger leisure trusts, if the local authority financial support changed, then facility closure would be likely to be immediate.

Secondly, the main practical conclusion for small leisure trusts is to pay attention to detail in managing costs and be sensitive, flexible and innovative in meeting local demand. This is facilitated by the small size of the organisation and the overlapping roles of trustees, managers and members of the community the centre's serve. Thirdly, from a local authority policy perspective, the broader context of asset transfer is the relationship between the public and voluntary sector in leisure provision. A traditional critique of the public sector is that it is impossible for it to anticipate the infinite range of individual choices of leisure, which is an inherently freely chosen activity. Therefore, the public sector will always be ineffective in meeting leisure needs (Gratton & Taylor, 1991) However, a strength of the voluntary sector is that it accurately reflects shared enthusiasms. In effect, the small leisure trusts led by local volunteers are able to combine collective provision with a sensitivity to local leisure needs, as the volunteers managing the facility are local people. As in other voluntary sector provision, the consumers and producers are the same people (Nichols, Holmes, & Baum, 2013). Local authorities could consider the progressive potential of these small trusts in meeting local needs effectively and efficiently. This adds strength to the case of community groups aiming to take public facilities on.

There are limitations to our research, as it is based on the eight North England-based trusts only, which limits its generalisability and whilst multiple volunteers were interviewed in some facilities, in others only one viewpoint was provided. Further research is merited on a wider range of facilities, plus small trust transfers that may have failed, to explore fully success and sustainability. The knowledge and skills requirements of paid staff and volunteers and the role of the local authority as support would be worthy of further exploration. Although political sensitivities would make this difficult, research could explore exactly how much had been saved by replacing paid staff by volunteers, and by how much other costs had been reduced. Simmons (2008) and Reid (2003) both explore the impact of transfer to trust on social inclusion, further research could explore the sensitivity to groups in the community and the balance between commercial and social objectives. Finally, a research question is the extent to which these transfers are a short-term political fix; avoiding facility closures; or are sustainable in the long-term.

Disclosure statement

No potential conflict of interest was reported by the authors.

ORCID

Lindsay Findlay-King http://orcid.org/0000-0001-5199-1797

References

Addicott, R. (2011). *Social enterprise in healthcare: Promoting organisational autonomy and staff engagement*. London: The Kings Fund.

Chief Cultural and Leisure Officers Association. (2015). Financial settlements for culture and leisure 15/16 and beyond. Retrieved from http://www.cloa.org.uk/images/stories/cCLOA_Financial_Survey_Findings.pdf

Conn, D. (2015, July 5). Olympic legacy failure: sports centres under assault by thousand council cuts. *The Guardian*. Retrieved from https://www.theguardian.com/sport/2015/jul/05/olympic-legacy-failure-sports-centres-council-cuts

Dey, P., & Steyaert, C. (2010). The politics of narrating social entrepreneurship. *Journal of Enterprising Communities: People and Places in the Global Economy*, 4(1), 85–108. doi:10.1108/17506201011029528

Farmer, J., & Kilpatrick, S. (2009). Are rural health professionals also social entrepreneurs? *Social Science & Medicine*, 69, 1651–1658. doi:10.1016/j.socscimed.2009.09.003

Fenwick, J., & Gibbon, J. (2016). Localism and the third sector: New relationships of public service. *Public Policy and Administration*, 31, 221–240. doi:10.1177/0952076715610413

Findlay-King, L., Nicholls, G., Forbes, D., & Macfadyen, G. (2018). Localism and the Big Society: The asset transfer of leisure centres and libraries – fighting closures or empowering communities? *Leisure Studies*, 37(2), 158–170. doi:10.1080/02614367.2017.1285954.

Gratton, C., & Taylor, P. (1991). *Government and the economics of sport*. Harlow: Longman.

Hall, K., Alcock, P., & Millar, R. (2012). Start up and sustainability: Marketisation and the social enterprise investment Fund in England. *Journal of Social Policy*, 41(4), 733–749. doi:10.1017/S0047279412000347

Hazenberg, R., & Hall, K. (2016). Public service mutuals: Towards a theoretical understanding of the spin-out process. *Policy & Politics*, 44(3), 441–463. doi:10.1332/147084414X13988685244243

Hodgkinson, I. R. (2013). Are generic strategies 'fit for purpose' in a public service context? *Public Policy and Administration*, 28(1), 90–111. doi:10.1177%2F0952076712440301.

King, N. (2014). Local authority sport services under the UK coalition government: Retention, revision or curtailment? *International Journal of Sport Policy and Politics*, 6(3), 349–369. doi: 10.1080?19406940.2013.825873

Mintel. (2018). *Leisure centres and swimming pools – UK – September 2018*. London: Mintel Oxygen. Retrieved from http://academic.mintel.com/display/859457/

Nichols, G. (1995). Competition for the management of local authority leisure services under compulsory competitive tendering. *Local Government Policy Making*, 21(5), 24–29.

Nichols, G. (1996). The impact of compulsory competitive tendering on planning in leisure departments. *Managing Leisure: an International Journal*, *1*(1), 105–114. doi: 10.1080/136067196376474

Nichols, G., Forbes, D., Findlay-King, L., & Macfadyen, G. (2015). Is the asset transfer of public leisure facilities in England an example of associative democracy? *Administrative Sciences*, *5*, 71–87. doi: 10.3390/admsci5020071

Nichols, G., Holmes, K., & Baum, T. (2013). Volunteering as leisure; leisure as volunteering. In T. Blackshaw (Ed.), *The Routledge Handbook of leisure studies* (pp. 456–467). London: Routledge.

Nichols, G., & Taylor, P. (1995). The impact on local authority leisure provision of compulsory competitive tendering, financial cuts and changing attitudes. *Local Government Studies*, *21*(4), 607–622.

Reid, G. (2003). Charitable trusts: Municipal leisure's "third way"? *Managing Leisure*, *8*(4), 171–183. doi: 10.1080/1360671032000149971

Reid, G. (2016). The politics of sport and social enterprise. In A. Balmer, J. Kelly, & J. W. Lee (Eds.), *Routledge Handbook of sport and politics* (pp. 401–416). London: Taylor and Francis.

Reid, G. (2017). A fairytale narrative for community sport? Exploring the politics of sport social enterprise. *International Journal of Sport Policy and Politics*, *9*(4), 597–611. doi: 10.1080/19406940.2017.1349827

Sheffield, H. (2018, May 21). Library offers playbook for communities taking control. *The Times*. Retrieved from https://www.thetimes.co.uk/article/library-offers-playbook-for-communities-taking-control-lmxbbqdzp

Simmons, R. (2004). A trend to trust? The rise of new leisure trusts in the UK. *Managing Leisure*, *9*(3), 159–177. doi: 10.1080/1360671042000273882

Simmons, R. (2008). Harnessing social enterprise for local public services. *Public Policy and Administration*, *23*(3), 278–301. doi: 10.1177/0952076708089977

Strauss, A., & Corbin, J. (1990). *Basics of qualitative research*. Newbury Park, CA: Sage.

Playing the climate game: climate change impacts, resilience and adaptation in the climate-dependent sport sector

Greg William Dingle and Bob Stewart

ABSTRACT
The aims of this study were to understand issues that climate change poses for major Australian sport stadia and the organizations that manage them, and any organizational responses to such issues. Like climate-dependent agriculture and tourism, the sport sector is potentially vulnerable to climate change impacts, yet has largely been overlooked in empirical research. The results reveal four primary climate change issues: organizational uncertainty; greater management complexity and cost risks associated with water and energy resources, and waste outputs. No revenue opportunities were evident. The results demonstrate that while most physical impacts are manageable, the primacy of commercial and operational imperatives determine organizational responses ahead of government climate policy, and any direct climate "signal" to adapt. Ten factors shape three organizational responses that we have typed using Berkhout's [2012, Adaptation to climate change by organizations. *Wiley Interdisciplinary Reviews: Climate Change*, 3(1), 91–106] adaptation framework. The results challenge the assumption that climate change impacts and responses are limited to non-sport and leisure industries.

Introduction

The impacts of climate change – a "long-term shift in the planet's weather patterns or average temperatures" (M.O., 2018) – present a range of strategic challenges for organizations. These challenges include the direct impacts of extreme weather events that can disrupt organization and industrial-level structures, and indirectly through regulatory and market responses to climate change (Linnenluecke, Stathakis, & Griffiths, 2011; Winn, Kirchgeorg, Griffiths, Linnenluecke, & Gunther, 2011). It has therefore been argued that organizations may be *vulnerable* to such impacts (Berkhout, 2012; Linnenluecke, Griffiths, & Winn, 2013; Winn et al., 2011), or *resilient* (Linnenluecke & Griffiths, 2010, 2012), or able to *adapt* their operations (Berkhout, 2012; Berkhout, Hertin, & Gann, 2006; Linnenluecke & Griffiths, 2010; Linnenluecke, Griffiths, & Winn, 2011; Linnenluecke et al., 2013; Linnenluecke, Stathakis, et al., 2011; Pinkse & Gasbarro, 2016). Organizations therefore have been described as "central actors" in the climate change adaptation process (Berkhout, 2012; Berkhout et al., 2006).

Whilst organizations play an important role in such adaptation, academic and media attention has to date focused on emerging carbon management regimes (Winn et al., 2011) and industrial sectors with significant greenhouse gas

(GHG) emissions. In management research, much less attention has been paid to the vulnerability, resilience and adaptive capacity of industries and organizations that depend directly on the resources of a stable climate system for their success. Compared to energy-intensive industries such as oil, gas, and electricity-generation, industrial sectors with "climate-dependent assets" (Packard & Reinhardt, 2000, p. 130) that rely on a narrow range of climatic extremes (Winn et al., 2011), have received little attention. Climate-dependant industries that are most vulnerable – aquaculture, forestry and tourism – are accompanied by another under-researched industrial sector: climate-dependant sport.

Similar to agriculture and tourism, sport is a predominantly outdoor activity relying on a stable climate to supply appropriate environmental conditions – temperatures, rainfall, snowfall, ice, humidity or winds – to facilitate the provision of the core sport product: sport events. Examples of this climate-sport relationship are the cold climate-dependence of downhill skiing, snowboarding and a variety of football codes, and the warm climate-dependence of major sports such as tennis, golf, baseball and cricket. By extension, grass turf sport surfaces, and the organizations that manage them, also depend on a stable climate to produce sport events.

Existing research literature exploring the climate change-sport relationship has four important limitations. First, barely a handful of studies exist, and these have given scant attention to vulnerability, resilience and adaptation. Second, these studies are limited to a small number of sports and climate zones. Third, little is known about GHG emissions associated with sport with the studies so far being limited to soccer events, amateur ice hockey and university sport. Surprisingly, no studies have investigated *what* impacts climate change might have on major sport stadia – the sites of sport's biggest events – the organizations that manage them, or *how* and *why* such organizations might respond to them. This is despite major sport stadia's significant, although mostly indirect, relationship with GHG emissions through their use of electrical energy for broadcast-quality lighting and other stadium services. This represents an important knowledge gap for the sport management discipline. We argue that research into climate-dependent sport facilities and organizations is important for what it can reveal about corporate experiences of climate change, vulnerability, resilience, adaptation and barriers to such adaptation. Such stadia are exemplars of climate-dependent facilities with the potential for operational disruption through either the physical impacts of climate change, or the regulatory and market responses to this phenomenon.

A fourth limitation is an absence of research on major sport stadia in national contexts with the potential for illuminating the sport management implications of climate change impacts. Accordingly, the major sport stadia sector in Australia was an ideal choice for this study for several reasons. First, Australia has an extensive and sophisticated stadia industry with climate-dependent playing surfaces, but which is also heavily reliant on carbon-intensive electrical energy production systems that are strongly associated with GHG emissions. Second, Australia is a nation that is both highly exposed to the physical impacts of climate change, and which has in recent years experienced significant public policy and regulatory change as a result. Defined as stadia with a seating capacity of 25,000 seats or greater that regularly host professional/commercial-level sport events, Australia's major sport stadia sector comprised 15 such facilities, that were managed by 12 organizations.

This paper therefore addresses the limitations of existing research by focusing on the bio-physical, regulatory and commercial impacts of climate change for such stadia, and the adaptive responses of the organizations that manage them. The broader *aim* of this study was to progress understanding of what climate change means when it intersects with climate-dependant sport. Within this general aim, our specific aims were to: (1) understand any *issues* that climate change poses for major Australian sport stadia (MASS) and the organizations that manage them; (2) explain *how* and; (3) *why* MASS organizations respond to any climate change issues. This included any attempts at GHG mitigation. In doing so, we considered the implications of climate change in a wider sense, that included any potential direct physical impacts, and any potential indirect impacts on the management of MASS organizations.

The structure of this paper therefore is as follows. The first section presents a review of current literature where we consider the reasons why organizations in the major sport stadia sector might include climate change within their strategic thinking. In this review, we integrate three bodies of literature pertaining to climate science, management, and sport management. Emerging from these literatures is the key argument of this paper: that the impacts of climate change present a range of strategic challenges for non-sport organizations, and for those in the major sport stadia industry. In particular, we focus on three concepts – *vulnerability*, *resilience* and *adaptation* – that originated in climate science literature, and which have in recent years extended into management literature. Consideration is then given to the impacts of climate change on Australia, and why research on major sport stadia and the organizations that manage them is important.

We then outline our research design and methods. For our study, we adopted a qualitative methodology and multiple-case design using both within-case and cross-case analysis. Our research design and methods section are followed by the presentation of the key findings of our research. In the discussion section that follows, we situate these findings within the prevailing literature. We conclude by discussing the implications for organizations that manage sport stadia, and potential avenues for future research.

Review of literature: climate change as a management issue for sport stadia

Climate change as a challenge for organizations managing major sport stadia is situated within a wider context of developments. Firstly, climate change is acknowledged to be a "wicked" problem on a global scale (Hulme, 2009; Winn et al., 2011). Human understanding of climate change is underpinned by a "vast preponderance of accumulated scientific evidence" (Mastrandrea & Schneider, 2010, p. 11) around which a clear "scientific consensus" has developed (Lewandowsky, Oreskes, Risbey, Newell, & Smithson, 2015). It is also now widely accepted that climate change is caused primarily by human activities (AASS, 2016; IPCC, 2014c; Steffen et al., 2015). Impacts of climate change include extreme weather events, sea-level rise, and coastal flooding (IPCC, 2014a, 2014c) that may be "severe, pervasive and irreversible" (IPCC, 2014b, p. 41) if GHG emissions continue at current levels.

In response to the scientific analysis of climate change, vulnerability and adaptation literature is now well established, and since the mid-2000s, has been marked by improved conceptual clarity (e.g. Füssel, 2007a, 2007b; Pinkse & Gasbarro, 2016). At the macro-level, climate change adaptation literature, in particular, is distinguished by a variety of foci. These include: types, societal sectors (industrial, civil and government), stakeholders, limits, barriers and conceptual linkages (e.g. Berkhout, 2012; Berkhout, 2014; Biagini, Bierbaum, Stults, Dobardzic, & McNeeley, 2014; Dow et al., 2013; Füssel, 2007a; Smit & Wandel, 2006). The emergence of risk-based frameworks has been an important development in the adaptation field (e.g. Arnell & Delaney, 2006; Berkhout, 2012; Berkhout et al., 2006; Dow et al., 2013; Hall, Berkhout, & Douglas, 2015).

At the industrial and organizational-levels, business and management literature has increasingly noted higher operating costs associated with climate change, and organizational vulnerability to disruption from physical impacts. Indirect cost risks include added regulatory burden and/or reputational damage, particularly for "high-salience" industries (Kolk & Pinkse, 2012) such as the oil, gas, electricity and automobile sectors (e.g. Haigh & Griffiths, 2012; Kolk & Hoffman, 2007; Kolk & Levy, 2004; Pinkse & Gasbarro, 2016; Pinkse & Kolk, 2007). In addition, organizational disruption through physical impacts include damage to business infrastructure from "extreme weather events" (e.g. cyclones, droughts and bushfires); "gradual impacts" (e.g. sea-level rise and higher ocean acidity); and "large-system changes" where gradual impacts exceed "critical thresholds" (Pinkse & Gasbarro, 2016; Winn et al., 2011, p. 158). As a consequence, it has been argued that climate change, and adaptation to its physical impacts, should be included in the strategic thinking of organizations (Hoffman, 2005; Kolk & Pinkse, 2012; Linnenluecke, Griffiths, & Mumby, 2015; Linnenluecke, Griffiths, et al., 2011; Winn et al., 2011).

Research on the vulnerability of organizations to climate change disruption is closely aligned with work on resilience, and adaptive capacity (e.g. Beermann, 2011; Charlton & Arnell, 2011; Hertin, Berkhout, Gann, & Barlow, 2003; Kiem & Austin, 2013). In particular, business research focused on organizational adaptation to climate change has seen important advances in recent years (e.g. Gasbarro, Rizzi, & Frey, 2016; Linnenluecke & Griffiths, 2010; Linnenluecke, Griffiths, et al., 2011; Weinhofer & Busch, 2013; Weinhofer & Hoffmann, 2010). A systematic review of existing studies has noted that they are spread across four levels of analysis (individual decision-maker, organizational, industry and institutional), but that knowledge gaps remain for each (Linnenluecke et al., 2013). For example, organizational adaptation studies have been criticized for overlooking changes in the natural environment such as extreme weather events (Linnenluecke et al., 2013), and management scholars have called for more progress (Linnenluecke & Griffiths, 2013; Linnenluecke et al., 2015; Linnenluecke et al., 2013; Patenaude, 2011).

Adding to the deficiencies in management literature is a limited range of empirical work investigating climate change impacts on industries with *climate-dependent assets* (Packard & Reinhardt, 2000). Climate-dependent assets have been defined as those that rely on particular temperatures and seasonal conditions (Pinkse & Gasbarro, 2016), or natural resources provided by the climate system (e.g. rainwater). Climate-dependent industries include agriculture, tourism, water and forestry, and whilst these industries have been empirically examined (Linnenluecke et al., 2013), there is very little research on the climate-dependant segment of the sport industry.

Like climate-dependant agriculture and tourism (Amelung & Moreno, 2012; Linnenluecke et al., 2013; Scott, Gössling, & Hall, 2012), outdoor sports typically rely upon the climate system for appropriate conditions (e.g. temperatures), but also for water resources. Specifically, the climate system – with the aid of water management infrastructure – provide sport facilities with the rainwater upon which they depend heavily (Kellett & Turner, 2009, 2011). However, modern sports' also rely heavily on energy resources for operations, lighting and transportation (Mallen & Chard, 2012; UNEP, 2018), and this illustrates another feature of the sport-climate relationship: indirect GHG emissions. In this context, the sport industry offers numerous opportunities to understand the vulnerability and/or resilience of sport infrastructure to climate change, *and* organizational adaptation, yet no studies have been carried out. This represents a significant knowledge gap for the sport management discipline.

The lack of empirical work about what climate change means for sport is particularly surprising given its cultural, commercial and historical significance. As a global commodity (Real, 1996), capturing the interest of billions of people across national, cultural and language boundaries (Miller, Lawrence, McKay, & Rowe,

2001), it has a market value of between $US620-700 billion, or approximately one per cent of global GDP (Collignon & Sultan, 2014). To date, existing studies into the climate change–sport relationship are limited to a handful of sports, issues and levels of analysis. Studies of sport with "climate-dependent assets" are limited to golf (Scott & Jones, 2006, 2007), snow and ice-based sports (e.g. Moen & Fredman, 2007; Scott & McBoyle, 2007; Wolfsegger, Gössling, & Scott, 2008), and the Winter Olympics (Scott, Steiger, Rutty, & Johnson, 2015). Aquatic facilities where swimming sport is staged is another example of such research (McDonald, Stewart, & Dingle, 2014). Other studies have overlooked vulnerability, resilience and adaptation (e.g. Chard & Mallen, 2012; Dolf & Teehan, 2015; Otto & Heath, 2010).

All but two of these studies were also limited geographically to the northern hemisphere – specifically, Europe and North America – and so little is known of the impact of climate change on the sport industry in equatorial or southern hemisphere regions. This is despite southern hemisphere nations such as Australia being among the worlds' most exposed and sensitive to climate change (CSIRO, 2009; Reisinger et al., 2014). Australian climate has already changed with average surface temperatures increasing 0.9°C. since 1910 (CSIRO & BoM, 2015), and is projected to warm a further 0.6–1.3°C. by 2030, and 1–5°C. by 2070 (CSIRO & BoM, 2015; Reisinger et al., 2014). Climate change impacts include more frequent and hotter days, more frequent severe droughts, increased evaporation, harsher fire weather and lower water supply reliability (CSIRO & BoM, 2015; Hennessy, 2011; Reisinger et al., 2014; Steffen & Hughes, 2013). The 12-year "Millennium Drought" of 1996–2008 was the worst in 110 years of meteorological records (Timbal, 2009). Against this background, Australia is an important site for researching the physical impacts on organizations, and adaptive organizational responses.

The research literature for sport stadia is rare, and consistently overlooks any direct or indirect impacts of climate change. Defined as, "athletic or sports ground(s) with tiers of seats for spectators" ("Stadium", 2017), the main purpose of major sport stadia is economic development, urban renewal and modernization (Ahlfeldt & Maennig, 2010; Feddersen, Grötzinger, & Maennig, 2009). They are the sites of "mega events" (Dolles & Soderman, 2010) such as the Olympic Games, and exemplify "iconic architecture" (Horne, 2011, p. 210). However, only one study explored the potential climate change–stadia relationship (i.e. Chard & Mallen, 2013), and vulnerability, resilience or adaptive responses to climate change were not considered. Given their water and energy-intensive nature, we argue that major sport stadia are important sites for understanding the breadth and depth of organizational challenges posed by climate change.

The nature of managerial decision-making in relation to organizational responses to climate change in the sport industry is also poorly understood. This is an important gap in sport management literature because managerial decision-making is central to any organizational responses to climate change. Whilst some sport management studies have canvassed managerial decision-making more generally (eg. Kikulis, Slack, & Hinings, 1995; Merigó & Gil-Lafuente, 2011), and others have considered managerial decision-making in relation to environmental sustainability (eg. Babiak & Trendafilova, 2011; Trendafilova, Babiak, & Heinze, 2013), none of have considered its role in sport organizations in response to climate change issues. In relation to major sport stadia specifically, no such studies are reported.

To address these knowledge gaps, we adopted a qualitative methodology and methods. Qualitative research is accepted as suitable for sport management research (Andrew, Pedersen, & McEvoy, 2011; Edwards & Skinner, 2009), is particularly suitable for answering complex "how" and "why" questions (Andrew et al., 2011; Yin, 2011), and has been applied previously in studies that have investigated impacts of climate change on climate-dependent assets (Kiem & Austin, 2013; Rickards, 2012). As a consequence, this study addresses knowledge gaps around climate change vulnerability, resilience and organizational adaptation in the climate-dependent major stadia segment of the sport industry.

Research design and method

Our study applied qualitative methods featuring a multiple-case, case study research design using replication logic. A multiple-case design was appropriate because it allows more powerful and valid conclusions to be drawn than a single-case design (Andrew et al., 2011; Miles, Huberman, & Saldana, 2014; Yin, 2009), and it expands external generalisability (Cresswell, 2009). The units of analysis for our study were organizations that own and/or manage MASS.

Sampling

To identify such organizations – and in the absence of a single, nationally or internationally agreed definition of major sport stadia – it was first necessary to create our own definition of MASS. Our definition was based on three criteria drawn from sport management literature, and a legislative definition of major sport stadia: (1) Sport stadia, where sport is defined as a *competitive, physical* activity *structured* according to rules or laws (Nicholson, Kerr, & Sherwood, 2015). (2) Stadia regularly host *professional/commercial-level sport* (Hoye, Smith, Nicholson, & Stewart, 2015) such as national sport leagues, championships and international events, and; (3) Stadia with a *minimum seating capacity of 25,000 spectators*. This threshold was based on the Queensland (state) Government legislative definition of major sport events as being those having 25,000 or more spectators (QLDG, 2001). MASS organizations were therefore those that managed stadia meeting these criteria. MASS organizations are typically small to medium-sized enterprises (SME) as 11 of the 12 (92%) met the European Commission (2018) definition of SME's based on either turnover or staff "head count" criteria. The twelfth MASS organization met the definition of a large business.

Twelve MASS organizations, out of a total of 14, were chosen as our case studies using a two-stage purposeful sampling method (Miles et al., 2014; Sarantakos, 2013). These 12 organizations represented 85 per cent of the total study population. The first stage involved *selective sampling* (Coyne, 1997; Sandelowski, Holditch-Davis, & Harris, 1992) where a "preconceived, but reasonable initial set of criteria" (Sandelowski et al., 1992, p. 628) was used to select a sample of cases. Sport facilities more generally were of interest because their climate-dependence suggested that they would be the most likely to have sport organizations that could reveal insights about climate impacts and adaptation. MASS organizations were of particular interest for three reasons: (1) their grass playing surfaces depend on the climate to provide rainwater to maintain them; (2) they were thought likely to be large users of water resources and; (3) electrical energy. Water use was of particular interest because water availability is a key climate issue in Australia (CSIRO & BoM, 2015; Hennessy, 2011). Electrical energy use at MASS was also of interest because electricity in Australia is predominantly generated by fossil fuel-based, carbon-intensive, greenhouse gas-emitting generators (AEMO, 2018).

Our second stage of purposeful sampling involved *theoretical sampling* (Sandelowski et al., 1992). The typology revealed three potential theoretical categories of MASS organizations covering the entire MASS industrial sector: (1) public-ownership, not-for-profit; (2) private-ownership, not-for-profit and; (3) private-ownership, for-profit. These three categories (conceptualizations) of MASS organizations were the "analytic grounds" (Sandelowski et al., 1992) for sampling the 12 MASS organizations. Replication logic (Andrew et al., 2011; Yin, 2009) was used to target a sample of MASS organizations within each of the three theoretical categories. The 12 replications/cases were spread across the three theoretical categories as follows: Category One (5 cases); Category Two (4 cases); Category Three (3 cases). With 85 per cent of the study population participating in the study, all theoretical categories had sufficient replications to enable confidence in our findings, and in the external generalization of our findings. The geographic locations of our sample also spanned three of the six major Australian climate zones identified under the Köppen climate classification system (BoM, 2018). The cases were anonymous and we refer to them by alphabetical codes (i.e. "A", "B", "C", etc.). An overview of the MASS cases/replications is presented in Table 1.

Data collection and analysis

As advocated by Yin (2009), each organizational case was developed from multiple sources. This included "focused" (in-depth) interviews with well-placed informants, documents and observation data. Interviews with 21 participants produced over 14 hours of data, and 63 historical documents were collected and analysed. All interviewees were given alphanumeric codes (i.e. "A1", "A2", "B1", "B2", etc.) to ensure their anonymity, and that of their organizations. Thematic coding (Miles et al., 2014) of interview transcripts and documents was used. Once the case studies were compiled, a further round of within-case, and cross-case analysis (Bazeley, 2007; Eisenhardt, 1989) was used to finalize the major themes.

Data reliability was achieved by using a case study protocol, checking data sample congruence with the research questions, and coding checks. External validity was achieved through the multiple-case research design, thick description, and cross-case analysis, while internal validity was achieved by the use of pattern matching (Yin, 2009, 2012). In addition, to make sense of any adaptive responses to climate by MASS organizations, Berkhout's (2012) adaptation framework was applied.

Results

Physical impacts of climate change on MASS – and associated policy, regulatory and market impacts on MASS organizations – were evident

Table 1. Overview of MASS organizations (cases).

Theoretical categories ($n = 3$)	MASS organizations/cases ($n = 12$)	Types of MASS organization ($n = 5$)	No. of MASS owned ($n = 13$)	No. of MASS managed ($n = 15$)
Category One –Publically-owned, not-for-profit	Case A	Government-owned statutory authority	5	3
	Case D	Government-owned statutory authority	2	2
	Case E	Government-owned statutory authority	1	1
	Case I	Government-owned statutory authority	1	1
	Case J	Local government	1	1
Category Two –Privately owned, not-for-profit	Case B	Not-for-profit governing body	0	1
	Case G	Not-for-profit governing body	1	1
	Case H	Not-for-profit governing body	1	1
	Case K	Not-for-profit, membership-based club	0	1
Category Three –Privately-owned, for-profit	Case C	Privately-owned for-profit company	0	1
	Case F	Privately-owned for-profit company	1	1
	Case L	Privately-owned for-profit company	0	1

in both interviews and organizational documents. Two direct climate change impacts on the stadia were consistently reported: (1) higher rates of water evaporation from the grass playing surfaces due to a warmer, drier climate; (2) the inadequacy of traditional grass varieties for coping with the persistently above average temperatures that now characterize the climate zones in which the stadia are located. Disruption from flooding caused by extreme weather events (i.e. storms) was reported by only two cases (A and L). The key organizational issues were uncertainty about long-term public policy for climate change; higher costs and added complexity for managing water and energy resources, and waste outputs. The three major organizational responses to these issues were water, energy and waste management strategies.

Organizational perceptions of climate change

Climate change has been a subject of intense debate in Australia in recent years, yet only just over half of the MASS cases (7/12) reported having discussed it as a management issue. The remaining five cases had not discussed it. The ownership-management categories of these organizations did not influence whether or not climate change had been discussed. In all cases, no formal corporate view of climate change was evident. For cases that had not explicitly discussed climate change, it was managed through environmental strategies. Nevertheless, climate change was consistently perceived as an important issue even if it wasn't the *most* important one.

All 12 MASS cases understood the basic science of climate change. That is, global climate was warming, and that this warming was caused principally by GHG's associated with human activities. This was evident across all three categories of MASS organizations. MASS organizations based their understanding of climate change overwhelmingly on media reportage, although other information sources were reported. Nine of the 12 cases were primarily influenced by media discussion of climate change, especially television and newspaper coverage. This was evident across all three categories of MASS organizations. Governments were the next most important influence.

The crucial role that the media plays in shaping organizational understandings of climate change has been illustrated in research over the last decade. For example, von Storch and Krauss (2005) argued that while national culture is a key influence on how people perceive climate change, media interpretations are also important in both Germany and the United States where "frameworks(s) of vulnerability" are used. The role of media interpretations of climate change in how the building industry makes sense of it is also known (Hertin et al., 2003). This is consistent with the media's well established role in influencing corporate responses to environmental issues more generally, and beyond climate change itself (Bansal, 2005).

One-third of all cases reported state government agencies as an influence while a minority of cases cited the Australian Government (Case E) and local governments (Case B and H) as important influences. surprisingly, only one case cited the influence of the Australian Government Department of Environment (Case E), while none reported the influence of the Australian Bureau of Meteorology despite both agencies having extensive information about climate change on their websites. Significantly, all MASS organizations interpreted climate change through existing strategic frameworks. Although some plans provided for "sustainability" and "environmental" management, none were specific to climate change.

Limited vulnerability and significant resilience

Despite the reported physical climate change impacts on the stadia, only two MASS organizations thought their stadia were vulnerable (H & K). Such vulnerability was limited to Theoretical Category Two. In contrast, vulnerability's antithesis – resilience – was reported for 13 of the 15 stadia, and so was evident across all three theoretical categories of MASS organizations. Enabling factors for stadia resilience were stadium design, and water and energy management infrastructure. Organizational resilience to climate change impacts, as distinct from the resilience of the stadia, was reported by all 12 MASS cases. A summary of the key climate change issues is presented in Table 2.

Issue 1: Organizational uncertainty about public policy for climate change

Whilst MASS organizations largely understood the basics of climate change, they were less certain about long-term government policy, and what that would mean commercially. This uncertainty was evident across all theoretical categories. In particular, most were uncertain about longer term government policy for GHG emissions and carbon pricing.

Issue 2: Water issues

The major problems arising from the physical impacts of climate change for MASS involved water. This was true for all three categories of MASS organizations. As organizations whose stadia rely heavily on water resources, they were concerned about significantly reduced rainfall over the past two decades. Seven of the 12 MASS cases reported significant declines in rainfall in recent years, which they described as an issue of high importance. MASS managers described water shortages as "drought", a phenomenon linked by Australian climate experts to climate change (BoM & CSIRO, 2017). Restrictions on water supply, and increasing water costs associated with these restrictions, were vulnerabilities repeatedly identified by MASS interviewees. All 12 cases reported it as a climate change issue, with 80 per cent of interviewees (17/21) referring to it.

Water issues for MASS organizations were thus multi-dimensional. These issues spanned *physical impacts* (lower rainfall, higher evaporation, difficulty maintaining grass playing surfaces), *commercial impacts* (higher water prices, infrastructure and compliance costs), and the *policy, legislative and organizational responses* to climate change in Australia (government-mandated water restrictions, harvesting, storage, efficiency, recycling, treatment and planning). All 12 cases reported major investment in water management infrastructure in response to government-mandated water efficiency laws that were introduced during the "Millennium Drought" (1996–2008), an unprecedented dry period in Australia. Case E's multi-million dollar water recycling plant was a notable illustration of such investment. Accordingly, water issues were strongly linked to higher costs.

Issue 3: Energy issues

All 12 MASS cases reported climate change issues around energy, and this was evident across the 3 categories of MASS organizations. MASS organizations consistently reported

Table 2. Key climate change issues.

Issue	Description
Uncertainty about climate change implications	Uncertainty about long-term national government climate policy; carbon pricing; compliance obligations.
Water issues	Increased average temperatures; higher water evaporation from grass playing surfaces; traditional grass varieties inadequate for a warmer climate; higher water costs; limited flood risk.
Energy issues	Higher energy costs, largely indirect GHG emissions, carbon pricing, energy efficiency, energy and GHG emissions reporting compliance.
Waste issues	GHG emissions from landfill, higher solid waste disposal costs.

electrical energy use in particular, as a climate change issue. One major energy issue was the need to reduce energy consumption, with "energy conservation" being the strategy for minimizing electrical energy costs. 11 of the 12 MASS cases recognized an indirect link between their energy use and GHG emissions. This suggests these organizations understand the problematic nature of electricity production in Australia where suppliers rely heavily on coal-fired electricity generators. 11 of the 12 MASS cases also reported direct GHG emissions, mainly from diesel or gas-powered vehicles and kitchens with gas cooking equipment. Such emissions were a small proportion of their total carbon footprint.

Seven of the 12 MASS cases reported programmes for reducing energy consumption as a response to climate change. These stadia are large users of electrical energy which peaks on event days but reduces dramatically on non-event days. Two MASS cases (A and E) used sufficient energy to meet the reporting thresholds of the National Greenhouse and Energy Reporting (NGER) Act (2007), a national law aimed at recording the GHG emissions of Australia's largest energy users. However, as only two MASS cases met the NGER thresholds, the emissions (direct and indirect) of most of these organizations are relatively small compared to large non-sport facilities such as oil refineries, coal mines, airlines and waste disposal sites.

Interestingly, the desire of MASS organizations to conserve energy was not driven primarily by concerns about climate change. Rather, energy conservation was driven primarily by the need to reduce operating costs. Like water inputs, energy use was seen as a cost issue. However, most MASS organizations also identified energy conservation as a strategy for mitigating GHG emissions associated with energy use even if it was a *second-order* priority. Purchasing renewable energy was another strategy for mitigating GHG emissions, but with limited application. One-quarter of MASS cases (A, E and F) reported purchasing "green" energy from electricity suppliers to mitigate GHG emissions. Only one case (A) reported using solar panels, which met up to 20 per cent of electricity demand at their stadium.

Although MASS organizations clearly linked energy use as a climate change issue, the prioritization of reducing energy costs ahead of reducing GHG emissions related to energy use is highly significant. Whilst these organizations were consistent in stating their credentials as good corporate citizens (a "responsibility" to "do the right thing" for the "community"), they were also consistent in reporting that energy management programmes and infrastructure spending had to be first justified to senior management with a strong "business case". Whilst climate change was a priority, it was only one of a range of issues to be managed, and it was largely secondary to operational imperatives (i.e. staging major sport events) and financial management. Energy use, while clearly linked to climate change, was framed primarily as a cost issue in much the same way as in other industries such as oil production, car manufacturing (Kolk & Levy, 2004) and aviation (Gössling & Upham, 2009).

Finally, 5 of the 12 MASS organizations reported that carbon pricing, through either a carbon tax or an Emissions Trading Scheme (ETS), as a cost issue. Carbon pricing is a cost issue for MASS organizations in two ways: (1) where their energy use is sufficient to meet the NGER thresholds, a direct carbon liability is created; (2) through higher electricity costs passed on by carbon-intensive electricity generators who themselves owe a carbon liability.

Issue 4: Waste issues

Nine of the 12 MASS cases reported stadium waste as a climate change issue. This was evident across all three categories of MASS organizations. The only exceptions were cases C, F and G. Waste is a climate change issue because of the link between waste disposal and GHG emissions such as methane (CH_4). Specifically, when solid waste is disposed of as landfill at Solid Waste Disposal Sites (SWDS), it decomposes and releases CH_4. This release of GHG emissions, sometimes referred to as "landfill gas", is a concern recognized by multiple domestic and international environment agencies (DCCEE, 2007; DEE, 2012; IEA, 2008; USEPA, 2018; VEPA, 2018). With the introduction of the carbon tax in 2012, SWDS began charging higher fees for waste to landfill, and such costs added to the commercial imperative to reduce solid waste.

Ten of the 12 MASS organizations had sophisticated solid waste recycling systems that enabled them to reduce their solid waste, and thus their contribution to landfill gas/GHG emissions. One-third of MASS cases reported using a Closed Loop Recycling system where recyclable material is eliminated from disposal at SWDS. MASS organizations divert recyclable materials from landfill through recycling processes including metal and plastic drink containers, and all paper and cardboard waste.

Managerial agency

However, across all four climate change issues, the personal agency of middle-to-senior-level managers in adaptive responses was noteworthy. Managers at five of the 12 MASS cases were individually responsible for initiating water, energy and waste management processes that were reported as climate change responses. Examples of this managerial agency include: advocating for organizational consideration of climate change; developing a climate change adaptation strategy; researching and proposing a water treatment strategy; hiring energy consultants and; proposing a green ticketing system. Motivating such initiatives were concern for "doing the right thing" by the environment and society, although having a "business case" that led to lower costs was crucial to winning approval from senior management. A summary of the key climate change issues for MASS, and MASS organizations, is presented in Table 3.

Discussion

The results of this study point to a multifaceted picture of climate change issues and responses for MASS organizations. We found that all MASS cases – regardless of their ownership structure – interpreted climate change as a cost issue for water and energy resources, and waste outputs. Some additional management complexity was evident, but the key concern was higher operational and capital costs associated with these issues. These issues were consistently evident regardless of the organizational size, ownership structure, or fundamental purpose. Water, energy and waste management strategies were therefore key responses.

How organizations respond to climate change begins with how they interpret it. It has been argued that organizational responses to climate change are shaped by how its impact on their core business is perceived (Kolk & Pinkse, 2012; Porter & Reinhardt, 2007), and by management uncertainty about the external market and policy environments (Lee & Klassen, 2015). Consistent with these studies, MASS organizations perceived the physical impacts to the stadiums from climate change as risks to their core product: sport event management. However, these impacts were generally interpreted as manageable within existing management resources, capabilities and strategies. These organizations were also uncertain about the longer-term government climate policy. One study has also concluded that organizational responses are shaped by whether opportunities or risks are perceived in climate change (Kolk & Pinkse, 2005). For MASS organizations, most saw risks, especially commercial ones.

Media reportage, especially in television and newspapers, was the primary influence on how MASS organizations understood climate change, especially their view that it was a cost issue. This cost-centric interpretation of climate change is consistent with much of the business media reportage in Australia that

Table 3. Climate change issues for MASS, and MASS organizations.

Climate change issue	Cases and categories showing strong evidence	Illustrative quotes
Uncertainty about longer-term climate change policy.	Cases A, B, C, D, E, F, G, H, I, J, K and L. All theoretical categories.	Well the uncertainty it causes me particularly is that we can't develop a strong strategic plan unless the government does so ... [Interviewer]: So there's a policy uncertainty? Correct. There's a bit of a wait for us and the thing that I'm fearful of with us is while you've got this hiatus of [government] people trying to make up their mind how they're going to deal with the climate change, this organization could actually say well we don't think is an issue anymore (E1, p. 9).
Water	All cases. All theoretical categories.	The thing that we notice more than anything else with turf and some of those things on the ground is the level of evaporation we have. The humidity is much lower than what it was, we've got drying days here that, and it's something, it's a subject that never gets talked about in terms of environmental change. People talk about °C increase and some of those things, but the air is much dryer ... We're putting more water on than what we ever have in terms of that because the evaporation levels are so high (E1, p. 9). Well it is in the product of climate change so for example in ... , we had a drought here last year and so there have been restrictions placed on local authorities relating to water management and so the good old days of just turning on the sprinkler and everything getting green are rapidly becoming a thing of the past (B1, p. 1). As it gets drier we need to water more, as we water more it increases the costs and it's not just a standard. As it's getting hotter, we have to water more (H1, P. 2) Yeah, our water bills are pretty high. Within the region we were considered an extremely high user. I think we were number two behind [company] only. So we were using somewhere around 20 mega litres a year on the field itself, just the field. All said and done, I think we were using about 50 mega litres a year. By taking the field offline we're down to 30 mega litres per year. So we've saved a massive amount of water just from that (J1, p. 5).
Energy	All cases. All theoretical categories.	I guess our organization sees climate change as important. Probably not of critical importance, but certainly elements of climate change as I mentioned before, the water initiatives and moving forward toward energy initiatives, we've recognized that they are important elements, issues that the organization needs to address and consider (A1, p. 1). Absolutely, as I say we report, we're over 25,000 tonnes [of GHG emissions] so that puts us in I think one of the top 700 or 800 contributors in the country (E1, p. 14). [E1]: At $20 a tonne, [a carbon price] would cost us about $600,000 a year. [Interviewer]: So that's $20 a tonne of CO_2 ... [E1]: If we wanted to then be ... if we wanted to be carbon neutral, or I shouldn't ... not carbon neutral. If we wanted to offset 100 per cent, that's what our cost would be (E1, pp. 10-11). We introduced [mobile] lighting rigs at the venue, the first to do it within Australia. Those lighting rigs use around $120,000 worth of power a year and we didn't want to be perceived as an organization that was having lights on 24 hours a day to stimulate grass growth without offsetting that grass growth with a green energy provider. So we use a green energy provider (F1, p. 1).
Waste	Cases A, B, D, E, H, I, J, K & L. All theoretical categories.	Our things that we've looked at in regards to mitigating any emissions are reducing waste. So obviously with the recycling programmes and separating glass, cardboard and bulk recycling from waste which has been, I mean we were looking at moving around 40 cubic metres of just general waste beforehand, that's what we'd do after every AFL game. Now we move about 35 cubic metres of recycling in general and about 10m of rubbish or general waste. So that's probably where we're looking at mitigating greenhouse gas emissions (J1, p. 11). Waste management again is a big part of reducing that carbon footprint (H1, p. 5)

focuses on financial costs, rather than revenue opportunities. It also is consistent with management research that confirms that media interpretations of climate change shape corporate understandings of climate change (Hertin et al., 2003), and corporate responses more generally (Bansal, 2005; Bansal & Clelland, 2004; Henriques & Sadorsky, 1996). Our finding is significant because it demonstrates that the media's influence on how organizations interpret climate change is wider than previously thought: it now extends to SME's and large organizations in the sport industry.

The link drawn by MASS organizations between climate change and water issues is also consistent with scientific work on climate change impacts in Australia (CSIRO & BoM, 2015; Reisinger et al., 2014). This link is explained by three factors: (1) their experience with the 12-year "Millennium Drought", Australia's longest and most severe in 110 years of meteorological records (Timbal, 2009); (2) state government regulatory responses to the resulting water scarcity requiring water efficiency and reporting for large water users and; (3) higher water costs associated with such scarcity. Given the role of media coverage of climate change in shaping their corporate perceptions of this phenomenon, this link was likely reinforced by extensive media coverage of water scarcity during this period.

Together, these factors were the drivers of the most comprehensive of the adaptive responses by MASS organizations: major investment in water management infrastructure. The investment of millions of dollars in water harvesting, storage, efficiency, treatment and recycling reflects a sector-wide pattern of adaptation to Australia's hotter and mostly drier climate, and its emergent regulatory framework for water resources. All three factors are consistent with existing literature that argues adaptation to water scarcity is a key climate change issue, and that organizational adaptive responses are strongly influenced by market and regulatory contexts (Arnell, van Vuuren, & Isaac, 2011; Berkhout et al., 2006; Charlton & Arnell, 2011). Understanding water scarcity as a climate change issue is significant because it establishes that water-intensive and climate-dependent sport is vulnerable in the longer term (Kellett & Turner, 2009, 2011; WADSR, 2007). It also confirms the importance of earlier studies of adaptive responses in sport (Rutty, Scott, Steiger, & Johnson, 2014; Scott & McBoyle, 2007).

Equally, the linking of climate change and energy issues by MASS organizations is a significant finding of this study for three reasons. First, the dependence of MASS on carbon-intensive Australian electricity suppliers establishes that they have a significant, although indirect, relationship with GHG emissions. The extent of this carbon footprint is illustrated by Cases A and E – whose largely indirect emissions use were smaller than large non-sport facilities such as oil refineries, coal mines, airlines and waste disposal sites – but were still sufficient to meet the reporting thresholds of the NGER legislation. Second, the climate-energy issues relationship establishes the primacy of costs, the absence of revenue opportunities, and confirms the secondary importance of GHG emissions for such organizations. Understanding this important managerial equation offers insight into the drivers of adaptive behaviours in service-based sectors of society. Thirdly, the climate-energy issues relationship establishes the sensitivity of such service-based organizations to carbon pricing. Although the change in carbon pricing legislation in 2014 reduced the cost impact of carbon pricing for MASS organizations, the results suggest that it is a new dimension for the management of operating costs for these sport industry organizations.

The link between climate change and waste issues made by MASS organizations is another significant finding of this study for different reasons. First, we have established a link between solid waste that accrues at MASS, its disposal and landfill waste GHG emissions. Second, we have established that the overwhelming majority of MASS organizations understand this relationship. Third, it is now clear that MASS organizations use their existing solid waste recycling processes to manage indirect GHG emissions from their solid waste, and to adapt to higher costs associated with carbon pricing. This study, therefore, extends existing studies that have addressed waste issues in sport, but not GHG impacts.

However, for water, energy and waste issues, the agency of senior-to-middle-level managers in adaptive responses was crucial. The internal advocacy of these managers for strategies to address climate change issues was consistent with research focused on small business (Williams & Schaefer, 2013), and other studies documenting the key role of managers in environmentally responsible management (Bansal & Roth, 2000; Winn, 1995).

MASS organizations and adaptation to climate change

Recent advances in adaptation literature offer deeper insights into these responses by MASS organizations. (2012). Berkhout's (2012) analysis of earlier adaptation literature revealed five possibilities that can all be seen as part of "deeper" organizational strategy that focuses on risk. (1) "Do nothing"/"wait and see" – a deferral strategy based on scepticism or uncertainty about the possible climate change impacts and benefits of adaptation. (2) "Assess" risk/"risk assessment and options appraisal" – a strategy of appraising options to prepare for adaptation of organizational routines. (3) "Reduce" risk/"bearing and managing risks" – a strategy for managing risks and opportunities arising from climate impacts using organizational resources and capabilities. (4) "Share" risk/"sharing and shifting risks" – externalizing climate change risks through insurance and collaboration. (5) "Diversify risk" (Berkhout, 2012). A summary of these adaptation strategies and their application to MASS organizations is presented in Table 4.

Responses to climate change by MASS organizations fall into three of the five types identified in Berkhout's (2012) typology, and are shaped by 10 factors. The three responses are: (1) do nothing (wait and see/business as usual); (2) adaptation/assess risk, and; (3) adaptation/reduce risk. The 10 factors shaping these organizational responses divide into seven internal and three external. The 10 factors are summarized in Table 5.

Only one MASS organization (Case G) adopted a "do nothing"/"wait and see" strategy. Case G had essentially no awareness of the actual or potential impacts of climate change on their organization or their stadium, direct and indirect, and showed little interest in the potential for strategic, commercial or technological adaptation. A lack of organizational resources was the key factor underlying this attitude.

For 10 of the 12 MASS cases, "reduce" risk/"bearing and managing risks" best describes their adaptive response. These 10 cases spanned all theoretical categories. To the extent that they adapted explicitly to climate change, they did so cautiously and within existing non-climate change-specific strategic plans. Translated into Berkhout's (2012) terms, these cases *reduce* risk by applying and adjusting existing commercial and environmental strategies. This finding is significant because it establishes for the first time that this climate-dependent and water and an energy-intensive segment of the sport sector is responding in ways that are similar to non-sport industrial sectors elsewhere in the world.

Table 4. Responses by MASS organizations expressed in Berkhout et al's (2006) and Berkhout's (2012) terms.

Adaptation strategies		
Berkhout (2012)	Berkhout et al. (2006)	MASS cases
Do nothing	Wait and see	G
Assess [risk]	Risk assessment and options appraisal	B, E and J
Reduce risk	Bearing and managing risks	A, B, C, D, E, F, H, I, J, K and L
Share risk	Sharing and shifting risks	Nil
Diversify		Nil

Table 5. Ten factors shaping organizational responses to climate change at Major Australian Sport Stadia.

Types of factors	Factors
External factors (climate change issues)	1. Physical impacts (hotter, drier climate, water evaporation) 2. Market changes (increased supplier costs in business-to-business segment) 3. Stakeholder [external]: • Government legislation [GHG emissions reporting (e.g. NGER Act) and Emissions pricing (e.g. Carbon Tax/ETS)] • Government legislation (water and energy efficiency) • Attitudes to CC of sport governing bodies and commercial partners
Internal factors (MASS organizations)	1. Energy use: • Big users, carbon intensive • Basis for GHG mitigation 2. Climate Change Sensemaking (interpretation): • Media as key influence shaping climate change interpretations • Uncertainty • Climate change perceived as cost issue • Outside-in over inside-out (CC as secondary issue) Waste as GHG issue 3. Resources (water, manufactured, financial, staff capabilities) 4. Stakeholders [internal]: • Managerial *agency* of staff 5. Corporate Social Responsibility (CSR) ethos: • Genuine commitment 6. Vulnerability and resilience to climate change 7. Barriers to climate change responses (money and uncertainty)

However, for 3 of these 11 cases (B, E and J), cautious water, energy, waste and cost management responses to climate change indicate they were moving beyond merely "bearing and managing risk" to undertaking "assess" risk/"risk assessment and options appraisal". This response spanned Theoretical Categories 1 and 2 but not the privately owned cases in Category 3. Case B did not have an integrated climate change plan, but their sustainability assessment, energy monitoring and climate change adaptation strategy revealed their concerns about climate change. Similarly, while Case J – the largest of all MASS organizations – did not have an integrated climate change plan, after the prolonged "Millennium Drought" of the late 1990s to mid-2000s, they consciously adapted their water, energy and turf management practices to work in a hotter, drier climate where higher water, energy and turf risks were significant concerns.

Case E also appeared to be actively *assessing* the risks posed by climate change and its associated regulatory and market changes, and *appraising* strategic options. This is reflected in their clear understanding of climate change – the most sophisticated of all MASS organizations – and its associated regulatory impact on energy use, GHG emissions reporting, carbon liability and their operating costs. Their significant investment in water management and energy efficiency occurred after extensive analysis of the direct and indirect climate change risks, and the preparation of a detailed business case that was later approved by senior management. Notably, Case E's *certainty* about climate change as a long-term management issue shaped their attitude to GHG mitigation, and facilitated their understanding of climate policy and its cost implications for their organization. This contrasts with the *uncertainty* about climate change of most of their peers in the stadia industry who prioritized reduction of energy-related costs over the mitigation of GHG emissions. These contrasting attitudes are consistent with Lee and Klassen's (2015) argument that management uncertainty about climate change shapes the adoption of carbon-specific mitigation practices.

Despite the insights afforded by the Berkhout (2012) and Berkhout et al. (2006) typologies, there is nothing in the actions of MASS organizations that is consistent with either of the "share risks"/"sharing and shifting risks", or with the "diversify" risks adaptation strategies. For them, it was inconceivable that they could share either direct or indirect climate change risks with their commercial or government partners, or diversify risk through their insurers. This finding is significant because it establishes for the first time a clear difference with non-sport industrial organizations who are either more aware, or more willing, to adapt in these ways.

Berkhout (2012, p. 92) noted that to understand what climate change means for organizations, analysis needs to start with the, "complex" reality of organizations themselves, rather than starting with the "climate signal" and then seeking to trace its presumed influence on organizational behaviour. The analysis needs to be done inside-out, rather than outside-in. For MASS organizations, their adaptations were a function of a complex interplay between multiple internal and external factors. That is, their adaptations are not explained solely by "direct signals" of climate change to adapt (Berkhout et al., 2006, p. 146) such as extended drought, higher temperatures and evaporation. As Berkhout (2012, p. 101) noted, organizations respond to "many stimuli, with climate risk and opportunity being but one". This was true for this industry: climate change was a priority, but it was only one of a range of issues to be managed, and so their adaptations typically occurred without climate change-specific strategies. A lack of financial resources at MASS organizations, and climate change-specific management capabilities, were the main barriers to having such strategies.

The influence of "indirect signals" like regulatory change, market change and an industry trend toward "greener" technologies coupled with internal factors including strategic goals, culture and managerial agency, illustrate a less "simple stimulus-response relationship" (Berkhout, 2012, p. 94) to climate change. Yet they also point to "incremental" (Pelling, 2011) adjustments for most MASS organizations rather than "transformational" changes that address the fundamental causes of climate change vulnerability (Agard et al., 2014; Eriksen, Nightingale, & Eakinc, 2015).

Finally, the scale and capabilities of these organizations must be factored into the interpretation of the mostly cautious nature of their adaptive responses. Eleven of the 12 organizations were SME's. All had relatively flat management structures, constrained financial resources and little or no formal education about climate change, or potential adaptive responses such as carbon management. Unlike large businesses, such as banks, insurance companies and airlines, they did not have the resources or capabilities to develop climate-specific strategic plans. This situation is typical of SME's who have "a tendency towards short-term planning" in relation to climate change (Halkos & Skouloudis, 2016, p. 3; Williams & Schaefer, 2013). This is significant because it suggests sport-industry SME's, as in other industries, would benefit from climate change-specific adaptation strategies.

Conclusion and implications for sport management

In this paper, we have argued that the phenomenon of climate change presents some strategic issues for the organizations that manage major Australian sport stadia. These issues are in the form of some physical impacts on the climate-dependent playing surfaces, and the water resources, of these stadia. However, the major issues are in the form of secondary impacts that flow from the climate change problem. These secondary impacts comprise a complex web of public policy, legislative and market responses to climate change that pose commercial risks in the form of higher operating costs for their water and energy resources, and waste outputs. Despite the climate-dependence of the grass playing surfaces of these stadia, major disruptions due to extreme whether events – of the kind experienced in other climate-dependent industries – were perceived to be manageable within existing resources and strategies. The stadia playing surfaces and buildings, therefore, have considerable resilience to the direct physical impacts of climate change due to their design and infrastructure resources. Mitigation of GHG emissions is a second-order priority relative to operational and commercial imperatives.

Adaptation is occurring at most MASS organizations, albeit in ways constrained by their scale and available resources. Whilst doing nothing about these risks is an option for these organizations, most choose to actively manage their climate change risks, while a minority go further and evaluate their strategic options. The organizational responses occurred despite their uncertainty about long-term public policy for climate change, and in the absence of climate change-specific plans. A lack of financial resources, and climate change management capabilities, were key barriers to having climate change-specific strategies. The findings of this paper suggest that climate change poses strategic issues for MASS organizations, and this challenges assumptions in the sport management discipline about the implications of climate change for sport organizations. Specifically, if climate change impacts and adaptation are occurring in the Australian stadia industry, is this happening in other national contexts?

Australia, as a nation that is among the worlds' most exposed and sensitive to climate change, but with a well-established and sophisticated sport stadia industry, was an ideal site for this study. And yet, a limitation of this research is that our findings are based on a single national context. We therefore conclude with some suggestions for future management research. First, the evidence of this study suggests that the impacts of climate change – both direct and indirect – on climate-dependent facilities and the organizations that manage them, are more widespread and complex than previously thought.

So we argue that business researchers should extend the scope of climate change vulnerability, resilience and adaptation inquiry to include other climate-dependent areas of the sport sector (e.g. professional sport staged outside of stadia, and community-level sport). Second, a pressing need for the organizations managing climate-dependent sport stadia is conceptual frameworks for preparing adaptation strategies that are both sport and climate change-specific, and practical tools for implementing them. Finally, as MASS organizations typically did not have the resources or capabilities to develop such strategies, further research is needed on how sport organizations with climate-dependent facilities might include climate change in their strategic thinking. Research is needed in other national contexts, particularly in the northern hemisphere where most of the world's major sport stadia are located, and where different public policy and regulatory responses to climate change apply. This inquiry is important because the interpretation of climate risks by sport managers is fundamental to informing effective adaptive responses.

Disclosure statement

No potential conflict of interest was reported by the authors.

References

AASS. (2016). *Thirty-one top scientific societies speak with one voice on global climate change*. Retrieved from https://www.aaas.org/news/intersocietyclimateletter2016

AEMO. (2018). *Fact sheet: National electricity market*. Retrieved from http://www.aemo.com.au/About-the-Industry/Energy-Markets/National-Electricity-Market

Agard, J. E., Schipper, L. F., Birkmann, J., Campos, M., Dubeux, C., Nojiri, Y., … Clair, A. L. S. (2014). *Annex II glossary, climate change 2014: Impacts, adaptation, and vulnerability. Contribution of Working Group III to the Fifth Assessment Report of the Intergovernmental Panel on Climate Change*. Cambridge, UK

Ahlfeldt, G., & Maennig, W. (2010). Stadium architecture and urban development from the perspective of urban economics. *International Journal of Urban and Regional Research*, *34*(3), 629–646.

Amelung, B., & Moreno, A. (2012). Costing the impact of climate change on tourism in Europe: Results of the PESETA project. *Climatic Change*, *112*(1), 83–100.

Andrew, D. P. S., Pedersen, P. M., & McEvoy, C. D. (2011). *Research methods and design in sport management*. Champaign, IL: Human Kinetics.

Arnell, N. W., & Delaney, E. K. (2006). Adapting to climate change: Public water supply in England and Wales. *Climatic Change*, *78*(2–4), 227–255.

Arnell, N. W., van Vuuren, D. P., & Isaac, M. (2011). The implications of climate policy for the impacts of climate change on global water resources. *Global Environmental Change*, *21*(2), 592–603.

Babiak, K., & Trendafilova, S. (2011). CSR and environmental responsibility: Motives and pressures to adopt green management practices. *Corporate Social Responsibility and Environmental Management*, *18*(1), 11–24.

Bansal, P. (2005). Evolving sustainably: A longitudinal study of corporate sustainable development. *Strategic Management Journal*, *26*(3), 197–218.

Bansal, P., & Clelland, I. (2004). Talking trash: Legitimacy, impression management, and unsystematic risk in the context of the natural environment. *Academy of Management Journal*, *47*(1), 93–103.

Bansal, P., & Roth, K. (2000). Why companies go green: A model of ecological responsiveness. *Academy of Management Journal*, *43*(4), 717–736.

Bazeley, P. (2007). *Qualitative data analysis with NVivo*. Los Angeles, CA: Sage.

Beermann, M. (2011). Linking corporate climate adaptation strategies with resilience thinking. *Journal of Cleaner Production*, *19*(8), 836–842.

Berkhout, F. (2012). Adaptation to climate change by organizations. *Wiley Interdisciplinary Reviews: Climate Change*, *3*(1), 91–106.

Berkhout, F. (2014). Adaptation to climate change by business organisations. In J. P. Palutikof, S. L. Boulter, J. Barnett, & D. Rissik (Eds.), *Applied studies in climate adaptation* (pp. 417–421). New York: John Wiley & Sons.

Berkhout, F., Hertin, J., & Gann, D. M. (2006). Learning to adapt: Organisational adaptation to climate change impacts. *Climatic Change*, *78*(1), 135–156.

Biagini, B., Bierbaum, R., Stults, M., Dobardzic, S., & McNeeley, S. M. (2014). A typology of adaptation actions: A global look at climate adaptation actions financed through the global environment facility. *Global Environmental Change*, *25*, 97–108.

BoM. (2018). *Bureau of meteorology climate zones*. Retrieved from http://www.bom.gov.au/iwk/climate_zones/map_2.shtml

BoM, & CSIRO. (2017). *State of the climate 2016*. Collingwood. Retrieved from http://www.bom.gov.au/state-of-the-climate/

Chard, C., & Mallen, C. (2012). Examining the linkages between automobile use and carbon impacts of community-based ice hockey. *Sport Management Review*, *15*(4), 476–484.

Chard, C., & Mallen, C. (2013). Renewable energy initiatives at Canadian sport stadiums: A content analysis of web-site communications. *Sustainability*, *5*(12), 5119–5134.

Charlton, M. B., & Arnell, N. W. (2011). Adapting to climate change impacts on water resources in England – an assessment of draft water resources management plans. *Global Environmental Change*, *21*(1), 238–248.

Collignon, H., & Sultan, N. (2014). *Winning in the business of sports*. Chicago, IL. Retrieved from https://www.atkearney.com/documents/10192/5258876/Winning+in+the+Business+of+Sports.pdf/ed85b644-7633-469d-8f7a-99e4a50aadc8

Coyne, I. T. (1997). Sampling in qualitative research. Purposeful and theoretical sampling; merging or clear boundaries? *Journal of Advanced Nursing*, *26*(3), 623–630.

Cresswell, J. W. (2009). *Research design: Qualitative, quantitative and mixed method approaches* (3rd ed.). Thousand Oaks, CA: Sage.

CSIRO. (2009). *The science of tackling climate change*. (p. 32). Retrieved from http://www.csiro.au/files/files/psvk.pdf

CSIRO, & BoM. (2015). *Climate change in Australia. Information for Australia's natural resource management regions: technical report*. Canberra, AUS.

DCCEE. (2007). *National greenhouse accounts: National inventory report 2007*. Retrieved from http://www.climatechange.gov.au/publications/greenhouse-acctg/~/media/publications/greenhouse-acctg/national-inventory-report-vol-2-part-h.ashx

DEE. (2012). *Waste emissions projections*. Retrieved from http://www.climatechange.gov.au/publications/projections/australias-emissions-projections/waste-emissions.aspx#solidwaste

Dolf, M., & Teehan, P. (2015). Reducing the carbon footprint of spectator and team travel at the University of British Columbia's varsity sports events. *Sport Management Review*, *18*(2), 244–255.

Dolles, H., & Soderman, S. (2010). Addressing ecology and sustainability in mega-sporting events: The 2006 Football World Cup in Germany. *Journal of Management and Organization*, *16*(2), 603–616.

Dow, K., Berkhout, F., Preston, B. L., Klein, R. J. T., Midgley, G., & Shaw, M. R. (2013). Limits to adaptation. *Nature Climate Change, 3*(4), 305–307.

Edwards, A., & Skinner, J. (2009). *Qualitative research in sport management*. Oxford: Butterworth-Heinnemann/Elsevier.

Eisenhardt, K. M. (1989). Building theories from case study research. *Academy of Management Review, 14*(4), 532–550.

Eriksen, S. H., Nightingale, A. J., & Eakinc, H. (2015). Reframing adaptation: The political nature of climate change adaptation. *Global Environmental Change, 35*, 523–533.

European Commission. (2018). *What is an SME?* Retrieved from http://ec.europa.eu/growth/smes/business-friendly-environment/sme-definition_en

Feddersen, A., Grötzinger, A. L., & Maennig, W. (2009). Investment in stadia and regional economic development: Evidence from FIFA World Cup 2006. *International Journal of Sport Finance, 4*(4), 221–239.

Füssel, H.-M. (2007a). Adaptation planning for climate change: Concepts, assessment approaches and key lessons. *Sustainability Science, 2*(2), 265–275.

Füssel, H.-M. (2007b). Vulnerability: A generally applicable conceptual framework for climate change research. *Global Environmental Change, 17*(2), 155–167.

Gasbarro, F., Rizzi, F., & Frey, M. (2016). Adaptation measures of energy and utility companies to cope with water scarcity induced by climate change. *Business Strategy and the Environment, 25*(1), 54–72.

Gössling, S., & Upham, P. (Eds.). (2009). *Climate change and aviation: Issues, challenges and solutions*. Sterling, VA: Earthscan.

Haigh, N. L., & Griffiths, A. (2012). Surprise as a catalyst for including climatic change in the strategic environment. *Business & Society, 51*(1), 89–120.

Halkos, G., & Skouloudis, A. (2016). *Bouncing back from extreme weather events: some preliminary findings on resilience barriers facing small and medium-sized enterprises*. Munich Personal RePEc Archive (December, Paper No. 75562).

Hall, J. W., Berkhout, F., & Douglas, R. (2015). Responding to adaptation emergencies. *Nature Climate Change, 5*(1), 6–7.

Hennessy, K. (2011). Climate change impacts. In H. Cleugh, M. Stafford Smith, M. Battaglia, & P. Graham (Eds.), *Climate change: Science and solutions for Australia* (pp. 45–57). Collingwood: CSIRO.

Henriques, I., & Sadorsky, P. (1996). The determinants of an environmentally responsive firm: An empirical approach. *Journal of Environmental Economics and Management, 30*(3), 381–395.

Hertin, J., Berkhout, F., Gann, D. M., & Barlow, J. (2003). Climate change and the UK house building sector: Perceptions, impacts and adaptive capacity. *Building Research & Information, 31*(3–4), 278–290.

Hoffman, A. J. (2005). Climate change strategy: The business logic behind voluntary greenhouse gas reductions. *California Management Review, 47*(3), 21–46.

Horne, J. (2011). Architects, stadia and sport spectacles: Notes on the role of architects in the building of sport stadia and making of world-class cities. *International Review for the Sociology of Sport, 46*(2), 205–227.

Hoye, R., Smith, A. C. T., Nicholson, M., & Stewart, B. (2015). *Sport management: Principles and applications*. London: Routledge.

Hulme, M. (2009). *Why we disagree about climate change: Understanding controversy, inaction and opportunity*. Cambridge: Cambridge University Press.

IEA. (2008). *Turning a liability into an asset: landfill methane utilisation potential in India*. Paris, France. Retrieved from http://www.iea.org/publications/freepublications/publication/India_methane.pdf

IPCC. (2014a). *Climate change 2013: The physical science basis*. Retrieved from http://www.climatechange2013.org/

IPCC. (2014b). *Climate change 2014: Synthesis report. Approved summary for policymakers*. Geneva, Switzerland.

IPCC. (2014c). *Climate change 2014: Synthesis report. Contribution of working groups I, II and III to the fifth assessment report of the intergovernmental panel on climate change*. Geneva, Switzerland.

Kellett, P., & Turner, P. (2009). *Managing sport in drought-new stakeholders and new governance issues: A case study*. Paper presented at the NASSAM 2009: North American society for sport management conference, Columbia, South Carolina.

Kellett, P., & Turner, P. (2011). CSR and water management in the sport sector: A research agenda. *International Journal of Sport Management & Marketing, 10*(1/2), 142–160.

Kiem, A. S., & Austin, E. (2013). Drought and the future of rural communities: Opportunities and challenges for climate change adaptation in regional Victoria, Australia. *Global Environmental Change, 23*, 1307–1316.

Kikulis, L. M., Slack, T., & Hinings, B. (1995). Does decision making make a difference? Patterns of change within Canadian national sport organizations. *Journal of Sport Management, 9*(3), 273–299.

Kolk, A., & Hoffman, V. (2007). Business, climate change and emissions trading. *European Management Journal, 25*(6), 411–414.

Kolk, A., & Levy, D. (2004). Multinationals and global climate change: Issues for the automotive and oil industries. In S. Lundan (Ed.), *Multinationals, environment and global competition* (pp. 171–193). Oxford: Elsevier.

Kolk, A., & Pinkse, J. (2005). Business responses to climate change: Identifying emergent strategies. *California Management Review, 47*(3), 6–20.

Kolk, A., & Pinkse, J. (2012). Multinational enterprises and climate change strategies. In A. Verbeke & H. Merchant (Eds.), *Handbook of research on international strategic management* (pp. 1–16). Cheltenham: Edward Elgar.

Lee, S. Y., & Klassen, R. D. (2015). Firms' response to climate change: the interplay of business uncertainty and organizational capabilities. *Business Strategy and the Environment, 25*(8), 577–592.

Lewandowsky, S., Oreskes, N., Risbey, J. S., Newell, B. R., & Smithson, M. (2015). Seepage: Climate change denial and its effect on the scientific community. *Global Environmental Change, 33,* 1–13.

Linnenluecke, M. K., & Griffiths, A. (2010). Beyond adaptation: Resilience for business in light of climate change and weather extremes. *Business & Society, 49*(3), 477–511.

Linnenluecke, M. K., & Griffiths, A. (2012). Assessing organizational resilience to climate and weather extremes: Complexities and methodological pathways. *Climatic Change, 113*(3-4), 933–947.

Linnenluecke, M. K., & Griffiths, A. (2013). Firms and sustainability: Mapping the intellectual origins and structure of the corporate sustainability field. *Global Environmental Change, 23*(1), 382–391.

Linnenluecke, M. K., Griffiths, A., & Mumby, P. (2015). Executives' engagement with climate science and perceived need for business adaptation to climate change. *Climatic Change, 131*(2), 321–333.

Linnenluecke, M. K., Griffiths, A., & Winn, M. I. (2011). Extreme weather events and the critical importance of anticipatory adaptation and organizational resilience in responding to impacts. *Business Strategy and the Environment, 21*(1), 123–133.

Linnenluecke, M. K., Griffiths, A., & Winn, M. I. (2013). Firm and industry adaptation to climate change: A review of climate adaptation studies in the business and management field. *Wiley Interdisciplinary Reviews: Climate Change, 4*(5), 397–416.

Linnenluecke, M. K., Stathakis, A., & Griffiths, A. (2011). Firm relocation as adaptive response to climate change and weather extremes. *Global Environmental Change, 21*(1), 123–133.

Mallen, C., & Chard, C. (2012). "What could be" in Canadian sport facility environmental sustainability. *Sport Management Review, 15*(2), 230–243.

Mastrandrea, M. D., & Schneider, S. H. (2010). Climate change science overview. In S. H. Schneider, A. Rosencranz, M. D. Mastrandrea, & K. Kuntz-Duriseti (Eds.), *Climate change science and policy* (pp. 11–27). Washington: Island Press.

McDonald, K., Stewart, B., & Dingle, G. (2014). Managing multi-purpose leisure facilities in a time of climate change. *Managing Leisure, 19*(3), 212–225.

Merigó, J. M., & Gil-Lafuente, A. M. (2011). Decision-making in sport management based on the OWA operator. *Expert Systems with Applications, 38*(8), 10408–10413.

Miles, M., Huberman, A. M., & Saldana, J. (2014). *Qualitative data analysis: A methods sourcebook.* Thousand Oaks, CA: Sage.

Miller, T., Lawrence, G., McKay, J., & Rowe, D. (2001). *Globalisation and sport: Playing the world.* London: Sage.

M.O. (2018). *What is climate change?* Retrieved from http://www.metoffice.gov.uk/climate-guide/climate-change

Moen, J., & Fredman, P. (2007). Effects of climate change on alpine skiing in Sweden. *Journal of Sustainable Tourism, 15*(4), 418–437.

National Greenhouse and Energy Reporting Act 2007, 175 Stat. 60 (Commonwealth of Australia 2007 September 16 2008).

Nicholson, M., Kerr, A., & Sherwood, M. (2015). *Sport and the media* (2nd ed.). Oxford: Taylor & Francis.

Otto, I., & Heath, E. T. (2010). The potential contribution of the 2010 Soccer World Cup to climate change: An exploratory study among tourism industry stakeholders in the Tshwane metropole of South Africa. *Journal of Sport & Tourism, 14*(2-3), 169–191.

Packard, K. O., & Reinhardt, F. (2000). What every executive needs to know about global warming. *Harvard Business Review, 78*(4), 129–135.

Patenaude, G. (2011). Climate change diffusion: While the world tips, business schools lag. *Global Environmental Change, 21*(1), 259–271.

Pelling, M. (2011). *Adaptation to climate change: From resilience to transformation.* London: Routledge.

Pinkse, J., & Gasbarro, F. (2016). Managing physical impacts of climate change: An attentional perspective on corporate adaptation. *Business & Society.* doi:10.1177/0007650316648688

Pinkse, J., & Kolk, A. (2007). Multinational corporations and emissions trading: Strategic responses to new institutional constraints. *European Management Journal, 25*(6), 441–452.

Porter, M. E., & Reinhardt, F. L. (2007). A strategic approach to climate. *Harvard Business Review*, 85(10), 22–26.

QLDG. (2001). *Major sport facilties Act 2001*. Brisbane: Queensland Government. Retrieved from http://www.legislation.qld.gov.au/LEGISLTN/CURRENT/M/MajorSpFacA01.pdf

Real, M. R. (1996). The postmodern Olympics: Technology and the commodification of the Olympic movement. *Quest (grand Rapids, Mich)*, 48, 9–24.

Reisinger, A., Kitching, R. L., Chiew, F., Hughes, L., Newton, P. C. D., Schuster, S. S., … Whetton, P. (2014). Australasia. In V. R. Barros, C. B. Field, D. J. Dokken, M. D. Mastrandrea, K. J. Mach, T. E. Bilir, … L. L. White (Eds.), *Climate change 2014: Impacts, adaptation, and vulnerability. Part B: Regional aspects. Contribution of working group II to the fifth assessment report of the intergovernmental panel on climate change* (pp. 1371–1438). Cambridge: Cambridge University Press.

Rickards, L. (2012). *Critical breaking point: The effects of climate variability, climate change and other pressures on farm households*. A report for Birchip Cropping Group and Sustainable Agriculture Initiative Platform Australia.

Rutty, M., Scott, D., Steiger, R., & Johnson, P. (2014). Weather risk management at the Olympic Winter Games. *Current Issues in Tourism*, 18(10), 931–946.

Sandelowski, M., Holditch-Davis, D., & Harris, B. G. (1992). Using qualitative and quantitative methods: The transition to parent-hood of infertile couples. In J. F. Gilgun, K. Daly, & G. Handel (Eds.), *Qualitative methods in family research* (pp. 301–323). Newbury Park, CA: Sage.

Sarantakos, S. (2013). *Social research*. (4th ed.). Hampshire: Palgrave MacMillan.

Scott, D., Gössling, S., & Hall, C. M. (2012). International tourism and climate change. *Wiley Interdisciplinary Reviews: Climate Change*, 3(3), 213–232.

Scott, D., & Jones, B. (2006). The impact of climate change on golf participation in the Greater Toronto Area (GTA): a case study. *Journal of Leisure Research*, 38(3), 363–380.

Scott, D., & Jones, B. (2007). A regional comparison of the implications of climate change for the Golf industry in Canada. *The Canadian Geographer/Le Géographe Canadien*, 51(2), 219–232.

Scott, D., & McBoyle, G. (2007). Climate change adaptation in the Ski industry. *Mitigation and Adaptation Strategies for Global Change*, 12(8), 1411–1431.

Scott, D., Steiger, R., Rutty, M., & Johnson, P. (2015). The future of the Olympic Winter Games in an era of climate change. *Current Issues in Tourism*, 18(10), 913–930.

Smit, B., & Wandel, J. (2006). Adaptation, adaptive capacity and vulnerability. *Global Environmental Change*, 16(3), 282–292.

Stadium. (2017). In J. Simpson (Ed.), *Oxford English dictionary*. Oxford: Oxford University Press.

Steffen, W., & Hughes, L. (2013). *The critical decade 2013: Climate change science, risks and responses*. Canberra, Aust.

Steffen, W., Richardson, K., Rockström, J., Cornell, S. E., Fetzer, I., Bennett, E. M., … Sörlin, S. (2015). Planetary boundaries: Guiding human development on a changing planet. *Science*, 347(6223), 736–748.

Timbal, B. (2009). *The continuing decline in South-East Australian rainfall: Update to May 2009*. Hobart, Aust.

Trendafilova, S., Babiak, K., & Heinze, K. (2013). Corporate social responsibility and environmental sustainability: Why professional sport is greening the playing field. *Sport Management Review*, 16(3), 298–313.

UNEP. (2018). *Impact of sport on the environment*. Retrieved from http://www.unep.org/sport_env/impactSport_Env.aspx

USEPA. (2018). *Methane*. Retrieved from http://www.epa.gov/methane/

VEPA. (2018). *Landfill gas: Factsheet*. Retrieved from http://www.epa.vic.gov.au/~/media/Publications/1479.pdf

von Storch, H., & Krauss, W. (2005). Culture contributes to perceptions of climate change. *Nieman Reports*, (Winter). Retrieved from http://www.nieman.harvard.edu/reports/article/100600/Culture-Contributes-to-Perceptions-of-Climate-Change.aspx

WADSR. (2007). *Climate change is no longer just a concept: How climate change could affect sport and recreation now and in the future*. Perth, WA: Western Australia Department of Sport and Recreation (WADSR). Retrieved from http://www.dsr.wa.gov.au/assets/files/Research/Climate_Change.pdf

Weinhofer, G., & Busch, T. (2013). Corporate strategies for managing climate risks. *Business Strategy and the Environment*, 22(2), 121–144.

Weinhofer, G., & Hoffmann, V. H. (2010). Mitigating climate change: How do corporate strategies differ? *Business Strategy and the Environment*, 19(2), 77–89.

Williams, S., & Schaefer, A. (2013). Small and medium-sized enterprises and sustainability: Managers' values and engagement with environmental and climate change issues. *Business Strategy and the Environment*, 22(3), 173–186.

Winn, M. I. (1995). Corporate leadership and policies for the natural environment. In D. Collins, & M. Starik

(Eds.), *Research in corporate social performance and policy* (pp. 127–161). Greenwich, CT: JAI Press.

Winn, M. I., Kirchgeorg, M., Griffiths, A., Linnenluecke, M. K., & Gunther, E. (2011). Impacts from climate change on organizations: A conceptual foundation. *Business Strategy & Environment, 20*, 157–173.

Wolfsegger, C., Gössling, S., & Scott, D. (2008). Climate change risk appraisal in the Austrian ski industry. *Tourism Review International, 12*(1), 13–23.

Yin, R. K. (2009). *Case study research: Design and methods* (4th ed.). Thousand Oaks, CA: Sage.

Yin, R. K. (2011). *Qualitative research from start to finish* (1st ed.). New York, NY: Guilford Press.

Yin, R. K. (2012). *Applications of case study research* (3rd ed.). Thousand Oaks, CA: Sage.

Understanding the growth in outdoor recreation participation: an opportunity for sport development in the United Kingdom

C. Mackintosh, G. Griggs and R. Tate

ABSTRACT
This paper examines the growth in importance and scale of the outdoor recreation sector in the United Kingdom. It establishes a five-component model to help understand the growth in this sub-sector of the wider sport and physical activity industry. The paper is based on a narrative literature review of the importance of outdoor recreation and also sets the position of the sector in terms of sport policy in the UK. From determining the factors that are underpinning the growing importance of the sector the article goes on to establish implications for policy and practice in sport policy and development in the UK and beyond. It seeks to establish lesson learning between industry and academia that has underpinned the evolution of outdoor recreation policy development in recent years. Furthermore, it establishes future research agendas and directions for those working in outdoor recreation and physical activity spaces and places.

Introduction

Participation in physical activities which are alternative or adaptations to traditional mainstream activities have increased rapidly across both North America and Europe in the last decade (Booth & Thorpe, 2007; Hindley, 2018; Sport England, 2016a, 2017; Tomlinson, Ravenscroft, Wheaton, & Gilchrist, 2005), with "increased visibility across public and private space" (Gilchrist & Wheaton, 2011, p. 113). Within the UK this represents a significant cultural shift where such activities have already both challenged and replaced traditional team sports (Booth & Thorpe, 2007; Green, 2010; Griggs, 2012; Howell, 2008; L'Aoustet & Griffet, 2001). The concern of this paper is with that of the shifts and growth in outdoor recreation participation. Likewise, the outdoor recreation sector was estimated to be worth an estimated £21 billion in 2012/2013 (Comley & Mackintosh, 2014) and an estimated 3.12 billion visits to the great outdoors in 2014–2015 (SRA, 2017). The wider European outdoor sector also experienced considerable growth in 2017, according to the European Outdoor Group (EOG) State of Trade report (OIA, 2017). This State of Trade report indicates that the wholesale outdoor market grew by 7.2 per cent in value and 6.7 per cent in volume with the wholesale outdoor market worth €5.86bn (OIA, 2017). The sector is now acknowledged by various government departments in the United Kingdom (UK) as fundamental to delivering central government cross-cutting goals in health, education and the economy. Later in this paper, the size of individual aspects of sports and physical activities in the broader outdoors sector will be presented. In recent years The Outdoor Industries Association (OIA) report (2015) established that using MENE data from 2013/2014 the outdoor recreation sector has grown with an overall upward trend in visits taken for health or exercise. This motivation was cited for around two-fifths of visits taken in 2013/2014. Furthermore, the OIA suggest the British Mountaineering Council reported an increase in climbing competitions (18% increase from 2012 to 2013). It was also illustrated by Sport England that Snowsport England recently reported a 12% increase at domestic slopes for the period February to April 2013–2014 and a 11% increase for the period May to August 2013–2014. As a wider proxy measure of growth the OIA report (2015) highlights The Mountain Training Association has grown 15% in 2014–2015 demonstrating an example of the growth in independent niche providers.

This paper will consider the underlying drivers that are shaping the potential growth in the outdoor recreation field as an area of restorative health policy in the UK (DCMS, 2015; DEFRA, 2018). The paper outlines underlying developments in this area of sport policy as part of a shift towards the adaptation of traditional sporting formats, styles and cultures during an era of "second modernity". This conceptual term will be discussed in more detail later after we examine the UK outdoor recreation sector. The paper is not intended as a comprehensive chronological historical map of sport policy in the subfield of outdoor recreation. However, the paper does have the central aim of examining the key societal and individual factors that underpin the growth in outdoor recreation sport and leisure participation. Furthermore, it locates UK outdoor policy and strategy developments alongside wider sociological theoretical understanding of outdoor and alternative sporting activity use, choice and behaviour. By doing so we present a framework for understanding better the growth in outdoor recreation sport and leisure participation growth in the UK and beyond. Finally, the paper considers the implications of the growth of the UK outdoor recreation sport and leisure management sector.

The appropriation of outdoor recreation spaces for alternative formats of traditional running, wild swimming, and other competitive club-centred sports offer a useful case study for considering why governments and other agencies are attempting to employ them to address wide-ranging issues in the UK and beyond. This paper is an attempt to stimulate a new research agenda, shape future understanding and provide a starting point for the sport development industry to examine why, how and in what ways growth is occurring. It provides a new model, to begin to explore the diverse, complex and multi-tiered layers of the sector. The geographical focus of the paper is predominantly the UK context and the management and implementation of outdoor recreation in this setting. However, it is also hoped that given the potential application of growth in global outdoor recreation (OIA, 2017) and diverse geographical interests of the sector, it may also have wider application in other international sport and leisure management contexts.

It will also consider how this area of sport and leisure management is conceptualised by practitioners and academics. To help scholars, managers and government policy makers in this area we propose a new framework for beginning to understand the growth of this area based on a narrative review of the literature, several years of working in policy advocacy and as a collective of authors working across academia, practice and policy.

The challenge with some of the emergent outdoor activities in the last decade such as open water swimming, obstacle courses, geocaching and hybrid forms of "traditional" recreation formats (for example "challenge" events involving canoeing, mountaineering, cycling and rafting) is that they do not neatly fall within clear categories of sport, recreation or existing typologies of government and national governing bodies (NGBs). Indeed, they may well "fit" no typology, dualistic traditional-alternative, outdoor-indoor or new-traditional binary theorisation. In some ways, they do "fit" better with being considered "alternative", in the physical context of taking place in the open spaces and places of the great outdoors (Hindley, 2018).

It is clear that socially constructed "traditional outdoor recreation" sport and physical activity is worth acknowledging here. In terms of the kayaking, canoeing, walking, mountaineering, cycling and rock climbing mainstream activities significant numbers of participants now "do this". The consumption of such sports is captured in Table 1 taken from a specifically run set of statistics as part of the Reconomics project using the former Active People survey in 2014. This is the most comprehensive set of statistics government have "run" from their ten-year Active People Survey (2005–2015). These statistics were "run" by the research team at Sport England, and were for the first time broken down into the smaller activities that are not representative due to very small numbers. However, it does give a sense of the breadth of what we might see from outdoor recreation. Note, however, how it is also hard to "categorise" events such as open water swim, forest night running groups and obstacle and multiple format events (swim, raft, team challenge formats).

Early identification and academic study of alternative sporting activities is often credited to the work of Nancy Midol (Midol, 1993). Midol and Broyer (1995, p. 210) suggest that for such activities, "the culture is extremely different from the official one promoted by sporting institutions… These groups have dared to practice transgressive behaviours and create new values." Examples of research in this broad field has explored the practices of participants in Parkour (Atkinson, 2009; Camoletto, Sterchele, & Genova, 2015; Puddle, Wheaton, & Thorpe, 2018) and Ultimate Frisbee (Crocket, 2013, 2016; Griggs, 2009a, 2009b, 2011). Findings of what are sometimes called "alternative sports" or events suggest that they present a challenge to the traditional way of doing and understanding sport and physical activity (Wheaton, 2000, 2004) and strongly adhere to practices which foster a close and supportive ethos (Bale, 1994; Eichberg, 1998; Rinehart & Sydnor, 2012). To date, this realm of the literature has not been positioned alongside that of outdoor recreation and management. We consider this a useful step in better conceptualising this "market" and set of related management practices and emergent area of policy.

Table 1. Average monthly participation in sport and recreation in England*, October 2012-October 2013 (Source: Sport England, 2014, Active People Survey).

Activity	Number of people (14+) participating monthly*	Percentage of the adult population (14+)
Outdoor Recreation Group**	25,703,100	59.3
Recreational walking	23,313,500	53.8
Outdoor Recreation Group (excluding walking)	7,707,500	17.8
Cycling	3,524,400	8.1
Running	2,791,500	6.3
Recreational cycling	2,159,800	5
Outdoor swimming	826,700	1.9
Mountain biking	736,900	1.7
Coarse fishing	632,800	1.4
Other horse riding	301,700	0.7
Sea fishing	245,900	0.6
Outdoor climbing/trekking	191,200	0.4
Game fishing	155,800	0.4
Canoeing	133,300	0.3
Alpine skiing	95,900	0.2
BMX	54,000	0.1
Cruising sailing	47,600	0.1
Water-based rowing	47,500	0.1
Pony trekking	35,300	0.1
Snowboarding	29,100	0.1
Cycle-Cross	27,300	0.1
Freestyle skiing	22,300	0.1
Windsurfing	19,400	0.03
Nordic skiing	17,400	0.03
Orienteering	11,800	0.02
Total	68, 831, 700	100

*At least 1 session, any duration, any intensity in last 28 days (October 2012–October 2013).
**The activities listed under the outdoor recreation group represent those from within the group that can be reported individually. It is not an extensive list of what is included in the APS.

A specific example of such growth in an activity, which has soared in popularity in the UK in just a few short years, is that of obstacle course challenges. Events labelled Tough Mudder, Warrior Dash, Spartan Race, Rat Race, Wolf Run and Mucky Races have drawn hundreds of thousands of participants to stagger through mud troughs, crawl under barbed wire, scale high walls and attempt to swim across pits filled with ice cold water. Globally, since 2010 the Tough Mudder series alone has gone from just three races worldwide to over fifty, spanning USA, Australia and Western Europe and grossing over $100 million dollars (Fitzpatrick, 2013; Martin, 2013). The origins of obstacle races can be backdated to the Tough Guy challenge in England, first staged in 1987, originally billed as the toughest race in the world (Triggs, 2008). Organisers of such events attribute their use of social media as the primary catalyst for the industry's contemporary unprecedented growth and the considerable uptake of participants. Initial development of such pursuits obviously occurred pre-internet era. In a recent interview Michael Mendenhall, head of marketing at Walt Disney, credited with the building the X Games explains that "social media has allowed an idea like this to be adopted at a speed and scale we've never seen before ... It used to take a decade or longer for something like this to take hold. Now you can do it in less than two years" (Kennedy, 2012). Such activities exist largely outside the domain of traditional government department, quasi-non-governmental organisation (QUANGO) and NGB jurisdiction.

However, for such ideas to take hold and develop the socio-cultural conditions must also be right for events to develop at such a rapid rate. Insights have yet to be offered as to why this shift within movement culture has occurred. The paper will briefly, outline the emergence of outdoor recreation as a policy field within UK sport policy and management, secondly, it offers a new theoretical framework to help provide better explanation, understanding and management of this sport and leisure phenomenon. Finally, it considers the implications for the management and policy implementation of outdoor recreation as a growing agenda within government in the United Kingdom and in the wider global context.

Background UK policy context

Defining the outdoors is challenging, complex and problematic making it difficult to define clear boundaries for a sphere of public life, a professional industry and to estimate its economic, social and cultural value. As such the definition and conceptualisation of outdoor recreation is always evolving. Natural England's outdoor recreation strategy (Henley Centre, 2005) highlighted that a concise definition of outdoor recreation is difficult to establish as it includes many different activities.

In this paper, we take outdoor recreation to mean physical activities which take place in the natural environment. Furthermore, our definition of the natural environment does not include outdoor pitches, which can be considered purpose-built, and as such, our definition does not incorporate sports such as football, rugby or golf. We recognise that some of the activities included within our definition can take place in purpose-built settings, for example, canoeing, skiing and climbing. However, we consider these as having their roots in the outdoor recreation and predominantly reliant on the natural environment – therefore in keeping with our definition. This definition itself was an agreed one formed through several rounds of consultation that formed part of the development of the *Reconomics* (2014) report by the Sport and Recreation Alliance (SRA) members from over 320 organisations. This process itself was a first for the industry as an attempt to build a definitional consensus and identity as part of moving forward as a collective of organisations with vested interests. Activities that we have included within this definition, as determined by this consultation process were categorised according to the natural environment in which they take place (Figure 1). This is illustrated in Figure 1 with a categorisation taxonomy across the six environmental contexts that emerged through the SRA consultation.

Given the close link between the identified benefits of outdoor recreation and the outcomes sought internationally by governments the increased focus on the potential of outdoor recreation as a policy tool has become evident in the last 15 years (DEFRA, 2018). More detail will be provided later in this paper around the identified benefits of outdoor recreation. Dating back now to its first publication in 2002, the UK's Governments *Game Plan strategy for sport (Cabinet Office and DCMS,* 2002) did not specifically mention outdoor recreation. In the UK, sport policy is driven by DCMS and the delivered by Sport England and many national partners such as County Sport Partnerships (CSPs), NGBs, local government and charity and social enterprise sector. This is not excluding the sizeable voluntary sector who "do" much of policy in this sector where much of the outdoor recreation sector sits. For a fuller explanation of the UK sport development system of relevance to outdoor recreation see Cutforth (2017).

Equally, outdoor recreation is a cross-cutting sub-sector of sport and physical activity policy that can equally embrace agencies as diverse as National Parks, the Forestry Commission, The National Trust, Natural England and sub-sector specific leisure providers working with more traditional policy makers such as Sport England and DCMS. Again, space does not permit a full outline of the historical map of these agencies and their inter-relationships in this paper.

It is worth acknowledging a little known document led by Natural England who did produce an outdoor recreation strategy (Countryside Agency, 2005). This strategy highlighted the potential variety of categories of outdoor recreational activities that make the interpretation of this sphere of sport and active recreation particularly complex. It is then thirteen years after the previous government sport strategy *Game Plan* (Cabinet Office/DCMS, 2002), that the latest incarnation *Sporting Future* (DCMS, 2015) specifically identified outdoor recreation as an asset in the effort to increase levels of physical activity. Within this latest strategy acknowledgement is given to the value that outdoor recreation contributes to the economy, and identified actions to improve monitoring of engagement in outdoor recreation and better understand behaviours. This alone was a significant policy landmark. But, policy also went beyond sport, to consider physical activity (bringing many forms of outdoor recreation within its remit) and also moving beyond a purely participation focused definition of success. Instead, *Sporting Future* defines five outcomes by which success will be measured: physical wellbeing, mental wellbeing, individual development, social and community development and economic development. These outcomes are reflected in Sport England's Toward an Active Nation strategy (Sport England, 2016b). Here, *Toward an Active Nation* recognises the potential of outdoor recreation to help achieve those targets, and, also sets an "increase in the percentage of adults using outdoor space for exercise/health reasons as one of its KPIs" (p. 25).

It is also worth being aware of wider policy agenda development and advocacy work that underpinned this emerging strategy. For example, the publication of *Reconomics: The Economic Impact of Outdoor Recreation in the UK – The Evidence* (Comley & Mackintosh, 2014) was led by the Sport and Recreation Alliance (known brand-wise hereon within this paper as "The Alliance") and was used in a House of Parliament debate (UK Parliament, 2015) to underpin and encourage a wider DCMS consultation in August 2015 on a potential Outdoor Recreation Strategy for the United Kingdom. DCMS asked the Alliance and

UNDERGROUND	**IN WATER**	**ON WATER**
eg caving and potholing	eg outdoor swimming, scuba diving	eg angling, canoeing, water-skiing
ON LAND	**HIGH UP**	**IN THE AIR**
eg walking, horse-riding, off-road cycling	eg mountain climbing, high ropes	eg gliding, sky diving

Figure 1. Typology of outdoor recreation based on the natural environment in which they take place.

Outdoor Industries Association (OIA) to consult with the outdoor recreation sector on what could be included in a national outdoor recreation strategy for England. Given that participation, physical activity development and promotion are core to this strategy consultation (DCMS, 2015a) it is surprising that previous government policy has not highlighted the role of outdoor recreation within sport development (Cabinet Office/DCMS, 2002). The presence of outdoor recreation within national policy is partly the product of such advocacy and the coalescing of various interest groups including The Alliance, outdoor recreation NGBs, the OIA and wider outdoor sector parties. The Alliance is the umbrella organisation for the sport and recreation sector in the UK with over 330 members including national governing bodies and other representative bodies. Established in 1935 and originally named the Central Council of Physical Recreation, the Alliance exists to protect, promote and provide for its members. Between them the Alliance members represent some 150,000 clubs and eight million regular participants.

Precise definition of this policy area is difficult, political by nature and driven by multiple vested interests. However, as part of the *Reconomics* policy advocacy and lobbying process (Comley & Mackintosh, 2014; Sport and Recreation Alliance, 2014) a series of debates in Parliament were generated (Sport and Recreation Alliance, 2017; UK Parliament, 2015). Within this set of debates a fairly traditional framework was proposed for setting boundaries around what was, and what was not outdoor recreation. This drawing of policy limits is critical to understand, but also to manage policy in this area. But, as this article shows further wider review of the conceptual sociological literature in this domain illustrates that such an overtly "tight", concrete and formalised set of named activities that fall within the sector is hard to delineate.

Furthermore, in the spirit of UK-wide, cross-government working, consideration of increased physical activity and outdoor recreation has not been limited to the sport strategy. Public Health England's *Everybody Active, Every Day report* (2014) aimed at tackling the estimated £7.4 Billion annual cost of physical inactivity identifies the benefit of improving ease of access to open space. Likewise, the government's 25 year Department of the Environment Forestry and Rural Affairs (DEFRA) environment plan contains an entire chapter on "connecting people with the environment to improve health and wellbeing" (2018). To assist in achieving all of this, Natural England's "Outdoors for All" programme is aimed at increasing access to the natural environment for people in England. It appears there is now a much greater awareness and appreciation of the benefits outdoor recreation can offer, and as a result outdoor recreation receives prominent consideration in government strategies to increase participation in physical activity and improve health and well-being across England. But, what remains is a need to better understand the levers, drivers and conceptual literature that potentially underpins this fast emerging policy domain.

Theoretical explanation of shift towards outdoor recreation

For the past seven years we have been engaged in this area of policy making, review and research (SRA, 2014, 2017) as well as open debate in Parliament (UK Parliament, 2015). This seven-year process has involved undertaking multiple literature reviews, running consultation events with policy makers and engaging with stakeholders in wider outdoor recreation. Ontologically, we position ourselves as social constructivist policy interpretivist analysts (Bevir & Rhodes, 2010, 2011, 2018; Wagenaar, 2011). Epistemologically, this means we undertake such reflexivity in our research with an openness and awareness of how we ourselves are part of the process, part driving the processes of policy. But, in offering a framework this offers a tool kit for understanding wider literature, projects, industry documents and policy offers. It also allows us as researchers to reflect upon why outdoor recreation, of all policy "fields" is used, shaped and re-shaped to deliver outcomes for government. We believe it is partly, but never wholly driven by some of these five driving factors. These five factors emerge in part from our "practice", praxis and theoretical understanding in this area. But also from the narrative literature review undertaken in this area. Importantly, we aim to reduce the binary divide between higher education and industry and theory and practice (Best, 2009; Mackintosh, 2018). In each of the next sections, we illustrate five aspects of our new theoretical framework we propose for the growth in outdoor recreation as an alternative leisure phenomenon. Figure 2 illustrates this framework that we hope will stimulate debate, a new research agenda and provide a starting point for examining the great outdoors and its role within sport development and sport policy implementation and evaluation. The diagram is meant as a starting point for providing a theoretical framework for understanding the growth in outdoor recreation with each of the five components being considered drivers in the societal and industry growth. There are naturally also conceptual links between these five components too.

Restorative nature of outdoor recreation

Use of green and blue spaces for physical activity, movement and sport is not new. However, with growing use of this area of policy by the UK government (DCMS, 2015; DEFRA, 2018; Sport England, 2016a) it seems that greater attention is needed as to why people are seeking alternatives to the indoor club, gym space or the more traditional sporting endeavour. One area in the literature that appears to be prevalent is the notion of the outdoors as possessing restorative value. Green exercise differs from indoor exercise in several ways, including the idea of nature as an escape from everyday life (Gladwell, Brown, Wood, Sandercock, & Barton, 2013), and as a provider of restoration (e.g. from mental fatigue; Herzog & Strevey, 2008; Herzog, Black, Fountaine, & Knotts, 1997; Herzog, Chen, & Primeau, 2002; Ojala, Korpela, Tyrväinen, Tiittanen, & Lanki, 2018). It is perhaps more enjoyable and easier too, for many participants. Some studies have shown that exercising in the outdoors feels easier to participants than if they were to perform the same exercise indoors (Focht, 2009), possibly because of the diverting and attractive features of a green setting (Akers et al., 2012) and the idea of nature-based recreation as escape and refreshment (Morris, 2003; Ojala et al., 2018).

Figure 2. A framework for understanding the growth in outdoor recreation.

Exercising in nature also mediates the frequency with which participants choose to engage in exercise, with the restorative properties of nature cited as a reason for more frequent participation (Bowler, Buying-Ali, Knight, & Pullin, 2010) alongside improvements in mood (Barton & Pretty, 2010; Bratman, Daily, Levy, & Gross, 2015; Peacock, Hine, & Pretty, 2007; Pretty, Peacock, Sellens, & Griffin, 2005; ten Brink et al., 2016). Interestingly, the greatest improvements on mood and self-esteem appear to emerge in the first 5 min of green and blue exercise (Barton & Pretty, 2010), with long and short term benefits observed (Gladwell et al., 2013) with exposure to green exercise for short periods. Conversely, a failure to engage with nature on any level (e.g. a child living on an inner-city estate) has been named "nature deficit disorder" (Louv, 2005) leading to an upswing in the potential for greater levels of stress, anxiety, depression and other mood disturbances (alongside obesity) to occur.

The role of green exercise (exercising whilst being exposed to nature) in health is significant (Barton & Pretty, 2010; Barton, Griffin, & Pretty, 2012; Gidlow et al., 2016; Park, Tsunetsugu, Kasetani, Kagawa, & Miyakazi, 2010), with natural environments providing a means of relaxation and reducing stress as a natural by-product of the experience (Li, 2010). According to a recent systematic review, it also offers more mental benefits than indoor exercise (Thompson & Aspinall, 2011). Furthermore, it has been identified that,

> natural settings and stimuli such as landscapes and animals seem to effortlessly engage our attention, allowing us to attend without paying attention. (Kuo & Sullivan, 2001, p. 545)

Research identifies the restorative role of nature (Gladwell et al., 2013; Herzog & Strevey, 2008), with outdoor exercise referred to as a "useful natural medicine" (Gladwell et al., 2013, p. 5) that promotes happiness (Sugiyama, Leslie, Giles-Corli, & Owen, 2008), which carries the potential to provide positive emotional regulation, to alleviate stress, and allow emotional stress-recovery to occur (Bowler et al., 2010; Korpela, Borodulin, Neuvonen, Paronen, & Tyrvainen, 2014), partly via the use of rehabilitative intervention programmes such as gardening on depressed patients (e.g. Gonzalez, Hartig, Patil, Martinsen, & Kirkevold, 2011). A meta-analysis (Bowler et al., 2010) comparing urban and natural environments reported that the strongest restorative outcome of nature-based exercise was well-being, and a decrease in negative feelings such as sadness and anxiety. This supported the findings of previous research that also found greater positive changes in a wide range of behaviours associated with emotional well-being following nature-based (as opposed to non-nature-based) exercise (Berman, Jonides, & Kaplan, 2008; Gidlow et al., 2016; Korpela et al., 2014; Ryan et al., 2010). These findings reflect a growth in interest in the field of environmental psychology, which adopts "restoration perspectives" on the use of nature in restoring mental, physical and emotional health.

The restorative properties for urban dwellers appears striking if one considers a rather seminal body of work conducted by Ulrich (e.g. Ulrich, 1979, 1981, 2002; Ulrich, Simons, & Losito, 1991) who considers that the viewing of natural blue and green scenes goes far beyond an aesthetic appreciation to concrete improvements in stress and emotional well-being. Interestingly, many authors discuss that nature-based scenes carry such a strong psychological impact that simply viewing photographs of nature can alleviate stress (e.g. Kaplan, 1992; Morris, 2003; Ulrich & Parsons, 1992; White & Heerwagen, 1998). As observed by Korpela et al. (2014), walking in the outdoors, as opposed to indoors, "produces greater physiological changes toward relaxation, greater changes to positive emotions and vitality, and faster recovery of attention-demanding cognitive performances" (Korpela et al., 2014, p. 2). In fact, it is perhaps restoration, as opposed to exercise itself that provides the greatest benefits of outdoor exercise. As stated by Korpela et al. (2014, p. 5),

> the present result refers to the importance of experiencing everyday calmness, getting new spirit and vitality for the everyday routines, forgetting everyday worries, clarifying one's thoughts' and signifies the importance of moving "away from physical exercise per se in population groups who are inactive or insensitive to exercise prescriptions". (p. 5)

Such an observation holds with conceptualisations of outdoor-exercisers as "recreationists" for whom the experience of being outdoors dominates. Outdoor exercisers can benefit from exercise, whilst also relaxing in nature, enjoying the aesthetic beauty of their surroundings, and partaking of the physical benefits such as fresh air and an escape from everyday life (Barton, Hine, & Pretty, 2009; Hammitt, 2000). From considering how this international body of literature is framing outdoor recreation leads into a consideration of how "movement culture" per se has grown in what has been referred to as an era of second modernity. The next section will consider how and why such a wider culture has developed.

A shift in UK movement culture towards second modernity

Movement cultures within any country are rich and varied containing patterns of movement actions and interactions (sport, play, dance, or other fitness activities) that encompass a group's leisure (Crum, 1993). "Within the UK movement culture, 'sport' has occupied a dominant position, traditionally conceived of as highly competitive in which the achievement motive has remained dominant" (Griggs, 2012, p. 180). Historically the creation and maintenance of competitive sports clubs have done much to reinforce position this with the formation of league and cup contests. These developed exponentially during the Victorian era from well-established organisational structures of civil clubs founded largely around factories and churches (Walvin, 1975). Since the dominance of sport was established the broader cultural landscape has continued to shift and consequently "the movement-cultural landscape has drastically changed" (Crum, 1994, p. 118). In contrast to this it has been suggested that "outdoor recreation and, in particular, walking is a multi-sensual and stimulating experience which frees the mind and generates reflexivity, philosophical and intellectual thought, aesthetic contemplation and opens up a more 'natural' self" (Morris, 2003, p. 18).

Beck (2011) explains the wider societal shift as a move from first modernity to that of second modernity (see also Beck, Bonss, & Lau, 2003). In first modernity, the freedom and equality of its individuals are moulded by powerful social institutions to which they are strongly adhered and disciplined by such as the work place, school and the church (Beck et al., 2003). By contrast in second modernity, society is far more globalised exacerbated by developments in technology. In addition tradition patterns of family life, gender roles and working practices have also occurred (Beck & Beck-Gernsheim, 1995). With first modernity more reflective of societal needs and survival, second modernity has allowed considerable freedoms for more recent generations, raising "children of an excitement society" (Shulze, 1992). This period has seen more intense individualisation has also developed a more consumerist and choice-driven society which sees less legitimacy in traditional social institutions and has thus eroded many traditional prescriptive life patterns (Beck & Beck-Gernsheim, 2001). Beck (2011, p. 281) concludes that this leaves us with "a new kind of society and a new kind of personal life [that] are coming into being."

This new kind of personal life is reflected in the move to participate in alternative sporting activities such as parkour, Ultimate Frisbee and obstacle course challenges which have begun to be documented in sporting ethnographies (Puddle et al., 2018; Rinehart & Sydnor, 2012; Wheaton, 2004). In his analysis of a shift in movement culture and building upon the idea of what is referred to as a shift in post-materialist values, Crum (1993) offers three further aspects to explain its change namely, the craving for self-realisation, the trend towards individualisation and the rediscovery of the body through the outdoors. Though outlined by Crum however, these societal shifts remain largely unexplored and may offer some explanations as to why outdoor recreation potentially offer such a popular sport policy solution. These themes will now be discussed in turn.

The craving for self-realisation

First modernity was characterised by more rigid notions of authority and morality and identity (Giddens, 1991). By contrast second modernity has created "new patterns of family life, marriage and divorce, labour market participation, work and global economy" (Prout, 2000, p. 306). It has become epitomised by greater uncertainty (Beck, 1992) but this uncertain climate has proved to be fertile conditions in which people can shape their own lives through the formation and exercise of self-consciousness, creativity and agency (Griggs, 2009b; Prout, 2000). Within Western societies, which have enjoyed increased leisure time and money this has led to populations being irresistibly drawn along a path of self-realisation as they engage in an ever-evolving range of pursuits which have developed of which obstacle course challenges are one such example (Lubbe, 1988). As consumption has increased the leisure choices that people make increasingly serve as a source of identity (Puddle et al., 2018; Rinehart & Sydnor, 2012; Wheaton, 2004). Crum (1994) suggests that sport is the clearest illustration of this. "In modern societies there is no cultural domain which is more accessible as a medium for the experience and training of self-determination and self-realisation for so many people, irrespective of their sex, age, social class and level of education" (Crum, 1994, p. 119). However, while there may well be increased participation within the broader movement culture there continues a direction away from convention and regulation (Griggs, 2009b). Research suggests that the draw of participating in more alternative physical activities lies within their underpinning philosophies of encouraging self-expression and personal growth (Midol & Broyer, 1995; Rinehart & Sydnor, 2012). A further common feature is participants ongoing search for authentic experiences (Butts, 2001; Wheaton, 2000).

Nettleton and Hardey (2006) suggest that running events such as outdoor trail events, fun runs, marathons, obstacle course races are considered extraordinary among the routine lives of runners and within these events Shipway, Holloway, and Jones (2013) reports an abundance of authentically felt experiences. What might be best termed existential authenticity, sees participants engaging in a freer, less constrained social environment in search of their true self, as a counter dose to the loss of true self "in public roles and public spheres" (Wang, 1999, p. 358). Though it has long been known that distance running challenges are about managing experiences and feelings of pleasure and pain (Bale, 2003) these have long been the preserve of the committed and regular runner. The creation of events such as obstacle course challenges has opened up the potential experiences to wider groups of people. Importantly these events provide a dual motivational appeal, allowing some to focus on pushing oneself to a prescribed limit and allowing other simply to face and overcome new challenges against the backdrop of a cheering crowd or a scenic route (Shipway & Holloway, 2010).

Motivation in physical activity is popularly attributed to achievement goal theory where the primary motive is for learning, striving, and the desire to demonstrate competence (Roberts, Treasure, & Conroy, 2007). Individuals are said to be motivated by task, whereby individuals find success in working hard and improving or by performance by better compared to others or prescribed standards (Hagger & Chatzisarantis, 2005). Mullins (2012) indicates that these two perspectives are prevalent among core groups of obstacle race participants. Furthermore, from a psychologically perspective, obstacle course participation meets the three powerful needs of self-determination theory; acting with autonomy, developing competence and feeling socially connected (Caron, Hausenblas, & Estabrooks, 2003; Kilpatrick, Hebert, & Jacobsen, 2002). Uniquely perhaps obstacle course races provide entrants the ability to choose to compete to win, to be challenged or participate for fun, offer autonomy for a broad range of people in an environment where they can develop their own skills and assist others in need (Mullins, 2012). Kaydo (2013) suggest that use of marketing of obstacle course challenges, particularly through the use of social media has been focused across these differing psychological needs, appealing to the craving we appear to have for self-realisation within second modernity. The use of social media and our creation of identity within is also reflective a trend towards individualisation, a theme to which we move next.

The trend towards individualisation

In first modernity traditional collective organisations such as the church and labour unions were of major significance to many and commanded significant power (Giddens, 1990, 1991). This power was also reflected in significant role played by civil groups such as sports clubs (Lubbe, 1988). However in second modernity, rather than choosing to be seen to have prescribed or standard identities through memberships and affiliations there is an unabated trend towards people coming to think of themselves as unique individuals (Prout, 2000). Among young people Beck (1998, p. 78) suggests that within Western Cultures this concept of individualisation is so strong that they "...no longer become individualized. They individualize themselves. The biographization of youth means becoming active, struggling and designing one's own life" (Beck, 1998, p. 78). The values espoused by traditional sporting forms represent the antithesis of this viewpoint. Holland and Thomson (1999) indicate that the prevailing attitude on the part of young people in empirical findings thrives in new kinds of institutions in which authority, and allegiance, must be constantly renegotiated, re-established and earned. In short, in an increasingly individualised world, young people articulate an "ethic of reciprocity arguing that their respect could be won by anyone who respected them ... they tend to be very wary of claims to authority and respect on the basis of tradition, custom or force" (Prout, 2000, p. 308).

Consequently, it is argued identity is now more fragmented (Giddens, 1991; Mort, 1988). As such, fragmented discourses around identity construction offer the opportunity for the development and establishment of more varied identities, shaped increasingly away from those produced around work and career (Jackson, Stevenson, & Brooks, 2001; Whannel, 2002) and more around leisure choices (Featherstone, 1991). Wheaton (2004) suggests that participation in alternative physical activities represent opportunities for people to live out these individualised identities. Findings from Shipway and Holloway (2010) suggest that extraordinary running events such as outdoor obstacle course challenges are ideal vehicles for individual identity reinforcement. This is because running success is immediately recognisable and can be understood, where the standards of achievement can be seen by participants, family, work colleagues and other audiences. Again perhaps similar could be seen in wild swimming events, trail adventure and those seeking what we refer to earlier as the "restorative effects" of green or blue leisure. Excellence in physical performance is typically admired as is effort, especially when participants are new to running or participate for good causes (Kaydo, 2013). It appears that distance running events appear to have the ability to attract participants of both serious leisure (Stebbins, 1992) and casual leisure (Stebbins, 1997). Previously longer distances had been prohibitive either by application or by the level of training needed. Both 5 and 10 km races had also gained popularity but had largely catered for running clubs and focused on achieved times. However, obstacle course challenges have successfully made these environments open to all (Shipway & Holloway, 2010). The broader rise in popularity of similar events is also indicative of the next theme, the rediscovery of the body.

The rediscovery of the body

A negative aspect attributed to a move to a more individualised culture there is the rising incidence of reported mental health problems among young people. Rutter and Smith (1997, p. 307) indicate unequivocally that " ... the shift towards individualistic values, the increasing emphasis on self-realisation and fulfilment, and the consequent rise in expectations, should be studied as possible causes of disorders." The shift to second modernity has seen changes in our daily routines as we have moved to greater sedentary office based work practices and embraced the development of modern technologies. Consequently, our bodies have reflected this shift of "movement denial" by exhibiting increased stress and cardio vascular illnesses (WHF, 2011).

At the same time, the growth of the fitness industry and a trend towards health and wellbeing practices is illustrative of something of a "rediscovery of the body" (Bette, 1989). Despite accepting the sedentary lifestyle that we have created, we also appear to have a deep need to escape these shackles and engage in liberating behaviour, termed by sociologists Elias and Dunning (1986) as a quest for excitement. Illustrative of this phenomena are examples of highly respected white collar workers such accountants, lawyers, bankers and doctors who feel constrained by their office environments, engaging in violent and illegal behaviour by engaging in acts of football hooliganism at the weekend (Giulianotti, 1995). Thus engaging in obstacle course challenges would provide what has also been termed by psychologists as sensation seeking behaviour, which sees individuals participation in experiences which are varied, novel, complex, and intense (Zuckerman, 1983). While physical activity literature has often historically associated these behaviours with high-risk sports (Breivik, 1996; Rossi & Cereatti, 1993); Zuckerman (1994) suggests that individuals can still pursue personally intense and rewarding sensations without seeking extreme risks for their own sake.

Benefits can also be found for the more serious or dedicated athlete. Typically, training schedules are prescribed and largely uniform so the varied terrain can provide a form of interval training that can enhance both aerobic and anaerobic capacities (Cramer, 2008; Reuter & Hagerman, 2008). A more forgiving terrain can also soften regular high impact training and the movement diversity also distributes training stress over more muscles and joints, which may reduce risks of overuse injuries (Auvinen et al., 2008). This diversity of movement activities can also break the monotony of repetitive training schedules (Laursen, 2010).

The more recent importance of positive socio-affective environments during physical activity is also reflective of a more holistic view of health and wellbeing beyond the psychomotor domain (Rink, 2005). Empirical findings indicate that strong social bonds developed through a shared ethos common in alternative physical activities appear to create highly desirable environments for increased and sustained participation (Stebbins, 1992; Wheaton, 2007). This is reflective of the accounts obtained during obstacle course challenges (Mullins, 2012) and of other events that provide participants with a powerful sense of identity, community and belonging (Shipway & Jones, 2008).

Discussion

In this paper, we propose five key drivers that together build a new framework to help partially explain the growth in outdoor recreation as a tool, instrument and most malleable of policy vehicle for government. We also want to reposition the need to consider involvement of the policy researcher and advocate within the research process for enabling a reflexive account of how policy and practice is understood (Wagenaar, 2011). Indeed, the missing voices from this paper are those of the lobbyists, activists, club volunteers, participants and consumers of outdoor recreation, in its many multiple forms at different hierarchical levels in society. We suggest this is a future avenue of sport and leisure management research yet to be fully explored. In classifying, conceptualising and defining outdoor recreation we assume this in itself is a socially constructed process. Policy analysis of this sector is missing. Understanding why certain activities do and don't get funding is an increasingly crucially research agenda. Furthermore, our framework can only provide a partially constructed point of reference for understanding growth in a fluid domain of leisure and sport.

By better understanding this area of activities, management and policy interventions, managers, volunteers and communities can better plan, cooperate and innovate to build a more cohesive responsive to government policy language, strategies and funding (DCMS, 2015; Sport England, 2016a). The artificial spectrum of outdoor activities proposed by The Alliance (SRA, 2014) used in government outdoor recreation policy debates (UK Parliament, 2015) went on to frame government policy formulation (DCMS, 2015; Sport England, 2016a). For the first time in DCMS sport policy outdoor recreation had an acknowledged role to play. This opens doors for a diversity of agencies, communities groups, social enterprises and charities to access funds, support and strategy agendas. Similarly, it remains clear that whether a private profit-driven Tough Mudder event, inner-city dockland "Open Water Swim" activity run by the English swimming NGB or a micro-level community walking group, the boundaries, definition and liminal spaces of this policy field are increasingly complex. How we navigate at a national level an increasingly expansionary area of provision is where we must next build a clearer research agenda. The Alliance has a key role to play here, but also the far wider policy community too. This sector encompasses diverse partners such as the National Trust, The National Parks, local government parks and open spaces departments, NGBs and the ever more important collective "patchwork" of non-traditional providers. In hard economic terms, it seems we have a better feel for supply-side agencies and those who deliver and where they deliver. But, this paper maps the ever-nuanced demand-side factors that suggest why it may be that outdoor recreation is growing. In a period of second modernity, we suggest that it perhaps through the five key drivers that we identify that we can better grasp why it is growing.

In addition, it has been clearly recognised that the government has failed to meet the long-heralded expectations of the London 2012 participation boom (Mackintosh, Darko, & May-Wilkins, 2016). Likewise, that the multiple agencies that are being asked to respond to this much-vaunted crisis need to be increasingly innovative and seek collaborations and partnerships beyond their usual policy and practice bedfellows. It is clear that one of the policy landscapes that is bucking the trend, is that of the outdoor recreation. It is clear that there is an artificial binary divide between traditional and alternative outdoor recreation. The last government strategy for sport suggested the impetus for *Creating a Sporting Habit for Life* (DCMS, 2015). We are now no longer aiming to reach out for a mass participation legacy driven by securing global mega-events. But, as we move into the next phase of austerity-led policy making for sport and physical activity it seems that the outdoor recreation market, potentially offers some of the opportunities that constrain other areas of policy and programme development such as social and healthcare, mental health provision, education provision and prisons (BBC, 2018; Meek, 2018). More recent work by the Sport and Recreation Alliance (2017) has outlined the potential of the outdoor recreation sector. What is less clear is whether other sports, and their NGBs have recognised this opportunity as one they could learn from and see how success can be defined differently to traditional notions of mainstream sport culture. For example, Active Forests and partnerships between the Forestry Commission and diverse sports such as table tennis, volleyball, Nordic walking, fitness, climbing, wild running, archery and duathlon (O'Brien & Forester, 2017). A further example of the outdoor recreational growth capacity is how it has been facilitated through green spaces in the global phenomenon of Park Run (Hindley, 2018; Stevinson & Hickson, 2014). The Active Forest and various Park Run evaluations show that we cannot make blanket assumptions of impact across settings, formats and adaptations of sport and physical activity in outdoor spaces. Research and researchers in sport and leisure management have a clear role to play (Mackintosh, 2018) in breaking down the artificial boundaries of "evidence-based practice" and "policy-based evidence" social constructs between Higher education and "practice". Earlier sections of this paper have also begun to map out debates around the motivations, meanings and beliefs that may underpin this new area of movement culture and physical activity.

Conclusion

A new collective research agenda and national policy leadership are needed in this little understood domain. Policy research in this area, despite the growth in participation, provision and policy rhetoric is incredibly rare. Indeed the policy actors, agencies and organisations in this area have no single "national voice", or strategic vehicle for supporting each other and avoiding duplication of efforts. We consider it a fruitful and vital time for traditional and mainstream sports to learn from this sphere of activity that is thriving, to begin to reconceptualise what it is they want to achieve and how they can begin to affect the long-held status quo in sport participation (Carter, 2005; Houlihan & White, 2002; Mackintosh, 2014; Mackintosh & Liddle, 2015).

The opportunities may be greatest for small governing bodies of sport that embrace and focus on the outdoor recreation landscape, but who can adapt traditional formats of their codes to embody new versions of the modern, hybrid and developmental that appeals to the wider market. This could, for example, be in activities as diverse as orienteering, cycling, rugby, where there is a branded and themed challenge, and extreme element to the game adapted to this event-led version of activities using the great outdoor spaces of the UK. For some NGBs this simply means using the open spaces, places and landscapes of the outdoors for accessing new audiences. Research into lifestyle sport is becoming increasingly well established (Wheaton, 2013), but, as more NGBs become increasingly centrally focussed on delivery of activities (Kylton, 2013) so the potential for learning and cross over is greater. We question whether lifestyle, alternative or traditional are useful terms anymore. For the users, consumers, community groups and managers or sport and leisure we perhaps need to return to the spaces and places that determine who plays, enjoys and takes part and consider why, when and how they do so in better planning leisure provision. Traditional NGBs have much to learn from organic and more culture-led minority and "alternative" sports. Some have started to tackle this flow of engaging with learning such as table tennis launching PING! its outdoor street, bar and public space adaptation of an older format (Mackintosh, Griggs, & Cookson, 2014). From an original pilot around the Olympic stadium, this version of the event running mainly through summer months now has expanded to hundreds of tables in 19 UK cities in parks, forests and outdoor recreation spaces. In parallel to this, event-based activities in cricket such as Cage Cricket show that even the most parochial of NGBs are starting to lean towards demand and engage with alternative formats (Hopps, 2015).

Where this is a continued gap in academic and industry understanding is in understanding beliefs, motivations and participant behaviour centred on what others have referred to as at times a rather mystical latent demand for sport and physical activity (Bullough, 2012). The shift to individualisation and craving for self-realisation through informality and the lack of regular commitment required with organised sports shows the potential of outdoor recreation for DCMS, Sport England and wider government (DEFRA, DoH and DCLG). It seems that we need to consider how individuals and group aspects linked to communities, families and friends illustrate how outdoor recreation facilitates the inclusion of boarder demographic groups in co-participation. For example, minority groups who access outdoor recreation less need to be better considered to identify what barriers sport and leisure providers and organisational infrastructure agencies put in place. Spaces and places for leisure then need to be proactively managed better to encompass such views using a research-led approach (Medcalf & Mackintosh, 2019). The scope with which factors including (but not limited to) gender, ethnicity, disability and social class shape or constrain growth of the outdoor recreation community are a critical line of future enquiry for policy makers and academic researchers. We encourage both communities of interested parties alongside those managing outdoor recreation practice to begin to examine these areas beyond the "gaze" and experience of the white middle-class male.

We have mapped out a framework that we propose that may underpin the development and in one specific alternative to this broader stagnant trend. Considering activities such as The Tough Mudder-type event has currently limited understanding. Yet we see this and other alternative incarnations that have begun to be more systematically developed, in part as a response to linking monitoring of NGB sport participation levels with potential reward of future funding. If Tough Mudder-style events and similar outdoor recreation alternatives are becoming a participation success globally, we need to question what is it about them that both funding agencies, sport development practitioners and policy makers can learn from. The natural link is to other events that run in other models of delivery such as Park Run (Hindley, 2018) and Active Forests partnership by Sport England (O'Brien & Forester, 2017). As sport and leisure managers, this, perhaps simply put, can allow us to better meet the needs of the individual participant and our communities. Future research needs to examine emergent new formats of activities that.

Inflexibility in funding based on existing tiers of decision makers in NGBs and a failure to open access to these new potential exciting markets as examined in this paper are currently limiting future expansion and growth. If craving for self-actualisation amidst an increasingly individualised leisure experience is how societies and communities are organising themselves then it is for the leisure and sport providers to respond to this challenge. Exploring the communities, individuals and policy makers that are part of this movement in the UK and beyond is both an empirical and theoretical challenge that can offer considerable insights for the management and development of sport and leisure.

Disclosure statement

No potential conflict of interest was reported by the authors.

ORCID

G. Griggs http://orcid.org/0000-0002-0985-8244

References

Akers, A., Barton, J., Cosey, R., Gainsford, P., Griffin, M., & Mickelwright, D. (2012). Visual color perception in green exercise: Positive effects on mood and perceived exertion. *Environmental Science & Technology*, 46, 8661–8666.

Atkinson, M. (2009). Parkour, anarcho-environmentalism, and poiesis. *Journal of Sport and Social Issues*, 33(2), 169–194.

Auvinen, J., Tammelin, T., Taimela, S., Zitting, P., Mutanen, P., & Karppinen, J. (2008). Musculoskeletal pains in relation to different sport and exercise activities in youth. *Medicine Science and Sports Exercise*, 40, 1890–1900.

Bale, J. (1994). *Landscapes of modern sport*. Leicester: Leicester University Press.

Bale, J. (2003). *Sports geography*. London: Routledge.

Barton, J., Griffin, M., & Pretty, J. (2012). Exercise-, nature- and socially interactive-based initiatives improve mood and self-esteem in the clinical population. *Perspectives in Public Health*, 132, 89–96.

Barton, J., Hine, R., & Pretty, J. (2009). The health benefits of walking in greenspaces of high natural and heritage value. *Journal of Integrative Environmental Sciences*, 6(4), 261–278.

Barton, J., & Pretty, J. (2010). What is the best dose of nature and green exercise for improving mental health? A multi-study analysis. *Environmental Science and Technology*, 44, 3947–3955.

Beck, U. (1992). *Risk society: Towards a new modernity*. London: Sage.

Beck, U. (1998). *World risk society*. Cambridge: Polity Press.

Beck, U. (2011). The Cosmopolitan Manifesto. In D. Held & G. Brown (Eds.), *The cosmopolitanism reader* (pp. 217–228). Cambridge: Polity Press.

Beck, U., & Beck-Gernsheim, E. (1995). *The normal chaos of love*. Cambridge: Polity Press.

Beck, U., & Beck-Gernsheim, E. (2001). *Individualization*. London: Sage.

Beck, U., Bonss, W., & Lau, C. (2003). The theory of reflexive modernization. *Theory Culture Society*, 20(2), 1–33.

Berman, M. G., Jonides, J., & Kaplan, S. (2008). The cognitive benefits of interacting with nature. *Psychologicical Science*, 19(12), 1207–1212.

Best, J. (2009). What policy-makers want from research; what researchers want to tell them. *Journal of Policy Research in Tourism, Leisure and Events*, 1(2), 175–178.

Bette, K.-H. (1989). *Korperspuren; Zur Semantik und Paradoxie moderner Korperlichkeit*. Berlin: Walter de Gruyter.

Bevir, M., & Rhodes, R. A. W. (2010). *The state as cultural practice*. Oxford: Oxford University Press.

Bevir, M., & Rhodes, R. A. W. (2011). The stateless state. In M. Bevir (Ed.), *The SAGE handbook of governance* (pp. 203–217). London: Sage.

Bevir, M., & Rhodes, R. A. W. (2018). *Routledge handbook of interpretive political science*. London: Routledge.

Booth, D., & Thorpe, H. (Eds.) (2007). *Berkshire encyclopaedia of extreme sports*. Great Barrington, MA: Berkshire Reference Works.

Bowler, D. E., Buying-Ali, L. M., Knight, T. M., & Pullin, A. S. (2010). A systematic review of evidence for the added benefits to health of the exposure to natural environments. *BMC Public Health*, *10*, 456–556.

Bratman, G. N., Daily, G. C., Levy, B. J., & Gross, J. J. (2015). The benefits of nature experience: Improved affect and cognition. *Landscape and Urban Planning*, *138*(6), 41–50.

Breivik, G. (1996). Personality, sensation seeking and risk taking among Everest climbers. *International Journal of Sport Psychology*, *27*, 308–320.

British Broadcasting Corporation (BBC). (2018). Allow boxing in prisons, Ministry of Justice report says. Retrieved from https://www.bbc.co.uk/news/uk-45141149

Bullough, S. J. (2012). A new look at the latent demand for sport and its potential to deliver a positive legacy for London 2012. *International Journal of Sport Policy and Politics*, *4*(1), 39–54.

Butts, S. (2001). Good to the last drop: Understanding surfers' motivations. *Sociology of Sport Online (SOSOL)*, *4*(1), 1–7.

Cabinet Office/DCMS. (2002). *Game plan*. London: Cabinet Office/DCMS.

Camoletto, R. F., Sterchele, D., & Genova, C. (2015). Managing alternative sports: New organisational spaces for the diffusion of Italian parkour. *Modern Italy*, *20*(3), 307–319.

Caron, A. V., Hausenblas, H. A., & Estabrooks, P. A. (2003). Motivational theories of exercise and physical activity. In *The psychology of physical activity* (pp. 171–182). Boston, MA: McGraw-Hill.

Carter, P. (2005). *Review of national sport effort and resources*. Lord Carter of Coles Independent Review, London.

Comley, V., & Mackintosh, C. (2014). *Reconomics: The economic impact of outdoor recreation in the UK – The evidence*. Liverpool: Liverpool John Moores University/SRA.

Countryside Agency. (2005). *Demand for outdoor recreation in the English national parks*. Cheltenham: Countryside Agency.

Cramer, J. T. (2008). Bioenergetics of exercise and training. In T. R. Baechle & R. W. Earle (Eds.), *Essentials of strength training and conditioning* (3rd ed., pp. 21–39). Champaign, IL: Human Kinetics.

Crocket, H. (2013). 'This is men's ultimate': (Re)creating multiple masculinities in elite open Ultimate Frisbee. *International Review for the Sociology of Sport*, *48*(3), 318–333.

Crocket, H. (2016). An ethic of indulgence? Alcohol, ultimate Frisbee and calculated hedonism. *International Review for the Sociology of Sport*, *51*(5), 617–631.

Crum, B. (1993). Conventional thought and practice in physical education: Problems of teaching and implications for change. *Quest (Grand Rapids, Mich)*, *45*, 339–356.

Crum, B. (1994). Changes in movement culture: Challenges for sport pedagogy. Proceedings from the AISEP conference, volume 2, *Sport Leisure and Physical Education, Trends and Developments*.

Cutforth, C. (2017). Understanding the landscape of community sport. In R. Wilson & C. Platts (Eds.), *Managing and developing community sport* (pp. 15–29). London: Routledge.

Department for the Environment, Farming and Rural Affairs (DEFRA). (2018). *A green future: Our 25 year plan to improve the environment*. London: Author.

Department of Culture, Media and Sport. (2015a). *A new strategy for sport: A consultation paper*. London: Author.

Department of Culture, Media and Sport (DCMS). (2015). *Sporting nation*. London: Author.

Eichberg, H. (1998). *Body cultures: Essays on sport, space and identity*. London: Routledge.

Elias, N., & Dunning, E. (1986). *Quest for excitement: Sport and leisure in the civilizing process*. Oxford: Basil Blackwell.

Featherstone, M. (1991). *Consumer culture and postmodernism*. London: Sage.

Fitzpatrick. (2013). I felt like I was a road runner. *Telegraph*, 10th May 2013. Retrieved from https://www.telegraph.co.uk/lifestyle/wellbeing/outdoors/10050064/Tough-Mudder-2013-I-felt-like-I-was-Road-Runner.html

Focht, B. C. (2009). Brief walks in outdoor and laboratory environments: Effects on affective responses, enjoyment, and intentions to walk for exercise. *International Journal of Stress Management*, *14*(1), 88–98.

Giddens, A. (1990). *The consequences of modernity*. Cambridge: Polity Press.

Giddens, A. (1991). *Modernity and self-identity. Self and society in the late modern age*. Oxford: Polity Press.

Gidlow, C. J., Jones, M. V., Hurst, G., Masterson, D., Clark-Carter, D., Tarvainen, M. P., ... Nieuwenhuijsen, M. (2016). Where to put your best foot forward: Psycho-physiological responses to walking in natural and urban environments. *Journal of Environmental Psychology*, *45*(3), 22–29.

Gilchrist, P., & Wheaton, B. (2011). Lifestyle sport, public policy and youth engagement: Examining the emergence of parkour. *International Journal of Sport Policy and Politics, 3* (1), 109–131.

Giulianotti, R. (1995). Participant observation and research into football hooliganism: Reflections on the problems of entrée and everyday risks. *Sociology of Sport Journal, 12*(1), 1–20.

Gladwell, V. F., Brown, D. K., Wood, C., Sandercock, G. R., & Barton, J. L. (2013). The great outdoors: How a green exercise environment can benefit all. *Extreme Physiology & Medicine, 2*, 3–13.

Gonzalez, M. T., Hartig, T., Patil, G. G., Martinsen, E. W., & Kirkevold, M. (2011). A prospective study of group cohesiveness in therapeutic horticulture for clinical depression. *International Journal of Mental Health Nursing, 20*, 119–129.

Green, K. (2010). *Key themes in youth sport*. London: Routledge.

Griggs, G. (2009a). 'Just a sport made up in a car park?': The 'soft' landscape of ultimate Frisbee. *Social and Cultural Geography, 10*(7), 757–770.

Griggs, G. (2009b). 'When a ball dreams, it dreams it's a Frisbee': The emergence of aesthetic appreciation within Ultimate Frisbee. *Sport in Society, 12* (10), 1317–1326.

Griggs, G. (2011). 'This must be the only sport in the world where most of the players don't know the rules': Operationalizing self-refereeing and the spirit of the game in UK Ultimate Frisbee. *Sport in Society, 14*(1), 97–110.

Griggs, G. (2012). Why have alternative sports grown in popularity in the UK? *Annals of Leisure Research, 15*(2), 180–187.

Hagger, M., & Chatzisarantis, N. (2005). *The social psychology of exercise and sport*. New York, NY: Open University Press.

Hammit, W. E. (2000). The relation between being away and privacy in urban forest recreation environments. *Environment and Behaviour, 32*(4), 521–540.

Henley Centre. (2005). *Outdoor recreation strategy*. London: Natural England.

Herzog, T., Black, A., Fountaine, K., & Knotts, D. (1997). Reflection and attentional recovery as distinctive benefits of restorative environments. *Journal of Environmental Psychology, 17*(2), 165–170.

Herzog, T., Chen, H., & Primeau, J. (2002). Perception of the restorative potential of natural and other settings. *Journal of Environmental Psychology, 22* (3), 295–306.

Herzog, T. R., & Strevey, S. J. (2008). Contact with nature, sense of humor, and psychological well-being. *Environment and Behavior, 40*(6), 747–776.

Hindley, D. (2018). "More Than Just a Run in the Park": An exploration of Parkrun as a Shared Leisure Space, Leisure Sciences. (iFirst publication).

Holland, J., & Thomson, R. (1999). *Respect youth values: Identity, diversity and social change. ESRC children 5-16 research programme Briefing*. London: ESRC.

Hopps, D. (2015). *ECB seeks to reshape amateur game*. Retrieved March, 2019, from http://wwwespncricinfo.com/england/content/story/839459.html

Houlihan, B., & White, A. (2002). *The politics of sport development*. London: Routledge.

Howell, O. (2008). Skatepark as Neoliberal Playground. *Space and Culture, 11*(4), 475–496.

Jackson, P., Stevenson, N., & Brooks, K. (2001). *Making sense of men's magazines*. Cambridge: Polity Press.

Kaplan, S. (1992). The restorative environment: Nature and human experience. In D. Relf (Ed.), *The role of horticulture in human well-being and social development: A national symposium* (pp. 134–142). Portland, OR: Timber Press.

Kaydo, C. (2013). *How Tough Mudder uses social media to fuel its rapid growth*. Retrieved March 20, 2019, from https://www.bizbash.com/experiential/media-gallery/13480106/how-tough-mudder-uses-social-media-sharing-to-fuel-its-rapid-growth

Kennedy, S. (2012). Playing dirty. Outside. Retrieved from https://www.outsideonline.com/1908376/playing-dirty

Kilpatrick, M., Hebert, E., & Jacobsen, D. (2002). Physical activity motivation: A practitioner's guide to self-determination theory. *JOPERD, 73*(4), 36–41.

Korpela, K., Borodulin, K., Neuvonen, M., Paronen, O., & Tyrvainen, L. (2014). Analysing the mediators between nature-based outdoor recreation and emotional wellbeing. *Journal of Environmental Psychology, 37*, 1–7.

Kuo, F., & Sullivan, W. (2001). Aggression and Violence in the inner city. *Environment and Behavior, 33*(4), 543–571.

Kylton, K. (Ed.). (2013). *Sport development: Policy, process and practice*. London: Routledge.

L'Aoustet, O., & Griffet, J. (2001). The experience of teenagers at Marseilles' skate park. *Cities (London, England), 18*(6), 413–418.

Laursen, P. B. (2010). Training for intense exercise performance: High-intensity or high-volume training? *Scandinavian Journal of Medicine, Science and Sports, 20*(2), 1–10.

Li, Q. (2010). Effect of forest bathing trips on human immune function. *Environmental Health and Preventative Medicine, 15*(1), 9–17.

Louv, R. (2005). *Last child in the woods: Saving our children from nature-deficit disorder*. Chapel Hill, NC: Algonquin.

Lubbe, H. (1988). Menschen im Jahr 2000. Rahmenbedinggungen fur die kunftige Entwicklung des Sports. In K.-H. Giesler, O. Grupe, & K. Heinmann (Eds.), *Dokumentation des Kongresses 'Menschen im Sport 2000'* (pp. 32–43). Schorndorf: Hofmann.

Mackintosh, C. (2014). Dismantling the school sport partnership infrastructure: Findings from a survey of physical education and school sport practitioners. *Education 3-13*, 42(4), 432–449.

Mackintosh, C. (2018). Challenging the status quo. *Sport Management*, 32 (3), London, Leisure Media. Retrieved from http://www.sportsmanagement.co.uk/digital/index1.cfm?mag=&codeid=3447&linktype=homepage&ref=n

Mackintosh, C. I., Darko, N., & May-Wilkins, H. (2016). Unintended outcomes of the London 2012 Olympic Games: Local voices of resistance and the challenge for sport participation leverage in England. *Leisure Studies*, 35(4), 454–469.

Mackintosh, C., Griggs, G., & Cookson, G. (2014). Reflections on the PING! Table tennis initiative: Lessons and new directions for sports development? *International Journal of Public Sector Management*, 27(2), 128–139.

Mackintosh, C., & Liddle, J. (2015). Emerging school sport development policy, practice and governance in England: Big Society, autonomy and decentralisation. *Education 3-13*, 43(6), 603–620.

Martin, H. (2013). In big-money obstacle runs, mud and risks are par for the course. *Los Angeles Times*. Retrieved from http://articles.latimes.com/2013/sep/14/business/la-fi-mud-runs-20130914

Medcalf, R., & Mackintosh, C. (2019). *Researching difference in sport and physical activity*. London: Routledge.

Meek, R. (2018). *A sporting Chance: An independent review of sport in youth and adult prisons*. London: Ministry of Justice.

Midol, N. (1993). Cultural dissents and technical innovations in the 'Whiz' sports. *International Review for the Sociology of Sport*, 28(1), 23–32.

Midol, N., & Broyer, G. (1995). Toward an anthropological analysis of new sport cultures: The case of whiz sports in France. *Sociology of Sport Journal*, 12, 204–212.

Morris, N. (2003). *Health, wellbeing and open space: Literature review*. OPENspace: Research for the Inclusive Access to Outdoor Environments.

Mort, F. (1988). Boy's won? Masculinity, style and popular culture. In J. Rutherford (Ed.), *Male order: Unwrapping masculinity* (pp. 192–224). London: Lawrence and Wishart.

Mullins, N. (2012). Obstacle course challenges: History, popularity, performance Demands, Effective training, and course Design. *Journal of Exercise Physiology*, 15(2), 113–125.

Nettleton, S., & Hardey, M. (2006). Running away with health: The urban marathon and the construction of 'charitable bodies'. *Health: An Interdisciplinary Journal for the Social Study of Health, Illness and Medicine*, 10(4), 441–460.

O'Brien, L., & Forester, J. (2017). *Fun and fitness in the forest: Monitoring and evaluation of the three-year Active forest pilot programme*. Farnham: Report for Sport England, Forest Research.

Ojala, A., Korpela, K., Tyrväinen, L., Tiittanen, P., & Lanki, T. (2018). Restorative effects of urban green environments and the role of urban-nature orientedness and noise sensitivity: A field experiment. *Health and Place* (in press, open access).

Outdoor Industries Association (OIA). (2015). *Getting active outdoors*. London: Sport England/OIA.

Outdoor Industries Association (OIA). (2017). *New WOG research indicates strong growth*. Retrieved March 15, 2019, from http://www.theoia.co.uk/news/new-eog-research-group-indicates-strong-growth-outdoor-market-2017/

Park, B., Tsunetsugu, Y., Kasetani, T., Kagawa, T., & Miyakazi, Y. (2010). The physiological effects of Shinrin-yoko (taking in the forest atmosphere or forest bathing): Evidence from field experiments in 24 forests across Japan. *Environmental Health Preventative Medicine*, 15(1), 18–26.

Peacock, J., Hine, R., & Pretty, J. (2007). *Got the blues? Then find some green space: The mental health benefits of green exercise activities and green care*. Colchester: Centre for Environment and Society.

Pretty, J., Peacock, J., Sellens, M., & Griffin, M. (2005). The mental and physical health outcomes of green exercise. *International Journal of Environmental Health Research*, 15(5), 319–337.

Prout, A. (2000). Children's participation: Control and self-realisation in British Late modernity. *Children and Society*, 14, 304–315.

Puddle, D., Wheaton, B., & Thorpe, H. (2018). The glocalization of parkour: A New Zealand/Aotearoa case study. *Sport in Society*, 1–18.

Reuter, B. H., & Hagerman, P. S. (2008). Aerobic endurance exercise training. In T. R. Baechle & R. W. Earle (Eds.), *Essentials of strength training and conditioning* (3rd ed., pp. 489–503). Champaign, IL: Human Kinetics.

Rinehart, R., & Sydnor, S. (Eds.) (2012). *To the extreme: Alternative sports, Inside and out*. Albany: SUNY Press.

Rink, J. E. (2005). *Teaching physical education for learning*. (5th ed.). St. Louis, MI: McGraw-Hill Humanities.

Roberts, G. C., Treasure, D. C., & Conroy, D. E. (2007). Understanding the dynamics of motivation in sport and physical activity: An achievement goal interpretation. In G. Tenenbaum & R. C. Eklund (Eds.), *Handbook of sport psychology* (3rd ed., pp. 3–30). Hoboken, NJ: Wiley.

Rossi, B., & Cereatti, L. (1993). The sensation seeking in mountain athletes as assessed by Zuckerman's sensation seeking scale. *International Journal of Sport Psychology*, 24(4), 417–431.

Rutter, M., & Smith, D. J. (1997). Psychosocial disorders in young people: Time trends and their causes. *British Journal of Educational Studies*, 32(4), 306–307.

Ryan, R. M., Weinstein, N., Berstein, J., Warren Brown, K., Mistretta, L., & Gagne, M. (2010). Vitalising effects of being outdoors and in nature. *Journal of Environmental Psychology*, 30, 159–168.

Shipway, R., & Holloway, I. (2010). Running free: Embracing a healthy lifestyle through distance running. *Perspectives in Public Health*, 130(6), 270–276.

Shipway, R., Holloway, I., & Jones, I. (2013). Organisations, practices, actors, and events: Exploring inside the distance running social world. *International Review for the Sociology of Sport*, 48(3), 259–276.

Shipway, R., & Jones, I. (2008). The great suburban Everest: An 'insiders' perspective on experiences at the 2007 Flora London Marathon. *Journal of Sport & Tourism*, 13(1), 61–77.

Shulze, G. (1992). *Die Erlebnisgesellschaft*. Frankfurt: Campus.

Sport and Recreation Alliance. (2014). *Reconomics*. London: Author.

Sport and Recreation Alliance. (2017). *Reconomics Plus*. London: Author.

Sport England. (2016a). Active people survey. Retrieved from http://www.sportengland.org/research/active_people_survey/active_people_survey_1.aspx

Sport England. (2016b). *Towards an active nation*. London: Sport England.

Sport England. (2017). Active people survey. Retrieved from http://www.sportengland.org/research/active_people_survey/active_people_survey_1.aspx

Stebbins, R. A. (1997). Casual leisure: A conceptual statement. *Leisure Studies*, 16(1), 17–25.

Stebbins, R. (1992). *Amateurs, professionals and serious leisure*. London: McGill Queens.

Stevinson, C., & Hickson, M. (2014). Exploring the public health potential of a mass community participation event. *Journal of Public Health*, 36(2), 268–274.

Sugiyama, T., Leslie, E., Giles-Corli, B., & Owen, N. (2008). Associations of neighbourhood greenness with physical and mental health: Do walking, social coherence and local social interaction explain the relationships. *Journal of Epidemiology and Community Health*, 62(5), e9.

ten Brink, P., Mutafoglu, K., Schweitzer, J. P., Kettunen, M., Twigger-Ross, C., Baker, J., … Ojala, A. (2016). *The health and social benefits of nature and biodiversity protection. A report for the European Commission (ENV.B.3/ETU/2014/0039)*. London: Institute for European Environmental Policy.

Thompson, C., & Aspinall, P. A. (2011). Natural environments and their impact on activity, health, and quality of life. *Applied Psychology: Health and Wellbeing*, 3, 230–260.

Tomlinson, A., Ravenscroft, N., Wheaton, B., & Gilchrist, P. (2005). Lifestyle sport and national sport policy: An agenda for research. Report to Sport England (March). Retrieved from http://www.sportengland.org/search.aspx?query=lifestyle+sport+and+national+sport+policy

Triggs, J. (2008). The toughest race on earth. Retrieved from http://www.express.co.uk/expressyourself/33358/The-toughest-race-on-earth

UK Parliament. (2015). Hansard parliament debate record from Westminster Hall – Outdoor recreation, 28th October 2.30 pm, 2015. Retrieved from https://hansard.parliament.uk/commons/2015-10-8/debates/15102834000003/OutdoorRecreation

Ulrich, R. S. (1979). Visual landscapes and psychological wellbeing. *Landscape Research*, 4, 17–23.

Ulrich, R. S. (1981). Natural versus urban scenes: Some psychophysiological effects. *Journal of Environment and Behaviour*, 13(5), 523–556.

Ulrich, R. S. (2002, May 14). *The therapeutic role of green space*. Paper presented at the Green space and Healthy Living National Conference, Manchester.

Ulrich, R. S., & Parsons, R. (1992). Influences of passive experiences with plants on individual well-being and health. In D. Relf (Ed.), *The role of horticulture in human well-being and social development* (pp. 93–105). Portland, OR: Timber Press.

Ulrich, R. S., Simons, R. F., & Losito, B. D. (1991). Stress recovery during exposure to natural ad urban environments. *Journal of Environmental Psychology*, 16, 3–11.

Wagenaar, H. (2011). *Meaning in action: Interpretation and dialogue in policy analysis*. New York, NY: M. E. Sharpe.

Walvin, J. (Ed.) (1975). *Leisure and society 1830–1950*. London: Longman.

Wang, N. (1999). Rethinking authenticity in tourism experience. *Annals of Tourism Research*, *26* (2), 349–370.

Whannel, G. (2002). *Media sport stars: Masculinities and moralities*. London: Routledge.

Wheaton, B. (2000). "Just Do It": Consumption, commitment, and identity in the windsurfing subculture. *Sociology of Sport Journal*, *17*, 254–274.

Wheaton, B. (Ed.) (2004). *Understanding lifestyle sports: Consumption, identity and difference*. London: Routledge.

Wheaton, B. (2007). After sport culture. *Journal of Sport and Social Issues*, *31*(3), 283–307.

Wheaton, B. (2013). *The cultural politics of lifestyle sports*. London: Routledge.

White, R., & Heerwagen, J. (1998). Nature and mental health: Biophilia and biophobia. In A. Lundberg (Ed.), *The environment and mental health: A guide for clinicians* (pp. 175–192). Mahwah, NJ: Lawrence Erlbaum Associates.

World Heart Foundation (WHF). (2011). Cardio vascular disease. Retrieved from http://www.bhf.org.uk/heart-health/conditions/cardiovascular-disease.aspx

Zuckerman, M. (1983). Sensation seeking and sports. *Personality and Individual Differences*, *4*(3), 285–292.

Zuckerman, M. (1994). *Behavioural expressions and biosocial bases of sensation seeking*. New York, NY: Cambridge Press.

OPEN ACCESS

Rationalities of goodwill: on the promotion of philanthropy through sports-based interventions in Sweden

David Ekholm and Magnus Dahlstedt

ABSTRACT
Organised in public–private partnerships, sports-based interventions for social inclusion are often seen as sites of strategies involving sport associations, social entrepreneurs, volunteers and sponsors in the provision of welfare. Here, we spotlight two midnight football practices acted out in two mid-sized Swedish cities promoting social inclusion, examining, from a governmentality perspective, how supportive community actors conceptualise their charitable contributions enabling opportunities for under-privileged youth to participate in sports. Analysis outlines how actors articulate their particular background, experiences and social networks as resources to provide support, stressing that provision needs to make a difference and support the less fortunate in the community. The provision imbues a political potential, as a means of promoting social change, guided by certain notions of the good society and of the good citizen. Involvement provides a site for realising particular visions of social change, while animating the contributions provided as non-political acts of goodwill.

Introduction

Sports-based interventions have emerged as an integral feature of social policy, not least as part of strategies to promote social inclusion (e.g. Collins & Haudenhuyse, 2015). Organised in public–private partnerships, they are often seen as sites of strategies involving sport associations (e.g. Stenling & Fahlén, 2016), entrepreneurs (e.g. Peterson & Schenker, 2017) and volunteers (e.g. Reid, 2012), among others, in the provision of welfare. In this article, we highlight two specific sports-based interventions: midnight football (MF) practices in two mid-sized Swedish cities and promoting social inclusion specifically targeting youth in what are referred to in dominant political discourse as areas of exclusion (cf. Dahlstedt & Ekholm, 2019).

In particular, we investigate the roles and contributions of charitable community actors and financial supporters, focusing on their contributions that facilitate these activities. More precisely, the aim of this article is to examine how supportive and facilitating actors describe their charitable roles, collaborations and contributions in providing resources that enable sports-based interventions and thus facilitate opportunities for youth in suburban areas of exclusion to participate in community sports. Based on a governmentality perspective (cf. Dean, 2010; Foucault, 1982; Rose, 1999),

---

This is an Open Access article distributed under the terms of the Creative Commons Attribution-NonCommercial-NoDerivatives License (http://creativecommons.org/licenses/by-nc-nd/4.0/), which permits non-commercial re-use, distribution, and reproduction in any medium, provided the original work is properly cited, and is not altered, transformed, or built upon in any way.

highlighting neo-philanthropic governmental rationality (cf. Dean & Villadsen, 2016; Villadsen, 2007), we address the following research questions: How do these community actors describe, motivate and legitimise the goodwill and contributions provided? How are the rationales of means and ends of social change articulated in relation to the goodwill and contributions provided? These questions are investigated through an analysis of statements made by representatives of the community actors involved and financial supporters. From this point of view, we examine how notions of goodwill, charitable contributions and rationales of philanthropy are embedded in strategies of providing social support and in promoting social change. Consequently, we explore how welfare provision is formed (and transformed) today, how a variety of community actors engage in welfare and how rationales of neo-philanthropy are intertwined in contemporary society.

Setting the scene

In the wake of increasing socio-economic divisions, ethno-cultural segregation and intensified polarisation in the urban landscape in Sweden, there has in recent years been a heated debate concerning tensions and conflicts ascribed to and located in areas of exclusion (Sernhede, Thörn, & Thörn, 2016). In Sweden, there has been a particular focus on the situation of youth in suburban residential areas of exclusion, where a range of interventions have been proposed as means of responding to social exclusion (Dahlstedt & Ekholm, 2019). In influential political discourse, these areas have been constructed as sites of otherness and positioned as outside the mainstream Swedish society, supposedly constituting a threat to community and social cohesion (Sernhede et al., 2016). Segregation, urban polarisation and conflicts are not limited to a Swedish context; rather, these issues have been noted as recurrent challenges by policymakers in many countries and continually observed and discussed in scientific discourse (Dikec, 2017).

One of the problems addressed is the lack of participation in youth sport activities and other organised leisure activities in these areas, viewed as one of the results of unequal living conditions (cf. Stockholm Municipality, 2015). In this policy landscape, civil society has been highlighted as a site where social inclusion could be created, and even as a site of social policy implementation (Skille, 2011) – not uncommonly in short-term projects acted out in public–private partnerships (Herz, 2016). Sports associations, in particular, have been highlighted in this regard (cf. Stenling & Fahlén, 2016). In Sweden, expectations on sport associations to contribute to social policy objectives are formalised and are increasingly conditioning financial support (e.g. Norberg, 2011).

Internationally, this development has been conceptualised as part of a neo-liberal trend in sport and social policy (e.g. Hartmann, 2016), described in relation to austerity policies (e.g. Parnell, Spracklen, & Millward, 2017) sharpening the conditions for sport provision, especially in distressed residential areas (e.g. Bustad & Andrews, 2017). Such a development has also been observed in Scandinavia (Agergaard, Michelsen la Cour, & Treumer Gregersen, 2015) and in Sweden (Ekholm, 2018). Researchers have highlighted sports-based interventions, performed on the basis of expected social benefits, as sites of public–private partnerships involving for instance municipal agencies (Hoekman, Breedveld, & Kraaykamp, 2017), sport federations and local sport associations (Stenling & Fahlén, 2016), social entrepreneurs (Peterson & Schenker, 2017), market-based corporations as sponsors (Stinson & Pritchard, 2013), non-governmental organisations (Sherry, Schulenkorf, & Chalip, 2015), community groups (Rosso & McGrath, 2017) and charity organisations (Bunds, 2017), as well as parents and youth (Ekholm, 2018; Ekholm & Dahlstedt, 2017). Practitioners and providers of such interventions have been noted to be motivated by both a love of sport and the desire to make a difference in society (Peachey, Musser, Shin, & Cohen, 2017) – motivations not uncommonly underpinned by neo-colonial notions of aid and support and an evangelistic faith in the power of sport (e.g. Giulianotti, 2004; Peachey et al., 2017). Consequently, interventions risk being carried out on the terms of the providers rather than on the conditions of the recipients and participating youth (Giulianotti, 2004).

Philanthropy in Swedish social policy

In this article, we draw attention to the role of charitable contributions and philanthropic underpinnings of certain actors partnering in the sports-based interventions scrutinised, a dimension that so far has received rather little attention in the literature. Still, philanthropy is not primarily a question of to which extent voluntary actors are involved in social support; rather, the main objective is the epistemology of help and social support, i.e. how activities are thought about, how subjects are constructed and targeted and how interventions are formed (Villadsen, 2008b). We focus on how a range of representatives and promoters, in funding and supporting roles, articulate their roles and contributions facilitating the sports-based interventions. Philanthropic rationalities and technologies of welfare provision are regular features in contemporary Western societies, when it comes to social and individual support as well as in labour market policies (i.e. empowerment, moral responsibilisation, help to self-help and community ideals) (Villadsen, 2007, 2008b), primarily in more liberal and conservative welfare regimes (cf. Esping-Andersen, 1990).

Even though charity and philanthropy throughout the history of the Swedish and social-democratic welfare state have been present in the social support provided (Trädgårdh, 2013), charity and philanthropy in Swedish social policy is a conflicted topic. In the Scandinavian context, *philanthropy* often has a negative connotation associated with arbitrary provision of goods based on goodwill rather than egalitarian principles of social rights (cf. Trädgårdh, 2013; Villadsen, 2011a). Furthermore, *welfare* generally has a more positive connotation than in liberal welfare states, emphasising social rights and social solidarity by means of risk-collectivisation (cf. Esping-Andersen, 1990).

With respect to contemporary political debate and forms of welfare provision, philanthropy has explicitly been emphasised as an innovative way to revitalise social support provision. Social entrepreneurs, modern-day philanthropists, are sometimes seen as pioneers breaking ground and influencing welfarist social support (Palmås, 2011). In addition, philanthropists often exhibit less accountability with respect to their contributions than other actors (Weinryb, 2015). Importantly, as Villadsen (2011a, p. 1061) notes, analysing philanthropic provision of social support is not only about highlighting certain actors and their charitable roles, but more about interrogating "how their involvement may contribute to transforming social policy and our thinking about social problems". This makes exploring the (re-)emergence of philanthropic rationales and forms of involvement in the provision of welfare in a Scandinavian, and particularly Swedish, welfare-statist context an intriguing point of departure.

Empirical material

The analysis is based on interviews with representatives and promoters, in funding and supporting roles, explicitly addressing charity, financial or other forms of support, of the two sports-based interventions mentioned.

The MF practices were initiated by a national foundation specialising in sports-based interventions that promote social inclusion, involving local associations in carrying out the programmes. The foundation hosts, charitable, national and local corporate social responsibility (CSR) initiatives supporting the local programmes. The goals are described as "to promote integration through sport" and "to develop a sense of responsibility and participation in society as well as employability [...], to prevent social exclusion [and] to contribute to crime reduction". East City MF is run by a local sports club and an elite football club in collaboration with the foundation; West City MF is run by one local sports club in partnership with the foundation. Both activities are performed in suburban areas in the respective cities. The activities are funded primarily by local sponsors and sponsors within the national foundation, as well as by grants and subsidies from municipal administrations. The activities consist of organised, yet spontaneous, five-a-side football, held indoors on Saturday nights between 8pm and midnight. Participating youth are generally aged 12–25. Notably, almost all the youth participating in the activities are boys. The two MF activities are related to each other through the foundation, even though they are do not collaborate formally. Both MF activities have received significant media attention and both have been nominated for prizes for their contribution to social inclusion. Similar MF activities are carried out with the foundation as a partner in 10 additional cities.

The analysis is based on interviews with the following seven respondents. *The foundation executive* initiated the MF concept and was part of the social network that started the foundation initiating the practices. He describes himself as an "entrepreneur with a mission to build up" the foundation. *The foundation manager* is a former elite football player who is now responsible for collaborations between the foundation and the local partners. *The insurance company sponsor representative* manages the company's CSR efforts and sponsorships, in which the two MF activities are pivotal. *The sports gear CSR representative* is responsible for the social responsibility commitment of his company, supporting the two MF practices and the foundation initiating the practices. *The factory owner* supports West City MF financially and provides contacts within his social network.

He is the third-generation owner and managing director of a family business, which is now a major manufacturer of industrial goods operating in the global market. *The gentlemen's club secretary* represents a local subdivision of an international charity trust and fellowship, which supports charitable projects in West City, including the MF activity. *The elite club CSR representative* works for the elite club and is in charge of its CSR activities.

Semi-structured interviews were conducted with each representative at locations decided on by the respondents themselves, primarily workplaces and offices, during 2017. These interviews were conducted within the same period as interviews with the management and coaches of the interventions that laid the ground for mapping the overall organisation of the interventions. The respondents were deemed to be the most important for – and well-informed about – the intervention. The questions asked in the interviews concerned the interventions in particular, and sport as a means of social inclusion in general. There was a particular focus on how they understood the goals of the interventions and the problems addressed, the organisation of the interventions, the respondent's role and driving forces in relation to the interventions, and their collaboration and networks with other actors and agencies. One recurring topic concerned how all respondents highlighted their charitable contributions, goodwill and drive to make a difference in various ways. All interviews were transcribed verbatim.

Theoretical and methodological framework

Interventions aiming to promote social change and reform the conduct of subjects or conditions of inclusion imbue dimensions of governing. Analytically, we approach governing as a productive force performed by actors seeking to lead, guide or shape the behaviours and ways of thinking – the *conduct* – of individuals and populations (Foucault, 1982). Accordingly, ways of governing means structuring power relations and therefore needs to be approached as political practices (cf. Dean, 2010). From this perspective, analysing how practices imbue political dimensions become theoretically amenable.

Notably, social policy interventions such as the sports-based interventions investigated in this article are seen as assemblages of governing technologies designed to lead social change, by shaping the conduct of the targeted youth. Accordingly, governing imbues conceptualisations of problems as well as means and ends of social change, and the relationship interconnecting these constructions of problems, means and ends together forms a *governmental rationality* (Dean, 2010). A particular governmental rationality – characteristic of advanced liberal welfare states, and analytically important with respect to informing the analysis put forth in this article – is *neo-philanthropy*, theoretically elaborated on by Villadsen (2007, 2008b, 2009, 2011a, 2011b). The concept of neo-philanthropy draws attention to the re-emergence of both philanthropic social support *practices*, such as donations to those defined as being in need, and *knowledge* about and political faith in such support, often seen as innovative and authentic forms of welfare provision (Villadsen, 2007, 2011a, 2011b). Here, civil society and community have a certain significance, formed as arenas where governing interventions can be performed "at a distance" from the state and the public sector (Rose, 1999). From this perspective, civil society and community are analysed as discursive formations (Foucault, 1972), animated in discourse forming targets of governing interventions (Rose, 1999). It is within these domains, seen as autonomous from statist government, human beings can perceivably engage in free and voluntary activities, engage in community and ensure welfare provision (Villadsen, 2007, 2009). Importantly, it is the discourse about these domains that makes certain governing interventions (of philanthropy, for instance) possible. Therefore, we need to analyse the discourse intertwined with and underpinning these practices in order to understand the rationality, how they are formed and the role that charitable contributions play in this respect.

Philanthropic organisations were pivotal for social support and assistance at the end of the nineteenth century, providing for instance education, health care and poverty relief to those seen as being in need. Such practices later influenced the emerging welfare states (Donzelot, 1979; Villadsen, 2011a, 2011b). Importantly, such provision was often underpinned by notions of pragmatism in contrast to religious charity. Here, philanthropic support was seen as a strategic means to attain actual outcomes and the betterment of the beneficiary's living conditions, while religious charity was criticised for its way of conceptualising donations and support as an end in itself (Donzelot, 1979; Villadsen, 2011b). However, such support was based on goodwill rather than social rights, which, in turn, was the basic principle of welfarist governmental rationality of support during the twentieth century (Dean, 2010; Villadsen, 2007).

At the end of the twentieth century, welfarist rationality was criticised for its allegedly centralised and statist planning, social engineering and bureaucratisation, passivising its citizens and corrupting the moral fabric of the population, and furthermore stifling civil society – perceived as more authentic – forms of social support (Dean, 2010; Villadsen, 2007, 2008b). Accordingly, in recent decades, social policy and strategies of support have increasingly relied on public–private partnerships, voluntary work, community-based social work and the mobilisation of social networks, as well as on social change emphasising empowerment technologies, moral and spiritual nourishment and help to self-help strategies – all characteristics of neo-philanthropic governmental rationality

(Villadsen, 2007, 2008b). This development involves a normative state phobia, stressing that civil society provides more authentic alternatives to the authoritarian public sector (Dean & Villadsen, 2016) where the emphasis is on individual willpower and morality rather than structural explanations and social reform (Villadsen, 2007, 2008b, 2011a).

The strategies of analysis adopted concern analysing governmental rationality structuring the statements articulated in the interviews. In practice, this means interpretations guided by the theoretical framework presented. First, inspired by the theoretical conceptualisation of philanthropic support, we managed to elaborate on themes recurring in the empirical material. Three themes were constructed, highlighting positions and motives of goodwill as well as the political potential, significance and underpinning of the statements examined. Second, on the basis of these themes, the interpretation of the statements was elaborated on further and reworked using the theoretical concepts presented as analytical tools. The constructionist epistemology adopted allows for a critical approach by problematising how notions and ideas are formed and how they underpin the contributions made and the technologies of governing promoted, as well as the effects they enable (cf. Foucault, 2004). The rationality of the intervention is contingent and constructed in relation to the specific practices and needs to be critically assessed (cf. Dean, 2010).

Analysis

The analysis highlights three recurring and intersecting themes illustrating the governmental rationality imbued: First, we highlight how the respondents position themselves and articulate their particular background, experiences and social networks as powerful resources to provide for charitable contributions. Second, we interrogate the specific motives underpinning the contributions made. Importantly, a pragmatic rationale is highlighted stressing that provision needs to result in real social change. Notably, the will to do good articulated is elaborated on in relation to the responsibility to provide for the less fortunate and the desire to form and be an active force in community. Third, we paid attention to how the provision of charitable contributions imbue a political potential, as a means of promoting social change, of forming a good society and a good citizen. Altogether, this rationality highlights how goodwill and charitable contributions become means of governing social change.

The position of goodwill

In the interviews, the will to contribute, to do good and to help those in need is a recurring topic. Such desires are allowed to flourish within the realms of civil society engagement, according to a recurring figure of thought made explicit in statements. Notably, statements concerning such wills are articulated from similar positions. Even though the respondents represent a fairly diverse group of actors, they position themselves in similar ways with respect to their contributions. In one instance, respondents describe their own background and experience as the primary motive for their contribution. In another instance, the respondents emphasise their social networks and social position as resources that can be used to provide contributions to society.

In the following excerpt, *the foundation executive* of MF expounds on his particular background, characterised by exclusion and hardship being important for his engagement in MF and his understanding of the targeted youth.

> When I was 15, I burned down a gymnasium, stopped doing sports and started hanging around punk rockers. Then … there were hooligans, skinhead gangs. […] I use to say that it's a broken soul, kind of. How is a soul broken? You recognise these things. And that is

something I recognise so well among the kids out in the suburbs. It's the same. [...] So, you feel excluded ... you kind of connect with that.

Here, the foundation executive positions, and constructs, himself as part of the same community as the targeted youth. Thus, the mutual experience of being and feeling excluded provides a bond ("connect"), perceived as a particularly authentic bond, between the provider and recipient of social support. The bond and mutual experiences, resulting in a "broken soul", is described as the main motive for engaging in providing social support for the youth. Accordingly, given the fact that he has now left his previous life behind him and achieved another social position, he now has the resources to give something back. This voluntary engagement could be channelled through and associated with civil society.

In other excerpts, community is emphasised in other terms, not explicitly on the basis of recognition and shared experiences of exclusion, but rather on the experiences and position of being included and privileged in society. Also, in these cases, previous experiences form a basis for the contributions made. In the following excerpt, *the gentlemen's club secretary* describes his position as geographically as well as socially quite distant from the targeted youth. Moreover, he describes his networks and connections in society as resourceful and ready to be mobilised. The gentlemen's club secretary describes a distinctly different biography to the one presented in the previous excerpt.

> I am part of [the gentlemen's club], which is ... yes, it is a male fellowship. [...] I believe that it is important, that when you are privileged as we are, even though we are not financially wealthy members, we have social networks and we are well off enough to spend money on being in a fellowship ... So, then you have a responsibility, a social responsibility, I believe. [...] None of us live in [the area]. And ... so, it was part of a discussion about giving money ... there were thoughts about the integration challenge. What can we do about this? We are ... we have our social networks, as we grew up in and live in a certain part of the city. But there is a different part of the city, that we are not familiar with. And ... about the visit there ... really, it was like coming to another world.

In the excerpt, the members of the club are described as privileged members of society. Though not always necessarily rich in economic terms, the members are described as being sufficiently well off to spend money and time on club membership. Furthermore, none of the club members reside in the excluded area. Rather, they all live in other parts of the city. As stated in the excerpt, the members do not even know much about the non-privileged parts of the city. When talking about his recent experience of visiting the area during the MF activity, he makes his own position distinctly different by describing it more or less as visiting "another world".

Moreover, in the excerpt the geographic residence of the members is intertwined with their social connectedness and resourceful networks in civil society. As described, having these resources and networks, the members have a social responsibility to provide for the less fortunate, in a variety of ways. Accordingly, the sense of responsibility and the importance of integration recognised provide motivation for engagement from the position of the representative. Here, there is an explicit focus on "the integration challenge", by means of supporting and facilitating the MF initiative. As connectedness and resourceful social networks are powers of the privileged, living in the privileged parts of the city, the provision of social support is directed from the "inside", from those having the means of providing charitable contributions, to the excluded "outside", those who are in need. Even though the respondents position themselves differently in terms of their previous experiences and geographic residence, they all express an explicit and voluntary desire to provide – thus, governing provision – for those who are in need. They are all in the position of having the means of making such contributions, in terms of social networks and resources. Also, provision of support is articulated as a way to form community and moral recognition across the divisions. In this way, relationships and positions of *provider* and *recipient* of social support and charitable contributions are constructed in statements.

The motives of goodwill

The positions of goodwill elaborated on above are intertwined with certain motives and ways of understanding goodwill. The will to do good is guided by certain ethical underpinnings, not least involving an assessment of need and a willingness to help the less fortunate. Yet, at the same time, help is articulated as a means of forming moral bonds and relations in community.

In the interviews, the relationship between the resourceful providers and the less fortunate is constructed as a hierarchic form of goodwill, in two instances. This goodwill involves, first, assessing the "weak" areas and their challenges and, second, providing for the needs assessed. In the following excerpt, *the foundation manager* elaborates on the role of the foundation with respect to the help provided.

> We support and help get started … in various socio-economically weak areas, finding some alternative meeting places for the youth, so that they can be in safe spaces and in secure places at sensitive times, on Friday and Saturday nights … And the effect of this has been immense.

Here, certain areas are constructed as "weak", thus distinguishing different areas in the city from each other. According to the rationale, the "weak" areas have a certain need for safe places where youth can meet on Fridays and Saturdays, as an alternative to destructive surroundings. Such articulations further reinforce a distance between provider and those in need of support. Still, this distance could be overcome through the support provided, establishing moral bonds in the community – something that is illustrated in the next excerpt.

For the local elite sports club involved in East City MF, establishing such morality and community appear to be the primary motivation for involvement in the activities. Here, the help provided becomes a means of establishing moral bonds and relations within the community. For instance, as illustrated in the following excerpt, *the representative of the elite sport club* underscores the importance of both forming and playing an active part in the community, given the club's prominent position in the city.

> The driving force is to always have social engagement. It could be a bit philosophical … […] We have such a strong platform in this city, so we must be able to stand for more things than only during the 90 minutes of a football match […] What kind of engagement do we want from ourselves? That is something we have worked on for some years now. There are core values that our club stands for. […] There are connections to elite sports, if we talk about integration. We have over fifty nationalities in our youth teams. If these are challenges that the city, that is society at large, confronts … well, then maybe it is something that [the elite sports club] should be dedicated to as well. […] So, we felt that we could reach a target group that we believe is really important to reach. That is youth aged 18 to 25 in socio-economically vulnerable areas. […] And we have a role to play here, so of course we want to do that.

As described, the elite sports club, based in the city centre, support the clubs based in the "socio-economically vulnerable areas" to carry out MF as part of its CSR work. Accordingly, social inclusion and integration are issues that the club needs to deal with in its regular youth activities, as these are challenges faced by society at large. The representative stresses that such "core values" of the club, instigating engagement, concern health and integration, which are issues were sport has a formative role to play and that are objects that the club wants to be associated with. By reaching out to youth, particularly those from ethno-cultural minority backgrounds, concentrated in areas with challenges of social exclusion, the elite sports club can regain its central position in the local community.

Although faith in goodwill seems to be firm in the statements analysed, ambiguous reflections on moral concerns with respect to charity and goodwill recur. For instance, *the insurance company sponsor representative* stresses that it should not be "like some superheroes coming into the area saving the kids from the suburbs out there … that's not the real purpose, and it could be so wrong if they get to hear that way of talking about it". According to him, the kids "don't want our compassion … and that's not what it is about, at all". Such reflections concern how charitable actions are underpinned by notions of compassion and feeling good as well as how these actions relate to socio-cultural and socio-economic segregation and inequality. Reflections also concern navigating between different rationalities of goodwill, where goal-oriented and pragmatic provisions of goods (according to a philanthropic rationality) are repeatedly advocated, rather than value-based charity (associated with a more religious rationality of mercy and charity). In the following excerpt, *the gentlemen's club secretary* puts forward such argument, stressing the importance of pragmatism in the support provided.

> We can't donate football boots, that would be a bit "von oben". We want to do something, but it can't be … They don't want donations from us. They don't want that. What can we do, where we help out with stuff, but not like some kind of … I don't know … for us to ease our bad conscience and so on … It shouldn't be about that. […] There is still an inner conflict in me about being in this kind of fellowship. […] But, I was afraid that it would appear as if we would … that they would receive charity, and that we would appear only as … if you know what I mean … like the white man helping out with money and donations to relieve his conscience. And it wasn't like that, we really put our effort into making a difference. […] In the end, it is charity. Because we have the means to do this and they don't. […] It's a little weird with charity, because … it feels nice and in a way it's good that we've done something. But, at the same time, when you have given something, it feels like, damn, you could have done even more.

In the excerpt, it is clearly stated that support should *not* be provided only to ease one's conscience for having a privileged position or for making a good impression. Instead, by means of the support provided, the desire is to make a difference in the lives of the beneficiaries (and thus to govern the social change envisioned), and it is to be "making a difference" that provides the fundamental motivation of engagement. Importantly, the provider explicitly disassociates himself from a way of conceptualising charitable contributions as a condescending, "von oben", activity. Such reflections on the provision of charitable contributions clearly illustrate an emphasis of pragmatism. Still, the provider stresses that feeling good for providing charitable contributions is a notable by-product.

The political potential of goodwill

However, feelings and actions of goodwill are not isolated actions of charitable help. Rather, in the statements analysed, the charitable actions are rooted, explicitly or implicitly, in notions of an ideal society and citizenship, involving the promotion of social change, constructed as a will to make a difference in society and to influence community. They also imbue notions of how this ideal society and citizenship may be enacted, and how their contribution to provide means for enabling community youth sport may be part of this governmental project (acted out at a distance from statist intervention). Accordingly, notions of goodwill imbue a political potential.

Most notably, this political potential involves a will to make a difference. By means of the contributions provided, the respondents wish to facilitate social change, in terms of help to form a good society, inhabited by good citizens. In the following excerpt, *the sports gear CSR representative* illustrates a pragmatic notion of making a difference, when describing the desired result of the charitable provision.

> We aren't so active in the political debate, unfortunately. But where we can make a difference, with local entrepreneurs, we are active there. [...] It comes from "the heart", so to speak... because sport and exercise can change the world. It sounds a bit cheesy, but if you want an answer, then that is what it is about. [...] There are different levels of philanthropy... [...] Within the industry, sports and sports in fashion, we make efforts for local entrepreneurship, to make sure that kids get the chance to be physically active at an early age, and not being out vandalising and making trouble on Fridays and Saturdays. If we can provide some money and contributions that would make a difference, then we should do that. [...] I can see the need here. It becomes very clear. We can see and feel that we actually make a difference. I can come back to the office and give a report from real life, which is valued very highly in this company, that you are not only making donations, but that you were also engaged and have visited there.

Here, making a difference and promoting social change is not explicitly described as a political project. However, by means of taking an active role in promoting social change and by being an active force in society, the technologies of provision promoted are indeed a way of engaging in a project to make a better society. Not least, supporting entrepreneurship within civil society becomes a way to empower and activate the local community. Such engagement is not described in terms of political involvement. The engagement is underpinned by genuine ambitions to do good and to promote a better society. Most notably, the contributions provided are associated with "heart" and a sense of generosity. However, at the same time the contributions provided are underpinned by a pragmatic and goal-oriented rationale. These seemingly contradictory notions of charitable contributions illustrate quite well how a good society, desired and formed as a result of "making a difference", is construed as a society characterised by personal and reciprocal relations between provider and those in need (i.e. a moral local community). Specifically, the political potential depicted in the statements analysed takes two main expressions: the formation of *the good society* and *the good citizen*.

In the following excerpt, the characteristics of the good society are detailed by *the factory owner*. Importantly, civil society is constructed as a domain with a certain potential of community, authenticity, social relations, autonomy and an assumedly genuine solidarity. However, such anti-statist sentiments are reluctantly talked about in political terms.

> Our society becomes what we make it. And I'm not a big fan of the state and the municipality and that they should run everything. [...] I don't want to be political, but for me... [...] My beliefs are that if you integrate everything into the public sector, then you won't solve these problems. Because it has to be from one human being to another. I mean civil society, that is individuals, associations, families, that's all kinds of constellations based on voluntarism in some sense. [...] Municipal government... well, you can't live without the municipality in this country, but, please, makes us at least economically independent from them. [...] I mean, it is incredibly paralysing for people. [...] Then it is a forced solidarity. Solidarity in itself, I mean... the word as such means that you do things by the will of your heart. But, I think that we lost that... when the state and municipality... [...] You take away the will power of individuals, a will power I believe is genuinely good.

In this excerpt, the potential to form a good society is once more made explicit. As "society becomes what we make it", the specific form of this society becomes the target of governing. In this endeavour of providing social support, the provision becomes a way to promote activities conceptualised in terms of (and constructing) civil society, its authenticity and powers of voluntarism, in contrast to the powers of coercion associated with the municipality. Accordingly, social problems should be countered by genuine personal relations and community between moral subjects, preferably without public intervention. Thus, social inclusion should be provided by voluntary measures. In this respect, the MF initiative serves as a way to reform the provision of social support, to enact social change and to re-vitalise civil society.

Also, in the following excerpt, the good society is manifested as an assemblage of good citizens. Accordingly, as described by *the sports gear CSR representative*, the good society is built by good human beings, for good people.

> We want to create activities for children and youth. We want to make sure that children and youth at risk of social exclusion are prioritised. […] That is our ambition, the great vision and mission. And, we say that we want to create an active life for all, and absolutely, that is part of it all. In the strategy we have set up for our social initiatives, that is the basis for all that we do. […] Both in terms of being a good citizen, but also taking part in forming good citizens in some way and … so, I want to say, the concept of the good citizen is quite tellingly.

In this excerpt, the youth targeted by the MF initiative are described as being at risk of social exclusion. Here, the social support provided is focused on enabling social inclusion and an active life. Thus, being active and included is articulated as a good way of being a citizen. As described, by taking corporate social responsibility in providing for social support, the sports gear brand demonstrates what it means to be a good citizen and to be an active part of the community. This demonstration is described as being aimed at facilitating an educative and edifying activity that in turn may form good citizens.

Discussion and conclusion

In relation to how sport participation is legitimised as a social policy objective by means of the envisioned social benefits expected, we here discuss how philanthropy is introduced in social policy through the use of sports-based interventions such as those investigated. The analysis of how actors in supportive and facilitating roles articulate their charitable contributions in providing resources to enable sports-based interventions underscores how their goodwill allows youth in these particular residential areas to participate in football activities. We can reasonably assume that the charitable contributions made contribute by providing opportunities for youth to participate in sport – opportunities that would probably not have been available otherwise. This may be a benefit of the practices: providing opportunities for youth to participate in sport and to enjoy what they feel is a meaningful social and sporting activity (cf. Hartmann, 2016). However, this benign provision of opportunities raises at least three concerns regarding the rationality of goodwill and its political significance, beyond the obvious concerns about the projectification of welfare provision highlighted (Herz, 2016) following on from this analysis, that need to be addressed.

First, the analysis underlines that the targeted youth have unequal opportunities to participate in sports compared to youth living in other areas. Importantly, the conditions of participation for youth in areas of exclusion are underpinned by notions of need and social utility as well as conceptualisations of risk. Here, sport participation is articulated as a means provided for those in need of social support, as youth from these particular areas allegedly pose a risk both to themselves and to society (potentially resulting in delinquency, drug abuse and crime). Consequently, sport participation is provided as a means for social objectives rather than an end in itself (sport participation for fun and amusement) for the targeted youth.

Second, as these sport practices are conditioned by the anticipated social benefit, they become a means of welfare provision, as a part of the plethora of social policy measures and interventions promoted as a response to challenges of social exclusion (cf. Ekholm, 2016). In terms of welfare, the charitable contributions are based on goodwill rather than social rights. Accordingly, for the targeted youth, both welfare and sport participation are conditioned on the grace and goodwill of the provider, of being provided with opportunities for inclusion *in* and *through* sport (cf. Collins & Haudenhuyse, 2015).

Third, the above observation concerns how philanthropic rationales and forms of organisation influence social policy. By forming a kind of practice – sports (generally performed within the realm of civil society) as a means of providing for social support – corporate and civil society actors become involved in social interventions. In addition, the emphasis on goodwill and charitable provision rather than social rights and equal opportunities illustrates how philanthropic rationalities inform social policy in practice. Sports-based interventions performed in public–private partnerships become an opportunity for modern-day philanthropists to engage in social work practices. Such practices emerge through a philanthropic rationale and involvement.

These observations could be viewed in light of a discourse, predominant in relation to welfarist forms of governing, concerning the perceived threat of statist governing colonising civil society, as seen in both social policy and social research (Villadsen, 2008a, 2009). Although public sector and civil society sector divides are contingent and continually re-apprehended, there might be developments in social policy illustrating how (neo-)philanthropy informs public sector interventions and practices (Villadsen, 2009). Such a discourse animates the kind of contributions provided, and focused on in this article, as non-political and non-governmental acts of goodwill, community and provision of support for those in need – incidentally positioning the charitable contributors in various contexts in favourable ways, and establishing themselves as part of the local community (cf. Chouliaraki, 2010). Such discourse is instrumental for setting up the technologies steering the conduct of youth and instigating social change (cf. Foucault, 1982), not least by means of constructing moral relations (and by making the morality visible and explicit) between provider and recipient of social support (cf. Rose, 1999; Villadsen, 2009, 2011a) – based on notions of need, moral reform and supposedly authentic goodwill. Seemingly paradoxical, such discourse positions provider and recipient distant from each other – on the "inside" and on the "outside" of society – yet, with underpinning notions of forming moral community (but, with maintained and non-articulated power relations).

However, this discourse includes obvious political notions of social change and, importantly, the analysis highlights the power relations between provider and recipient embedded in the social support provided. The kinds of personal engagement and contributions illustrated in this analysis recognise injustices when it comes to poverty and exclusion; however, the form of intervention promoted does not address these problems or support collective actions and reform, but rather utilises them to legitimise a certain kind of provision of support and a particular form of governing social change (cf. Chouliaraki, 2010). In this sense, the motivations for charitable contributions highlighted could be seen to align with a neo-colonial discourse on the support provided to those deemed to be in need, when provided from the position of the included to those assumed to be in need, that is excluded youth (cf. Chouliaraki, 2010; Giulianotti, 2004). Involvement in sports-based social interventions such as the MF initiatives provides opportunities to realise particular visions of social change (albeit while maintaining these power relations) based on certain notions of a desired society and an ideal community rather than other alternatives; and that, essentially, is a matter of politics and contestation.

Disclosure statement

No potential conflict of interest was reported by the authors.

Funding

This work was supported by The Swedish Research Council for Sport Science [Grant Number 25-2016] and The Swedish Agency for Youth and Civil Society [Grant Number 1086/17].

ORCID

David Ekholm http://orcid.org/0000-0002-6252-9220

References

Agergaard, S., Michelsen la Cour, A., & Treumer Gregersen, M. (2015). Politicisation of migrant leisure: A public and civil intervention involving organised sports. *Leisure Studies*, *35*(2), 200–214.

Bunds, K. (2017). *Sport, politics and the charity industry*. New York: Routledge.

Bustad, J. J., & Andrews, D. L. (2017). Policing the void: Recreation, social inclusion and the Baltimore Police Athletic League. *Social Inclusion*, *5*(2), 241–249.

Chouliaraki, L. (2010). Post-humanitarianism. *International Journal of Cultural Studies*, *13*(2), 107–126.

Collins, M., & Haudenhuyse, R. P. (2015). Social exclusion and austerity policies in England: The role of sports in a new area of social polarisation and inequality? *Social Inclusion*, *3*(3), 5–18.

Dahlstedt, M., & Ekholm, D. (2019). Social exclusion and multi-ethnic suburbs in Sweden. In B. Hanlon & T. J. Vicino (Eds.), *The Routledge companion to the suburbs* (pp. 163–172). New York: Routledge.

Dean, M. (2010). *Governmentality*. London: Sage.

Dean, M., & Villadsen, K. (2016). *State phobia and civil society*. Stanford, CA: Stanford University Press.

Dikec, M. (2017). *Urban rage*. New Haven, CT: Yale University Press.

Donzelot, J. (1979). *The policing of families*. London: John Hopkins University Press.

Ekholm, D. (2016). *Sport as a means of responding to social problems. Rationales of governing, welfare and social change* (PhD thesis). Linköping studies in arts and science, no. 687. Linköping University, Linköping.

Ekholm, D. (2018). Governing by means of sport for social change and social inclusion: Demarcating the domains of problematization and intervention. *Sport in Society*, *21*(11), 1777–1794.

Ekholm, D., & Dahlstedt, M. (2017). Football for inclusion: Examining the pedagogic rationalities and the technologies of solidarity of a sports-based intervention in Sweden. *Social Inclusion*, *5*(2), 232–240.

Esping-Andersen, G. (1990). *Three worlds of welfare capitalism*. Cambridge: Polity Press.

Foucault, M. (1972). *The archaeology of knowledge*. London: Tavistock.

Foucault, M. (1982). The subject and power. *Critical Inquiry*, *8*(4), 777–795.

Foucault, M. (2004). Polemics, politics, and problematizations. In P. Rabinow (Ed.), *The Foucault reader* (pp. 381–390). London: Penguin Books.

Giulianotti, R. (2004). Human rights, globalization and sentimental education: The case of sport. *Sport in Society*, *7*(3), 355–369.

Hartmann, D. (2016). *Midnight basketball*. Chicago, IL: University of Chicago Press.

Herz, M. (2016). 'Then we offer them a new project'— The production of projects in social work conducted by civil society in Sweden. *Journal of Civil Society*, *12*(4), 365–379.

Hoekman, R., Breedveld, K., & Kraaykamp, G. (2017). Providing for the rich? The effect of public investments in sport on sport (club) participation of vulnerable youth and adults. *European Journal for Sport and Society*, *14*(4), 327–347.

Norberg, J. R. (2011). A contract reconsidered? Changes in the Swedish state's relation to the sports movement. *International Journal of Sport Policy and Politics*, *3*, 311–325.

Palmås, K. (2011). *Prometheus eller Narcissus?* [Prometheus or Narcissus?]. Göteborg: Korpen Koloni.

Parnell, D., Spracklen, K., & Millward, P. (2017). Sport management issues in an era of austerity. *European Sport Management Quarterly*, *17*(1), 67–74.

Peachey, J. W., Musser, A., Shin, N. R., & Cohen, A. (2017). Interrogating the motivations of sport for development and peace practitioners. *International Review for the Sociology of Sport*, *53*(7), 767–787.

Peterson, T., & Schenker, K. (2017). Social entrepreneurship in a sport policy context. *Sport in Society*, *21*(3), 452–467.

Reid, F. (2012). Increasing sports participation in Scotland: Are voluntary sports clubs the answer? *International Journal of Sport Policy and Politics*, *4*(2), 221–241.

Rose, N. (1999). *Powers of freedom*. Cambridge: Cambridge University Press.

Rosso, E. G. F., & McGrath, R. (2017). Community engagement and sport? Building capacity to increase opportunities for community-based sport and physical activity. *Annals of Leisure Research*, *20*(3), 349–367.

Sernhede, O., Thörn, C., & Thörn, H. (2016). The Stockholm uprising in context. In M. Mayer, C. Thörn, & H. Thörn (Eds.), *Urban uprisings* (pp. 149–173). Basingstoke: Palgrave Macmillan.

Sherry, E., Schulenkorf, N., & Chalip, L. (2015). Managing sport for social change: The state of play. *Sport Management Review*, *18*(1), 1–5.

Skille, E. (2011). The conventions of sport clubs: Enabling and constraining the implementation of social goods through sport. *Sport, Education and Society*, *16*(2), 241–253.

Stenling, C., & Fahlén, J. (2016). Same same, but different? Exploring the organizational identities of Swedish voluntary sports: Possible implications of sports clubs' self-identification for their role as implementers of policy objectives. *International Review for the Sociology of Sport*, *51*(7), 867–883.

Stinson, J. L., & Pritchard, M. P. (2013). Leveraging sport for social marketing and corporate social responsibility (CSR). In M. P. Pritchard & J. L. Stinson (Eds.), *Leveraging Brands in sport business* (pp. 221–238). New York: Routledge.

Stockholm Municipality. (2015). *Skillnadernas Stockholm* [Differences in Stockholm] (Commission for a socially sustainable Stockholm, Report No. 1). Retrieved from www.stockholm.se/PageFiles/1020704/Rapport%20 1%20Skillnadernas%20Stockholm,%20juni%202015. pdf

Trädgårdh, L. (2013). Den nya välfärden [The new welfare]. In K. Almqvist, V. Ax:son Johnson, & L. Trädgårdh (Eds.), *Non-profit och välfärden* [Non-profit and welfare] (pp. 117–124). Stockholm: Axel och Margaret Ax:son Johnsons stiftelse för allmännyttiga ändamål.

Villadsen, K. (2007). The emergence of 'neo-philanthropy'. *Acta Sociologica*, *50*(3), 309–323.

Villadsen, K. (2008a). Doing without state and civil society as universals: 'Dispositifs' of care beyond the classic sector divide. *Journal of Civil Society*, *4*(3), 171–191.

Villadsen, K. (2008b). Freedom as self-transgression: Transformations in the 'governmentality' of social work. *European Journal of Social Work*, *11*(2), 93–104.

Villadsen, K. (2009). The 'human' touch. *Public Management Review*, *11*(2), 217–234.

Villadsen, K. (2011a). Modern welfare and 'good old' philanthropy. *Public Management Review*, *13*(8), 1057–1075.

Villadsen, K. (2011b). Neo-Philanthropy. *Social Work & Society*, *9*(2), 1–3.

Weinryb, N. (2015). *Free to conform* (PhD thesis). Uppsala University, Uppsala.

Developing workreadiness; a Glasgow housing association sports-based intervention

Catherine Mary Walker

ABSTRACT
The contribution of sport-based interventions to individual, societal and cultural development has been debated extensively since 2007. Community organisations increasingly employ these programmes to develop participant aspirations and employment choices. Housing Associations are one of the agencies to utilise this approach and there is a growing academic acknowledgement of the value of sport and physical activity to this work. This article examines a Glasgow Housing Association project using rugby to promote the personal development of unemployed individuals, combining employability and behaviour change approaches. Consisting of end of programme focus groups and interviews of four cohorts of the programme, the article investigates potential improvements in work readiness. The Housing Association plays a unique role in driving forward the intervention. Participants perceived an increased sense of belonging, autonomy, relatedness and competencies required for future employment. The programme provides a key step towards work readiness, benefitting individuals and the Housing Association community investment activities.

Introduction

According to the Office of National Statistics (2017) there are still 3.1 million households in the UK (14.9%) where no member of the household is in employment. This concern for worklessness in parts of the UK, exacerbated by austerity (Dwyer & Wright, 2014; Hastings, Bailey, Gannon, Besemer, & Bramley, 2015) presents a continuing challenge to policy makers (Barnes, Garratt, McLennan, & Noble, 2018). Policy responses to worklessness have varied by context: in the United States there has been compulsory "'workfare' – work for benefit programmes"; in Europe the focus has been on Active Labour Markets (ALM) including training and work experience, whereas a hybrid model emerged in the UK "Welfare to work" Bambra (2011, p. 8). The UK model evidences reforms in the welfare benefits system. These labour market policies will be discussed in detail later.

Worklessness and the subsequent problems resulting from this, such as poverty, create accumulative complex welfare problems for communities and Government alike in the UK (Bambra, 2011). Spaaij, Magee, and Jeanes (2013) propose that increasing employment opportunities for the workless is a key focus of government welfare reform and an integral part of regenerating disadvantaged communities. In fact, HM Treasury and the Department for Work and Pensions state that addressing worklessness is a key tenet of current policy in the UK (cited in Gardiner & Simmonds, 2012). "Workless" individuals are unwillingly excluded from the labour market, (Barnes et al., 2018) and worklessness can be defined as "detachment from the formal labour market in particular areas, and among particular groups" (Ritchie, Casebourne, & Rick, 2005, p. 11). "Workless" is measured by being in receipt of benefit such as Jobseeker's Allowance (JSA), Incapacity Benefit or Severe Disablement Allowance (IB/SDA), Income Support for lone parents (IS-LP), Carer's Allowance (CA) or other out-of-work benefits including Disability Premium, or Pension Credit under State Pension age. Consequently, worklessness is a complex phenomenon that is affected by an amalgamation of personal, household, community, institutional and labour market factors (Spaaij et al., 2013). Moreover structural worklessness (Bambra, 2011) is a term used to describe large numbers of individuals who have been unemployed and in receipt of benefit for some time.

Bambra (2011) cites Siegrist and Marmot (2004) who suggest that having a "positive experience of self, is an important motivation in an individual engaging in his or her own environment" (p. 75). Bambra further recounts that in order to achieve this positive experience of self, that the "psychosocial environment must offer opportunities for autonomy, belonging, interacting, contributing and receiving feedback" (Siegrist & Marmot, 2004 as cited in Bambra, 2011, p. 75). Corresponding positive psychosocial environments can increase self-esteem by providing areas for positive social interaction. Conversely, negative or alienating environments can impact on a constricted sense of self. This results in individuals often lacking motivation, self-efficacy and educational attainment and exhibiting problematic experiences of work (Ritchie et al., 2005). Increased self-efficacy, hope, and resilience are often used as constituents of positive psychological capital, an amalgamation of both human and social capital (Luthans, Avolio, Avey, & Norman, 2007). These concepts are often proposed as key to the development of work motivation (Luthans et al., 2007) and thus a vital predisposition for employment and work-readiness. Impetus PEF (2014) define work readiness as having self-awareness, being receptive, driven, self-assured, resilient and informed. In the 2013 report "Work Readiness Standards and Benchmarks," ACT, Inc. (2013) defines work readiness as aligning education and training to current job-skill requirements. They propose

> a work-ready individual possesses the foundational skills needed to be minimally qualified for a specific occupation as determined through a job analysis or occupational profile. The skills needed for work readiness are both foundational and occupation-specific and vary in both importance and level for different occupations (p2).

To that end, the purpose of this article is to examine from the perspective of participants, the development of work readiness through a rugby-based sport intervention in North Glasgow. To do this, the author draws upon Basic Psychological Needs Theory (Deci & Ryan, 2002) to identify the programme components effective in engaging participants and to discern the role of a housing association in the delivery of the project.

Literature review

Since the 1990s, there has been discourse in western democracies regarding the debate about the welfare state, suggesting that "social policy" should change from passive labour market policies that result in benefit dependency and increasing unemployment, to active labour market programmes (ALMP) that propose investment in people to enhance their capacity to participate in the economic workforce (Rueda, 2015). These "Welfare to Work" programmes tend to comprise three areas: (1) Public employment services such as job centres and labour exchange; (2) training schemes such as apprenticeships; and (3) short-term measures such as employment subsidies, typically designed to allow the unemployed to build up experience and prevent skill deterioration (Rueda, 2015). An example in the UK is the New Deal polices of the 1990s (Cabinet Office, 2010). Although cost effective, the success of many of these programmes is questioned in terms of improving employment in the long term (Brown & Koettl, 2015). However, despite the global recession, the UK has fared better than many EU countries in terms of unemployment. The unemployment rate in the UK in June 2018 fell to 4%, below the lowest level since February 1975 (The ONS, 2018). These notable figures, however, come alongside falls in "real" wages and a large increase in part-time or insecure jobs (Myant, Theodoropoulou, & Piasna, 2016). More worrying, when examining the last 20 years, the UK has replaced more of the higher and medium-skilled jobs that have been lost with lower skilled jobs than other European countries (Holmes, 2014).

"Welfare to work" programmes have sought to support workless populations in gaining, sustaining and progressing into employment (Adam, Atfield, & Green, 2017). These have been focused principally on "individualised support, intensive services for those furthest from the labour market, work placements and co-ordination of local provision" (Adam et al., 2017, p. 1173). Furthermore, in terms of broader social policy in communities, Levitas (2005) suggests this evidences how a lack of social integration views social exclusion as arising mainly from unemployment, and this as a consequence of individuals' lack of knowledge and skills. Accordingly this underpins continuing poverty and social exclusion, since individuals are not able to breakout of the cycle of disadvantage. Lindsay (2010) goes further by explaining that for individuals finding themselves in a workless situation, they often become isolated and as a result may lose social networks, impacting on their ability to re-enter the job market. Sherry (2010) submits there is some suggestion employers are reluctant to employ long-term workless, specifically those with challenging backgrounds or individuals with a criminal past. Sherry (2010) argues that programmes are often more successful in achieving participants' work readiness when the participants have minimal "external constraints", such as mental health problems, addiction and/or criminal histories. Ironically these are the individuals that these welfare-to-work programmes should be targeting (Dean, 2003). These issues are the challenges that many of the participants of the Pitstops programme experience resulting in many, though not all, experiencing long-term unemployment, little personal motivation to change and limited education or qualifications.

Sherry (2010) and Walker, Hills, and Heere (2017) all propose that there should be a change in the underlying focus of employability programmes. They explain that many of these programmes are measured simplistically in terms of individuals securing regular employment. Often the individuals on these said programmes are not working ready at the end of programmes and therefore programmes are often deemed ineffective. Instead, Sherry (2010) and Walker et al. (2017) argue that programmes need to be more reactive to local conditions recognising other forms of social engagement such as volunteering which would effectively require a redefinition of the meaning of employment planning (Sherry, 2010). This evolution in redefining "work" is reinforced by Spaaij et al. (2013) in their acknowledgement of the Dutch workfare model which recognises unpaid and voluntary work as "activity fare" (Spies & Van Berkel, 2001) hence creating mechanisms to develop skills and social networks necessary for reengagement with the job market.

Sport has the capacity to act as a conduit for social inclusion with marginalised groups, by providing opportunities to develop social networks (Jarvie, 2003; Sherry, 2010) thus reducing isolation. Sports policy has reflected the belief that sport is culturally important in the UK (Piggin, Jackson, & Lewis, 2009). Government appears to sanction the role of sport in their policy documents. Indeed Houlihan and Lindsey (2012) suggest that there has been significant change in the importance of sport to government, as indicated by government funding associated with sport such as the 2012 Olympic bid and subsequent elite sports funding; and the recognition of the reducing levels of sport participation and high levels of inactivity and its implications to society as evidenced in the recent Sporting Future – A New Strategy for an Active Nation (HM Government, 2015). Accordingly these changes appear to reinforce a "blurring" of what sport policy in the UK is advocating.

Research by Collins (2014) and Haudenhuyse and Theeboom (2015) suggests that sport is often cited as an effective mechanism to lessen the impact of social exclusion, yet they are also critical about the long-term success of this approach. There is evidence that sports-based interventions can contribute to the development of social and human capital (Coalter, 2007; Hoye, Nicholson, & Brown, 2015). The discourse around this issue has become significant. Moreover, this suggests there appears an inherent belief that sport is always good and that sport can act as a vehicle for community and personal development (Coakley, 2015). What Coakley describes as the egocentric "ruling elites", commit individual and public resources to sport in "the belief that its purity and goodness is successfully transmitted to children, young people 'at risk', students in need of academic motivation and developmental experiences, and citizens seeking social integration and inclusion" (Coakley, 2015, p. 406). Coakley argues that this blind faith in sport for good is not useful and that as a sector, evidence-based strategies for the use of sport for good is vital. Coalter (2007) however maintains that confirmation for the reputed social impact of sport is contentious and ambivalent at best. These sentiments are echoed by Hartmann and Kwauk (2011) and Levermore (2011), who maintain that empirically there is contradictory evidence in the conviction of the impact of sport, which is often motivated by emotional discourses (cited in Harris & Adams, 2016). Coalter (2013) does not ignore the potential benefits of sports-based interventions but advocates the need to identity "sufficient conditions" which seek to highlight what works, why and in what circumstances. Consequently the relationship between social inclusion and sport has been paid increasing academic attention (Coalter, 2010; Nicholson & Hoye, 2008; Sherry, Schulenkorf, & Chalip, 2015; Williams, Collingwood, Coles, & Schmeer, 2015).

Still, organisations utilise these sports-based interventions (SBI's) to enhance personal development and employment opportunities, in addition to addressing educational inequalities and community cohesion previously delivered through "statutory" practises (Lindsay, McQuaid, & Dutton, 2007). Kelly (2011) argues that the "added value" that these sports programmes bring indicate that using sports activities to develop and improve skills can sometimes assist the workless in engaging in the job market more effectively. Moreover Spaaij et al. (2013) agree and identify that more sports-based initiatives are being utilised as a means of combatting worklessness [albeit predominantly in young people]. Fuller, Percy, Bruening, and Cotrufo (2013) argue that researchers have only recently begun to examine whether programmes espousing such employment aims are effectively achieving the overarching social goals they claim to remedy. There appears an increasing discourse about sports-based employability programmes where the key outcomes are employability rather than increased sports participation. Additionally there seems to have been a softening and shifting of the discourse from SBI's to Sport Employability Interventions (SEI) (Walker & Hayton, 2017). Promoting goals that work towards developing workreadiness and consequently employment reflects Levitas' (2005) redistributionist and social integrationist discourse. Social integration through (paid) work, as endorsed in these SEI's, views social exclusion as arising mainly from unemployment, which it attributes to deficiencies in the knowledge and skills of individuals.

Authors such as Schulenkorf (2012) suggest that academics could develop this research theme by undertaking longitudinal evaluations and case study examples to further critique the successful completion of programme goals supporting Coalters' necessary conditions and requirements.

Housing Associations have become one of a category of agencies to utilise this sports-based approach. Housing Associations act as "not for profit" providers of social housing which "incorporates government-owned council housing and other affordable accommodation" (National Housing Federation, 2017). Housing Associations are working with partners to improve learning in their communities, expanding on their social landlords' role and facilitating other services such as financial advice, employment support and welfare guidance (Robson, 2017). Providing support for work readiness and/or to provide skill development and qualifications has progressively become the concern of social housing providers. According to McKee (2015) greater importance is being placed on the third sector in delivering formerly core public services as there is a shift away from "a welfare state to a welfare society" (p3). Moreover, the Home Secretary in his speech to the National Housing Federation conference in 2017, announced the intention to bring forward a social housing Green Paper in late 2018, expanding the role and importance of Housing Associations in community investment activities. Housing Associations' primary role is to provide housing however, often their role extends beyond this. The Centre for Social Justice (2018) highlighted that in 2014 a third (39%) of Housing Associations offered employment and skills support, social housing and employment. Housing Associations are well positioned to make positive interventions in the lives of those seeking employment as they are often placed in disadvantaged areas in addition to the unique relationship they have with their residents. Moreover, they have a further advantage of being able to provide employment opportunities themselves (Centre for Social Justice, 2018). According to research (Rallings & Coburn, 2014), 88% of housing providers are offering help, advice, services or work opportunities to residents. Give us a Chance (GUAC), [a leading consortium of social landlords], propose increasing numbers of social landlords are working in partnership to influence the housing and employability agenda (GUAC, 2018). They go on to highlight that Housing Associations invest around £70 m a year in employment and training support programmes – £60 m of this is Housing Associations' own funding (GUAC, 2018). This is significant as almost half of working-age social housing residents are currently out of work and the unemployment rate among working-age social housing tenants is almost three times that of other tenures (Dromey, Snelling, & Baxter, 2018). What is more, within this sector there appears a growing acknowledgement of the value of sport and physical activity interventions as part of community investment activity (HACT, 2017), although academic research regarding the emerging partnerships between the housing sector and sports bodies is in its infancy.

Glasgow, the location for this research, is often acknowledged as being a disadvantaged community being in the 15% most deprived areas (Scottish Indices of Multiple Deprivation [SIMD], 2012), despite Scotland's renewal efforts (Robertson, 2014). Moreover, nearly 30% of households have no adults in employment (Eisenstadt, 2017). This figure has not changed appreciably in the last eight years and is significantly higher in comparison to other UK cities (Understanding Glasgow, 2017).

According to Deci and Ryan (2002) people are dynamic, developing organisms who endeavour to realise Basic Psychological Needs (BPN). They further suggest that achievement of these basic psychological needs in their lives underwrites personal development, reliability and wellbeing. Conversely if these needs remain unmet then self-motivation can diminish, potentially impacting negatively on that individual's wellbeing (Ryan & Deci, 2000). Gunnell, Crocker, Wilson, Mack, and Zumbo (2013) refer to this as psychological need thwarting. This Basic Psychological Needs theory (BPNT) posits that there are three BPN: competence; autonomy; and relatedness (Deci & Ryan, 2002). Vansteenkiste and Van den Broeck (2017) advise that individuals require these three aspects to thrive, Competence in gaining new skills, relatedness in establishing new relationships and autonomy to develop independence. It could be argued therefore that this developing autonomy and relatedness connect to self-efficacy and personal growth. The need for autonomy as proposed by deCharms (1968) establishes a sense of choice in participating in an activity. Autonomy requires self-efficacy and willing engagement (Ryan & Deci, 2017) and these capacities for self-regulation and decision making can be negatively impacted by unsupportive or personally challenging contexts therefore "need thwarting" (Gunnell et al., 2013). Equally, autonomy is sustained and heightened when an individual feels able to make their own choices and decisions about their conduct and the protocols that they choose to employ within a work or activity-based context (Deci, Eghrari, Patrick, & Leone, 1994).

A second psychological need, concomitant with autonomy, is the need for competence. Competence refers to the basic need for an individual to feel capable and proficient in life situations, thus leading to feelings of self-efficacy (Markland & Vansteenkiste, 2007; White, 1959). However, like autonomy, it can be circumvented. It weakens in situations that are deemed too challenging or when "feelings of mastery are diminished" (Ryan & Deci, 2017, p. 11). Moreover, the authors stress that feelings of competence will only increase intrinsic motivation to achieve when complemented by a sense of autonomy (2000).

Baumeister and Leary (1995) contended that relatedness, the third psychological need, refers to developing connections with others, belong to a group, be accepted and feel positive emotions while acting as a group member (Baumeister & Leary, 1995; Deci & Ryan, 2000). Individuals who become disconnected from communities often become socially isolated, resulting in mental health problems, feelings of loneliness, a perceived inadequacy and a lack of belonging (Van Baarsen, Snijders, Smit, & Van Duijn, 2001). Moreover, Timpone (1998) found that formal group membership was related to greater levels of relatedness and he also identified that education, income and age were also related to greater relatedness suggesting a sense of belonging, wellbeing, motivation and an increased sense of self-worth can be promoted through increased relatedness.

Researchers (Chatzisarantis & Hagger, 2009; Cheon, Reeve, & Moon, 2012; Ryan, Patrick, Deci, & Williams, 2008; Tessier, Sarrazin, & Ntoumanis, 2010) have utilised BPNT when investigating sport and health contexts and often undertaken quantitative measurement studies. However for this article the author followed a qualitative approach as outlined in the methodology. Research into relatedness has often focused on exploring questions around both the quantity and quality of relationships (Tessier et al., 2010). Hoye & Nicholson's (2012) study of social capital and country race clubs in Victoria, Australia, followed a qualitative method, utilising a number of semi-structured interviews across a range of stakeholders to understand social networks created through sport organisations. The author of this article has utilised a similar approach to Hoye and Nicholson (2012) and the emergent nature of the data was used to generate meanings in order to identify patterns and relationships in regards the development of relatedness, autonomy and competence resulting from the Pitstops programme.

The programme

Increasingly Rugby has been used as a vehicle for community development. Programmes such as "Try for Change", the RFU's social responsibility programme (Rugby Football Union, 2017), School of Hard Knocks Charity (SOHK, 2017) Premier Rugby and Scottish Rugby's CashBack schools Rugby scheme (2017), have all utilised the sport as part of their community development programmes. They argue that rugby can tackle truancy, help maintain a healthy active lifestyle, develop leadership and improve team work skills (SOHK, 2017). These programmes argue that the values synonymous with rugby such as respect, engagement, enjoyment, inclusivity, team work and fitness can aid community and personal development (SOHK, 2017). The Pitstops programme (the focus of this paper) argues that the use of challenging activities and values-based lessons helps participants take steps forward in their lives and take responsibility for their actions through completing modules such as values, attitudes and non-technical skills with the objective of getting each participant into sustainable employment. Many if not all of the participants have previously not played rugby so the challenge of a new sport is also attractive.

The Pitstops programme aims to develop individuals' personal and social development in addition to employability skills in economically inactive men and women in Glasgow. The programme combines "Workreadiness", developing employability services and behaviour change approaches to help participants with human and social capital development. Furthermore, the programme designs services to promote longer term skills and personal development including employability awards and community achievement award, as well as a number of optional additional qualifications including first aid and health and safety delivered by an education delivery partner. After an eight week programme participants are mentored and supported by programme staff through regular phone calls and face to face "personalised" support including interview and job application guidance.

Methodology

Research approach

In order to explore the subjective experiences of the participants in this study, a qualitative approach was employed and underpinned by a constructivist epistemology. Following a fusion of both inductive and deductive research design, this study adopts a case study approach and is the first part of a larger longitudinal study evaluating the "Pitstops project" over a number of cohorts. The first stage of data collection resulted in an iterative process exploring and continuously reviewing earlier stages of the research to generate conclusions (Thornberg & Charmaz, 2014).

What follows is a qualitative examination of cohorts 1–4 of the project. A case study enabled the researcher to explore new phenomena utilising a variety of data sources (Baxter & Jack, 2008) for the purposes of data triangulation, and to promote trustworthiness in and of the data. Moreover, the case study approach provides opportunities for participants to express their own experiences and enables the researcher following an interpretivist philosophy, to better understand their actions (Baxter & Jack, 2008). Case studies are often used to determine effectiveness of programmes (Lewis, 2015). Therefore, case study design is useful when one needs to answer the "how" and the "why" questions to construct validity, and is vital if the researcher requires an understanding of the contextual environment in which the participants are placed. Many past studies regarding the social outcomes of sport depend on qualitative examinations by interviews, observations, focus groups, poetry readings and video messages (Bailey*, 2005; Beutler, 2008; Jarvie, 2003).

Participants

After achieving ethical agreement, two methods of enquiry were utilised for this research. Firstly 4 focus groups (one per cohort×six participants in each group; $n = 24$ participants) as recommended by Lasch et al. (2010) and Fusch and Ness (2015) were undertaken. Secondly, unstructured interviews with three participants from each cohort ($n = 12$) were undertaken, reinforcing the triangulation with focus groups thus aiding data saturation (David & Sutton, 2011; Denzin, 2012). Focus groups enabled the researcher to identify emerging themes from the participants and the unstructured interviews provided an opportunity to explore these themes in more detail. A purposive criterion-based sampling strategy was identified (Smith, Sparkes, & Caddick, 2014). Participants attend one eight-week course which runs every three months. Participants were required to have attended at least seven weeks of the eight-week development programme so they were able to make informed judgements about the overall programme. Participants were approached by the researcher at the end of week eight of each cohort and the purpose of the research was explained. Those that agreed to participate indicated if they would prefer to participate in either an interview or focus group. Focus groups were selected to provide insight into the attitudes and beliefs of the participants, with regards to the perceived impact of the project on their personal development and job readiness (Silverman, 2006). Focus groups also enabled the researcher to gain rich information through flexible, unstructured dialogue with members, thereby fostering an openness of opinions thus eliciting multiple viewpoints on specific issues (Brockman, Nunez, & Basu, 2010). This also enables participants to discuss and challenge their own and their peers' views (Patton, 2002). Following the inductive design process as informed by the literature, themes generated from the focus groups provided additional question content for the interviews.

A basic framework for questions for the focus groups was established, generated from the literature from which the interview was guided. The respondents were given freedom to talk about their views in their own time. The researcher, where required, used probes to expand on information. Semi-structured interviews with selected participants allowed in-depth exploration of process issues and allowed the researcher to amend the tempo or question order, to garner comprehensive responses from the interviewees (Qu & Dumay, 2011). During the interviews the researcher verbally checked for clarification of participants' responses to improve the accuracy of comments.

Procedures

In the final week of each of the Pitstops course [week 8/8] the researcher visited the project to undertake the research. Before commencement of the focus groups the researcher was introduced to the participants and carried out informal conversations over lunch to build trust and rapport. This rapport building was deemed important in addressing any potential power imbalance between researcher and participants (Dickson-Swift, James, Kippen, & Liamputtong, 2007). At the start of both interviews and focus groups a brief explanation of the research was given to break the ice. Interview and focus group schedules were prepared using open ended questions and probes on job readiness, social networks, and perception of participants' personal development on the programme. The focus groups although facilitated by the researcher were participant led, guided only by a limited number of questions generated by the "a priori" themes from literature (Carey & Asbury, 2016). The researcher was cognisant of the limited educational attainment of some of the participants so changed the language of questions to match the social background of respondents (McLeod, 2014).

For the focus groups the researcher explained the aim and purpose of the study at a lunch break for participants and asked for volunteers to contribute. The first six participants were selected and taken to an adjoining room at the course location, where the focus groups were conducted. For the interviews participants who had attended for a minimum of seven weeks were identified and selected by the project manager, as they would have experienced the whole programme. The researcher then selected three participants [from each cohort] and invited them to participate in an interview. Each interview lasted an average of 33 min. The researcher promoted a "conversational" atmosphere to encourage participants to feel relaxed and able to share their stories (Long & Dart, 2001). All interviews and focus groups were recorded on digital recorders with the consent of participants. These recordings were later transcribed verbatim.

Data analysis

The thematic analysis incorporated both Boyatzis (1998) data-driven inductive approach generating themes and the "a priori" deductive approach outlined by Crabtree and Miller (1999). The analysis was informed by constructivist epistemology, where the researcher is making sense of the participant's personal accounts and experiences. The initial codes, the "a priori" categories selected for analysing the focus group data, consisted of key themes of relatedness, autonomy and competence contiguous with the literature highlighted earlier in this paper. This approach complemented the research questions by enabling a process of deductive thematic analysis while allowing for themes to be generated from the data using inductive coding. After transcription of the interviews and focus groups, this thematic analysis was carried out following Miles, Huberman, Huberman, and Huberman's (1994) interactive model for thematic analysis. Firstly, data was reduced by manual highlighting of the interview transcripts and organised using colour coding for a general summary of themes generated, by looking for patterns, themes, relationships, sequences and differences. So themes such as skill improvement, opportunity to learn new skills, certificated course attendance, previous limited education achievement and validation of knowledge became Workreadiness/Competence. Researcher comments/reflections in the form of memos were added in the text. Patterns were then explored through elaboration and small generalisations of the generated themes which were then linked to the body of literature, to construct arguments. Finally, informed by the context and theoretical framework of BPN, these specific categories were illustrative of, and therefore subsumed within, three core categories that encompass the data: Workreadiness/Competence, Relatedness, and Autonomy. Lastly as recommended by Smith and McGannon (2018), a "Peer debriefing" by a colleague not involved in the original data collection, acted as a critical friend to challenge the themes presented providing an opportunity for dialogue and reflexivity for trustworthiness in the research process. The resulting refined codes used in the discussion headings, arose as a result of this contextualising and parsimony. Selective quotations that were illustrative of the key themes generated from the data were then used to structure the discussion of the paper.

A limitation of the research process and a caveat to the analysis must be acknowledged. The qualitative data was grounded in the personal accounts of the participants experiences of the programme. To that end, the role of the researcher as interpreter of this information must be recognised in relation to the researchers' interpretation of the information. Although the research design attempted to diminish any power imbalances, these could still exist (Karnieli-Miller, Strier, & Pessach, 2009). The researcher could be perceived as an expert and any information shared could be influenced due to a variety of factors including gender, socioeconomic status, ethnicity and importantly, learned internalisation of the programme aims and objectives (Anyan, 2013). Further studies should utilise more visual methods of data collection such as video diaries or blogs, supplemented by quantitative data collection methods for triangulation. Additionally as a sole researcher this could have an impact on the range of information gained. Furthermore gathering wider accounts from the programme staff and employers involved in the programme would have been beneficial in providing corroborative accounts.

Analysis

The evidence generated from the data collection phase suggests that there were a range of positive outcomes emerging from the Pitstops programme that contribute to improved work readiness of the participants. These include additional education qualifications and training to develop current job-skill requirements. These qualifications evidenced a closer positioning towards employment (ACT, Inc., 2013). The participants also articulated a greater self-awareness, being receptive to new ideas, resilience when challenges occurred and increased self-confidence, all traits of demonstrating workreadiness. This section will discuss the core themes of Workreadiness/Competence, Relatedness, and Autonomy, in relation to contemporary literature and theory and example quotations will be provided from participant focus groups and interviews.

Workreadiness/Competence

A lack of transferable skills is a particular problem for the workless (Devins et al., 2011) and there is evidence that employment opportunities are restricted for those with limited employability or basic skills (Gardiner & Simmonds, 2012). Developing work readiness skills such as First aid, computer literacy, interview skills and CV preparation, prepares individuals to continue their education journey and is clearly important but these are often restricted by the individual's self-efficacy.

> I do part time work in the community and I am a carer, I always want to learn. I wasn't expecting much as I have been on lots of personal development course but this is the best thing I have done in years because alongside feeling better about myself I have some additional qualifications to add to my CV, the best of both worlds. They [the staff] are helping me to go back to college. I'm sure I would not have had the courage to do this before

This also evidences that the individuals perceive an increasing self-awareness and self-confidence from their participation.

It was clear from interviewing all the participants that the programme was providing them with "something different" than they had experienced before in terms of relevant training and also developing individuals aspirations for employment. A male participant from cohort 2 said:

> I did do a bit of volunteering cos I did na have anything [qualifications]. This was the first course I come across that was not full of shit – because usually when you get put on a course from the job centre its shit cos other courses I've been on, it's just they're talking I turned up, you never gain nothing. Here you're getting taught stuff that will help me get a job but you're mingling with people you never knew. I think it's that they want you to succeed and so do I now.

The "stuff" the participant mentioned involved activities such as personal goal setting, anger management and teamwork practised through Rugby. The participant above [a long term unemployed older male, who also had substance misuse challenges] elaborated that in previous courses, he felt judged and belittled by staff – that he felt like an outsider. He explained that he did not see the relevance of previous training programmes and that any "certificates" he had received did not help [he felt] assist him both identify what he wanted to do but also validate any knowledge he had gained. Again all these skills he now feels he has, are highlighted as qualities of workreadiness [self-awareness, being resilient and informed]. This focus of the "Pitstops" programme on creating a sense of belonging, integrated with setting goals for themselves and feeling valued, were highlighted as "different" from other courses attended, emphasising that relatedness provides the base for autonomy and competence (Ryan & Deci, 2017). Further research by Krabbenborg, Boersma, van der Veld, Vollebergh, and Wolf (2017) has demonstrated how quality of life is most strongly influenced with competence amongst homeless young adults. It is thought that within homeless young adults in particular, building their sense of competence is important as it can protect them from further negative outcomes such as substance abuse of low self-esteem (Fergus & Zimmerman, 2005).

Relatedness

Relatedness, the third psychological need, refers to developing connections with others belong to a group, be accepted and feel positive emotions while acting as a group member (Baumeister & Leary, 1995; Deci & Ryan, 2000). Individuals who become disconnected from communities often become socially isolated, resulting in mental health problems, feelings of loneliness, a perceived inadequacy and a lack of belonging (Van Baarsen et al., 2001). Moreover, Timpone (1998) found that formal group membership was related to greater levels of relatedness and he also identified that education, income and age were also related to greater relatedness suggesting a sense of belonging, wellbeing, motivation and an increased sense of self-worth can be promoted through increased relatedness.

Group membership appears to have a strong influence in people's life, behaviour and choices (Hoye et al., 2015). However, prior to the intervention, participants involved in the project tended to have limited or no group support structures on which to rely. This leads to a disconnection;

> "I moved here to look after my family and have a few mental health issues. A lot of this area has withdrawn since the 70's, the dual carriage way split the community, people are fed up it feels like the community was shaded in grey – there's no buses really in some areas and that difficult it's a rough area I had to walk miles to go to work. You feel you don't belong to anything" Female cohort three.

Individuals therefore who experience these issues can become quickly isolated and this is exacerbated by being in a workless situation (Lindsay, 2010). They become disconnected from others and therefore work around them and if already experiencing additional life challenges such as mental health issues or substance misuse, these are aggravated (Townsend & McWhirter, 2005).

Both the interview and the focus groups suggested that participants develop a sense of relatedness and an increase in their social connections through the programme (Deci & Ryan, 2008). This sense of relatedness is evidenced by participants articulating an increased sense of belonging facilitated by involvement in the programme. One participant [cohort 4 Female] shared their background

> I was often on my own after the meetings and rehab sessions and this made me think about drinking again. When I came here I made friends. Now you have someone to talk to.

Furthermore, participants communicate on the phone outside of the sessions suggesting a real development of the group relationship;

> Meeting new guys has been brilliant I would not have done that before. A great thing has been getting together so we now help each other. I've made mates that I now hang out with. I know I can ring him now if I get stuck and talk. [Cohort 4 Male]

This sense of feeling part of "something" – part of a community that values them was reiterated by many of the participants. Participants were attracted to the programme as they felt isolated and lonely. This was further emphasised by a male participant form cohort 3,

> I don't think I ever thought I belonged to anything before. I always felt on the outside from being here I feel part of something. The Facebook page has been great cos it lets you know what's going on. Sometimes it's just good to talk to someone who has gone through stuff like you, they sort of know what you're feeling. They put job adverts on there and about what is going on in college and stuff. That helps you still feel part of something.

Relatedness within this social environment provided through this programme is a key factor in developing the self-determination of these participants. Barker (2014) emphasised how within some homeless populations the strategy of relatedness can often be high and have unrealistic expectations in regard to their expectations with others. These high expectations have often led to the feelings of being let down or exploited by other people. Similarly the "pitstops" programme has the potential to allow for a more reliable and "safe" social network, where social connections are built through the programme rather than through the identity of being workless. Does it always follow however, that this increased relatedness leads to employment? Sports employability programmes such as this seem to suggest that gaining employment will be a "cure all" to participants' problems, supporting the social integrationist discourse. At the end of the course, participants feel a greater sense of belonging however is this transitory? Without the physical contact and interaction facilitated by attendance at the programme will this sense of belonging continue?

Autonomy

The interviews clearly demonstrated that participants are thinking about the future and starting to become autonomous and as individuals, increasingly driven (Markland & Vansteenkiste, 2007),

> I never really planned what I wanted to do cos everyone always told me I couldn't do stuff. I did na even finish school then ended up in prison, so I just thought about getting through just each day. I like being outside and since 'Pitstops' I have been given a chance to work [for the Housing Association], doing gardening and mowing the grass and stuff. I want to set up my own business so my kids will be proud of me. (Male participant cohort 4)

The unique position held by the Housing Association in both facilitating the programme development and being able to provide work placements for course alumni, provides at least some consistency and support once the eight week course has finished.

Although a key aim of the programme is work readiness and ultimately employment, the progress of individuals within the programme is not always consistent. Many of the individuals have additional life challenges such as overcoming substance abuse, poor numeracy and literacy, a criminal past or experiences of domestic violence. Whilst the support to these individuals ensures they stay with the programme there is a danger that they over rely on these support mechanisms and do not challenge themselves to be autonomous people (Deci & Ryan, 2008). Both during and on completion, programme staff attempt to act as signposters to other statutory support services such as welfare, social services, job centres or NHS services. However as positive relationships have been established the less empowered individuals, on occasion, struggle to become independent. It is vital therefore that the programme structures activities and management to support and facilitate participant's autonomy. Ironically the sense of belonging fostered by the programme to participants sometimes results in less confident individuals becoming over-reliant on staff due to their proximity and familiarity. This is a challenge the programme needs to grapple with in the future.

There is evidence from the research that participant's subsequent personal development through the programme can impact on "external constraints" such as mental health problems, addiction and/or criminal histories (Sherry, 2010).

> I was an angry wi man, running about doing stuff takes up energy, smashing into the rugby bag helps you get rid of shit and bad thoughts, it's all about a battle, the physical stuff is all well but as you constantly get knocked down doing the rugby, you have to keep getting up, that mentality. I know I can use this now when I am going for a job. (Cohort 2 Male)

The programme, whilst not specifically a mental health or substance misuse treatment programme, seems to combine work preparation development with personal support that assists individuals to start the process of overcoming the barriers they face. Specifically Rugby offers the opportunity for gaining new skills, improving fitness, cultivating self-confidence and targeting aggression. Uniquely therefore the programme combines a Rugby initiative such as "School of Hard Knocks" (a sports-based Intervention) with an employability invention resulting in a Sport Employability Intervention. As a consequence, individuals begin to aspire to employment and the responsibilities this entails.

The ability to become autonomous, grow resilience and improve self-efficacy (Deci & Ryan, 2008; Vansteenkiste & Van den Broeck, 2017) can develop independence through disciplined empowerment. One of the first participants on the programme articulated this:

> It's helped with simple things like getting up early and getting into some sort routine in my life. It really helps with confidence, when you are out on the street it's all about testosterone, but here you meet people with all backgrounds, you can see people's confidence building when they realise that they can do stuff on their own. We get support afterwards which is great but those that do best use that but then stand on their own 2 feet, I know that cos I know I'm the one that's got to do stuff – it's my life and I know I have to take these chances the course has given me but only me can do it. (Cohort 1 male)

Participant's perception of the enhancement in their resilience and self-confidence (linking to competence) was also highlighted:

> I used to doubt myself before and that someone empathises with you makes a difference cos they know what we are going through, The encouragement they give you is great, you believe that you can do it. Its Ok now if shite happens I know I can get through it. (Cohort 2 male).

The participant suggests that having poor esteem resulted in a feeling of being out of control. He went on to explain that he often felt ignored, excluded, and unimportant. However the data suggests that as a result of the programme individuals are able to exhibit hope, and increased self-efficacy resulting in many of the participants developing an ability to choose or value guidance and embracing trust. Emphasising that through the enhancement of autonomous behaviour and improving competence, then relatedness emerges. Participants identified that many of them are now undaunted with potential job interviews and after completion of the course either return to volunteer with the programme or are directed to other volunteering opportunities. Ironically though two participants identified that there is a fine line between tailored support leading to empowered individuals and creating dependent participants:

> Sometimes there is too much aftercare for some people. It's important that people don't get too dependent they don't really get going on their own. (Female participant Cohort 1)

The aftercare identified here is regular communication with staff arranging interviews or helping improve CV's. By acknowledging this, the participant is demonstrating that the programme has promoted autonomy and ownership in many of the individual participants if not all. Creating a sense of autonomy is one of the key factors in developing self-determined individuals.

Role of the Housing Association

Interestingly the role that the Housing Association plays in the delivery of the programme is significant (Rallings & Coburn, 2014). The participants acknowledge this and recognise that if they can improve self-efficacy and competencies, they are in a much better position to secure employment and thus pay rent. Many of the interviewees explained that being engaged in the programme had helped with housing advice and welfare support in addition to the increased social networks, employment guidance and training, supporting a holistic approach from the Housing Association to support and empower residents. As a result of austerity and the UK Government localism agenda, the role of organisations such as Housing Associations is becoming increasingly important in delivering services to communities and progressively a key focus for housing providers (Rees & Mullins, 2016). The "New deal for social housing" Green paper (August 2018) recently released from the Ministry of Housing, Communities & Local Government may assist in providing a strategy and framework for this.

Finally the importance of the programme staff was vital in both delivery and supporting the programme (Coalter, 2007; Nichols, 2010). The staff take time to talk with participants. The aftercare programme whereby staff keep in touch, advise and guide participants was mentioned by many of the participants as an important support system;

> The importance of the staff is really good, without them I would not have achieved anything. They have shown me what I can do, they support you when you need it but also push you to be independent to stand on your own two feet. (Male participant cohort 4)

It cannot be underestimated that a key success determinant of these programmes is the staff. A progressive staff approach can help to facilitate better engagement of participants, through supportive autonomy. Good relationships and inclusive, non-judgmental communication between staff and a respectful staff attitude towards participants are significant. It is not necessary that these staff be professional sports qualified coaches but that they demonstrate these competencies and may have some sports coaching experience. Positive relationships between staff and people who use services are vital to engaging participants. Certainly, social networks play an important part in influencing attitudes towards jobs and training and the staff involved in delivering these programmes must be cognisant of these.

Conclusion

The intention of this paper was to examine from the perspective of participants, the development of work readiness through a Rugby-based sport intervention delivered by a Housing Association based in North Glasgow. Concomitant to this was to identify the programme components effective in engaging participants and to discern the role of the Housing Association in the delivery of the project. Using Basic Psychological Needs theory as an approach to undergird the research, the data suggests that through the combination of Rugby, personal development, employability skills and supportive participants, relatedness, autonomy and competencies are improved. This sense of relatedness is evidenced by an increased sense of belonging. For participants an increased autonomy and perceived improved self-efficacy (in this case self-belief in an ability to undertake learning or get a job) was demonstrated by continuing volunteering and engagement in job searches and interviews. Participants also perceived greater self-awareness, they welcomed new ideas, were more self-assured, resilient and had knowledge of many other employment, training and recreational opportunities: all traits of increased

Workreadiness (ACT, Inc, 2013; Impetus PEF, 2014). Sport [in this programme Rugby] integrated with personal development was the vehicle to develop these basic psychological needs. It appears that relatedness is the most prominent with competence and autonomy being something that develops from this relatedness. This programme evidences a growing sport employability programme focus for interventions particularly aimed at long-term workless individuals. Whilst the research suggests that individuals do in fact gain relatedness and a sense of belonging from being involved in the programme, it is impossible to say at this point if this is transitory. Although support is provided post programme, this in itself could lead to a learned dependency from some of the participants and, while volunteering is built into the post-programme activities, these individuals may still not become close to regular paid employment. It is the intention of the author of this paper to continue the evaluation of the Pitstops project over the next three years to provide a more longitudinal focus to ascertain if this increased relatedness, and thus gainful employment, has continued on completion of the programme..

There is no "magic pill" resulting from these programmes and the very nature of the participants, as being so far away from employment and needing intensive support both personal and skill based, is not always recognised by statutory funders as a complex and long-term process. As a consequence of this programmes could be directed at those easiest to help, thus neglecting those with sophisticated needs. Many employability programmes are measured simplistically in terms of individuals securing regular employment and do not acknowledge the progress made by individuals in the journey towards employment. Other forms of social engagement such as volunteering should be recognised as part of the learning journey to regular employment. "Bridges" into work (Meadows, 2008) whereby volunteering is recognised as an environment for applying and developing work skills should be further explored by statutory funders.

Importantly Housing Associations are playing a key role in this work. Many Housing Associations have a specific, rational strategic role in helping residents into work, accordingly tackling worklessness both among their residents and with those living in wider communities. However, more research is required about the role that sport and physical activity can play, in not only enabling these work readiness programmes but also in facilitating the general health and wellbeing of their residents. This paper contributes to this burgeoning discourse. Further research should be undertaken in this area. Organisations such as the Housing Association Charitable Trust (an umbrella charitable organisation supporting housing trusts) are driving this agenda forward providing leadership, sharing ideas and working with both sporting and health-related service providers to identify areas of best practice. Specific research should be undertaken to maximise these developments and provide innovative projects harnessing the knowledge and resources of the housing and community sports sectors. This article presents a snap shot over a period of 2 years and contributes to concepts provided by previous academics in the broader topic of sport and employability.

Disclosure statement

No potential conflict of interest was reported by the author.

ORCID

Catherine Mary Walker http://orcid.org/0000-0001-9450-3191

References

ACT, Inc. (2013). The condition of work readiness in the United States. Retrieved from http://www.act.org/research/policymakers/pdf/ConditionWorkReadiness.pdf

Adam, D., Atfield, G., & Green, A. E. (2017). What works? Policies for employability in cities. *Urban Studies, 54*(5), 1162–1177.

Anyan, F. (2013). The influence of power shifts in data collection and analysis stages: A focus on qualitative research interview. *Qualitative Report, 18*, 36.

Bailey*, R. (2005). Evaluating the relationship between physical education, sport and social inclusion. *Educational Review, 57*(1), 71–90.

Bambra, C. (2011). *Work, worklessness, and the political economy of health*. Oxford University Press.

Barker, J. (2014). Alone together: The strategies of autonomy and relatedness in the lives of homeless youth. *Journal of Youth Studies, 17*(6), 763–777. doi:10.1080/13676261.2013.853874

Barnes, H., Garratt, E., McLennan, D., & Noble, M. (2018). [online] Research Report No 779 Understanding the worklessness dynamics and characteristics of deprived areas. Department for Work and Pensions. Retrieved from http://research.dwp.gov.uk/asd/asd5/rrs-index.asp

Baumeister, R. F., & Leary, M. R. (1995). The need to belong: Desire for interpersonal attachments as a fundamental human motivation. *Psychological Bulletin, 117*(3), 497–529.

Baxter, P., & Jack, S. (2008). Qualitative case study methodology: Study design and implementation for novice researchers. *The Qualitative Report, 13*(4), 544–559.

Beutler, I. (2008). Sport serving development and peace: Achieving the goals of the United Nations through sport. *Sport in Society, 11*(4), 359–369.

Boyatzis, R. E. (1998). *Transforming qualitative information: Thematic analysis and code development*. Thousand Oaks, CA: Sage.

Brockman, J. L., Nunez, A. A., & Basu, A. (2010). Effectiveness of a conflict resolution training program in changing graduate students style of managing conflict with their faculty advisors. *Innovative Higher Education, 35*(4), 277–293.

Brown, A. J., & Koettl, J. (2015). Active labor market programs-employment gain or fiscal drain? *IZA Journal of Labor Economics, 4*(1), 12.

Cabinet Office. (2010). *Building the big society*. London: Author. Retrieved February 13, 2019, from https://assets.publishing.service.gov.uk/government/uploads/system/uploads/attachment_data/file/78979/building-big-society_0.pdf

Carey, M. A., & Asbury, J. E. (2016). *Focus group research*. London: Routledge.

Centre for Social Justice. (2018). 'Helping social housing be the springboard to a better life': The Centre for Social Justice: London.

Chatzisarantis, N. L., & Hagger, M. S. (2009). Effects of an intervention based on self-determination theory on self-reported leisure-time physical activity participation. *Psychology and Health, 24*(1), 29–48.

Cheon, S. H., Reeve, J., & Moon, I. S. (2012). Experimentally based, longitudinally designed, teacher-focused intervention to help physical education teachers be more autonomy supportive toward their students. *Journal of Sport and Exercise Psychology, 34*(3), 365–396.

Coakley, J. (2015). Assessing the sociology of sport: On cultural sensibilities and the great sport myth. *International Review for the Sociology of Sport, 50*(4–5), 402–406.

Coalter, F. (2007). *A wider social role for sport: Who's keeping the score?* London: Routledge.

Coalter, F. (2010). The politics of sport-for-development: Limited focus programmes and broad gauge problems? *International Review for the Sociology of Sport, 45*(3), 295–314.

Coalter, F. (2013). 'There is loads of relationships here': Developing a programme theory for sport-for-change programmes. *International Review for the Sociology of Sport, 48*(5), 594–612.

Collins, M. (2014). *Sport and social exclusion*. Abingdon: Routledge.

Crabtree, B. F., & Miller, W. L. (Eds.). (1999). *Doing qualitative research*. Thousand Oaks, CA: Sage.

David, M., & Sutton, C. D. (2011). *Social research: An introduction*. London: Sage.

Dean, H. (2003). Re-conceptualising welfare-to-work for people with multiple problems and needs. *Journal of Social Policy, 32*(3), 441–459.

deCharms, R. (1968). *Personal causation*. New York: Academic Press.

Deci, E. L., Eghrari, H., Patrick, B. C., & Leone, D. R. (1994). Facilitating internalization: The self-determination theory perspective. *Journal of Personality, 62*(1), 119–142.

Deci, E. L., & Ryan, R. M. (2000). The" what" and" why" of goal pursuits: Human needs and the self-determination of behavior. *Psychological Inquiry, 11*(4), 227–268.

Deci, E. L., & Ryan, R. M. (2002). Self-determination research: Reflections and future directions. In E. L. Deci & R. M. Ryan (Eds.), *Handbook of self-determination research* (pp. 431–441). City Rochester, NY: University Rochester Press.

Deci, E. L., & Ryan, R. M. (2008). Self-determination theory: A macrotheory of human motivation, development, and health. *Canadian psychology/Psychologie canadienne, 49*(3), 182–185.

Denzin, N. K. (2012). Triangulation 2.0. *Journal of Mixed Methods Research, 6*(2), 80–88.

Devins, D., Bickerstaffe, T., Nunn, A., Mitchell, B., McQuaid, R., Egdell, V., & Lindsay, C. (2011). The role of skills: from worklessness to sustainable employment with progression: UK Commission for Employment and Skills Evidence Report no. 38.

Dickson-Swift, V., James, E. L., Kippen, S., & Liamputtong, P. (2007). Doing sensitive research: What challenges do qualitative researchers face? *Qualitative Research, 7*(3), 327–353.

Dromey, J., Snelling, C., & Baxter, D. (2018). Building Communities that work: The role of Housing Assciaitions in suppoting employment: Briefing paper; The Institute for Public Policy Research London.

Dwyer, P., & Wright, S. (2014). Universal Credit, ubiquitous conditionality and its implications for social citizenship. *Journal of Poverty and Social Justice, 22*(1), 27–35.

Eisenstadt, N. (2017). Independent Advisor on Poverty and Inequality. The Life Chances of Young People in Scotland. A Report to the First Minister.

Fergus, S., & Zimmerman, M. A. (2005). Adolescent resilience: A framework for understanding healthy development in the face of risk. *Annual Review of Public Health, 26*, 399–419. doi:10.1146/annurev.publhealth.26.021304.144357

Fuller, R. D., Percy, V. E., Bruening, J. E., & Cotrufo, R. J. (2013). Positive youth development: Minority male participation in a sport-based afterschool program in an urban environment. *Research Quarterly for Exercise and Sport, 84*, 469–482.

Fusch, P. I., & Ness, L. R. (2015). Are we there yet? Data saturation in qualitative research. *The Qualitative Report, 20*(9), 1408.

Gardiner, L., & Simmonds, D. (2012). *Housing providers' approaches to tackling worklessness*. London: Centre for Economic and Social Inclusion and HACT.

GUAC. (2018). Retrieved from [Online] https://www.giveusachance.co.uk/about/give-us-chance/

Gunnell, K. E., Crocker, P. R., Wilson, P. M., Mack, D. E., & Zumbo, B. D. (2013). Psychological need satisfaction and thwarting: A test of basic psychological needs theory in physical activity contexts. *Psychology of Sport and Exercise, 14*(5), 599–607.

HACT. (2017). Sport and Physical activity. Retrieved from https://www.hact.org.uk/sport-and-housing

Harris, K., & Adams, A. (2016). Power and discourse in the politics of evidence in sport for development. *Sport Management Review, 19*(2), 97–106.

Hartmann, D., & Kwauk, C. (2011). Sport and development: An overview, critique, and reconstruction. *Journal of Sport and Social Issues, 35*(3), 284–305.

Hastings, A., Bailey, N., Gannon, M., Besemer, K., & Bramley, G. (2015). Coping with the cuts? The management of the worst financial settlement in living memory. *Local Government Studies, 41*(4), 601–621.

Haudenhuyse, R., & Theeboom, M. (2015). Introduction to the special issue "sport for social inclusion: Critical analyses and future challenges". *Social Inclusion, 3*(3), 1–4.

HM Government. (2015). *Sporting future: A new strategy for an active nation*.

Holmes, C. (2014). Why is the decline of routine jobs across Europe so uneven? SKOPE issues paper no. 33, November 2014.

Houlihan, B., & Lindsey, I. (2012). *Sport policy in Britain* (Vol. 18). London: Routledge.

Hoye, R., & Nicholson, M. (2012). Life at the track: Country race clubs and social capital. *International Review for the Sociology of Sport, 47*(4), 461–474.

Hoye, R., Nicholson, M., & Brown, K. (2015). Involvement in sport and social connectedness. *International Review for the Sociology of Sport, 50*(1), 3–21.

Impetus: The Private Equity Foundation. (2014). *Ready for work: The capabilities young people need to find and keep work – and the programmes proven to help develop these*. London: Impetus – The Private Equity Foundation.

Jarvie, G. (2003). Communitarianism, sport and social capital: Neighbourly insights into Scottish sport'. *International Review for the Sociology of Sport, 38*(2), 139–153.

Karnieli-Miller, O., Strier, R., & Pessach, L. (2009). Power relations in qualitative research. *Qualitative Health Research, 19*(2), 279–289.

Kelly, L. (2011). 'Social inclusion' through sports-based interventions? *Critical Social Policy, 31*(1), 126–150.

Krabbenborg, M. A. M., Boersma, S. N., van der Veld, W. M., Vollebergh, W. A. M., & Wolf, J. R. L. M. (2017). Self-determination in relation to quality of life in homeless young adults: Direct and indirect effects through psychological distress and social support. *The Journal of Positive Psychology, 12*(2), 130–140. doi:10.1080/17439760.2016.1163404

Lasch, K. E., Marquis, P., Vigneux, M., Abetz, L., Arnould, B., Bayliss, M., … Rosa, K. (2010). PRO development: Rigorous qualitative research as the crucial foundation. *Quality of Life Research, 19*(8), 1087–1096.

Levermore, R. (2011). Evaluating sport-for-development: Approaches and critical issues. *Progress in Development Studies, 11*(4), 339–353.

Levitas, R. (2005). *The inclusive society?: Social exclusion and new labour*. London: Palgrave Macmillan.

Lewis, S. (2015). Qualitative inquiry and research design: Choosing among five approaches. *Health Promotion Practice, 16*(4), 473–475.

Lindsay, C. (2010). In a lonely place? Social networks, job seeking and the experience of long-term unemployment. *Social Policy and Society*, *9*(1), 25–37.

Lindsay, C., McQuaid, R. W., & Dutton, M. (2007). New approaches to employability in the UK: Combining 'human capital development' and 'work first' strategies? *Journal of Social Policy*, *36*(4), 539–560.

Long, J., & Dart, J. (2001). Opening-up: Engaging people in evaluation. *International Journal of Social Research Methodology*, *4*(1), 71–78.

Luthans, F., Avolio, B. J., Avey, J. B., & Norman, S. M. (2007). Positive psychological capital: Measurement and relationship with performance and satisfaction. *Personnel Psychology*, *60*(3), 541–572.

Markland, D., & Vansteenkiste, M. (2007). Self-determination theory and motivational interviewing in exercise. In *Intrinsic motivation and self-determination in exercise and sport* (pp. 87–99). Champaign, IL: Human Kinetics.

McKee, K. (2015). An introduction to the special issue–The big society, localism and housing policy: Recasting state–citizen relations in an age of austerity. *Housing, Theory and Society*, *32*(1), 1–8.

McLeod, S. A. (2014). The interview method. Retrieved from https://www.simplypsychology.org/interviews.html

Meadows, P. (2008). Local initiatives to help workless people find and keep paid work Joseph Rowntree foundation. Retrieved from https://www.jrf.org.uk/report/local-initiatives-help-workless-people-find-and-keep-paid-work

Miles, M. B., Huberman, A. M., Huberman, M. A., & Huberman, M. (1994). *Qualitative data analysis: An expanded sourcebook*. London: Sage.

Myant, M., Theodoropoulou, S., & Piasna, A. (Eds.). (2016). *Unemployment, internal devaluation and labour market deregulation in Europe*. Brussels: European Trade Union Institute (ETUI).

National Housing Federation. (2017). Retrieved from https://www.housing.org.uk/about-us/about-our-members/about-housing-associations

Nichols, G. (2010). *Sport and crime reduction: The role of sports in tackling youth crime*. London: Routledge.

Nicholson, M., & Hoye, R. (2008). Community sport/recreation members and social capital measures in Sweden and Australia. In *Sport and social capital* (pp. 185–206). London: Routledge.

Office for National Statistics. (2017). Retrieved from https://www.ons.gov.uk/employmentandlabourmarket/peopleinwork/employmentandemployeetypes/bulletins/workingandworklesshouseholds/jantomar2017

Office for National Statistics. (2018). Retrieved from https://tradingeconomics.com/united-kingdom/unemployment-rate

Patton, M. Q. (2002). Two decades of developments in qualitative inquiry: A personal, experiential perspective. *Qualitative Social Work*, *1*(3), 261–283.

Piggin, J., Jackson, S. J., & Lewis, M. (2009). Knowledge, power and politics: Contesting evidence-based' national sport policy. *International Review for the Sociology of Sport*, *44*(1), 87–101.

Qu, S. Q., & Dumay, J. (2011). The qualitative research interview. *Qualitative Research in Accounting & Management*, *8*(3), 238–264.

Rallings, M., & Coburn, J. (2014). Retrieved from http://www.hact.org.uk/sites/default/files/uploads/Archives/2014/7/Strategic%20approaches%20to%20employment%20-%20report%20July%202014.pdf

Rees, J., & Mullins, D. (Eds.). (2016). *The third sector delivering public services: Developments, innovations and challenges*. Bristol: Policy Press.

Ritchie, H., Casebourne, J., & Rick, J. (2005). *Understanding workless people and communities*. London: Department for Work and Pensions.

Robertson, D. (2014). Regeneration and poverty in Scotland: Evidence and policy review.

Robson, B. (2017). What work! HACT case study. Retrieved from http://www.hact.org.uk/blog/2017/06/21/what-works-helping-tenants-work-let%E2%80%99s-find-out-together

Rueda, D. (2015). The state of the welfare state: Unemployment, labor market policy, and inequality in the age of workfare. *Comparative Politics*, *47*(3), 296–314.

Rugby Football Union. (2017). Retrieved February 13, 2019, from https://www.englandrugby.com/about-the-rfu/rfu-charities/try-for-change/

Ryan, R. M., & Deci, E. L. (2000). The darker and brighter sides of human existence: Basic psychological needs as a unifying concept. *Psychological Inquiry*, *11*(4), 319–338.

Ryan, R. M., & Deci, E. L. (2017). *Self-determination theory: Basic psychological needs in motivation, development, and wellness*. New York: Guilford Publications.

Ryan, R. M., Patrick, H., Deci, E. L., & Williams, G. C. (2008). Facilitating health behaviour change and its maintenance: Interventions based on self-determination theory. *European Health Psychologist*, *10*(1), 2–5.

School of Hard Knocks. (2017). Retrieved February 13, 2019, from https://www.schoolofhardknocks.org.uk/

Schulenkorf, N. (2012). Sustainable community development through sport and events: A conceptual framework for sport-for-development projects. *Sport Management Review*, 15(1), 1–12.

Scottish Indices of Multiple Deprivation. (2012). Retrieved from http://www.understandingglasgow.com/indicators/poverty/deprivation

Sherry, E. (2010). (Re) engaging marginalized groups through sport: The homeless world cup. *International Review for the Sociology of Sport*, 45(1), 59–71.

Sherry, E., Schulenkorf, N., & Chalip, L. (2015). Managing sport for social change: The state of play.

Siegrist, J., & Marmot, M. (2004). Health inequalities and the psychosocial environment—two scientific challenges. *Social Science & Medicine*, 58(8), 1463–1473.

Silverman, D. (2006). *Interpreting qualitative data*. London: Sage.

Smith, B., & McGannon, K. R. (2018). Developing rigor in qualitative research: Problems and opportunities within sport and exercise psychology. *International Review of Sport and Exercise Psychology*, 11(1), 101–121.

Smith, B., Sparkes, A. C., & Caddick, N. (2014). Judging qualitative research. In L. Nelson, R. Groom, & P. Potrac (Eds.), *Research methods in sports coaching* (pp. 192–202). Abingdon: Routledge.

Spaaij, R., Magee, J., & Jeanes, R. (2013). Urban youth, worklessness and sport: A comparison of sports-based employability programmes in Rotterdam and Stoke-on-Trent. *Urban Studies*, 50(8), 1608–1624.

Spies, H., & Van Berkel, R. (2001). Workfare in the Netherlands: young unemployed people and the Jobseeker's Employment Act. *An Offer You Can't Refuse: Workfare in International Perspective*.

Tessier, D., Sarrazin, P., & Ntoumanis, N. (2010). The effect of an intervention to improve newly qualified teachers' interpersonal style, students motivation and psychological need satisfaction in sport-based physical education. *Contemporary Educational Psychology*, 35(4), 242–253.

Thornberg, R., & Charmaz, K. (2014). Grounded theory and theoretical coding. In *The SAGE handbook of qualitative data analysis* (pp. 153–169). London: Sage.

Timpone, R. J. (1998). Ties that bind: Measurement, demographics, and social connectedness. *Political Behavior*, 20(1), 53–77.

Townsend, K. C., & McWhirter, B. T. (2005). Connectedness: A review of the literature with implications for counseling, assessment, and research. *Journal of Counseling & Development*, 83(2), 191–201.

Understanding Glasgow. (2017). Retrieved February 13, 2019, from https://www.understandingglasgow.com/indicators/poverty/overview

Van Baarsen, B., Snijders, T. A., Smit, J. H., & Van Duijn, M. A. (2001). Lonely but not alone: Emotional isolation and social isolation as two distinct dimensions of loneliness in older people. *Educational and Psychological Measurement*, 61(1), 119–135.

Vansteenkiste, M., & Van den Broeck, A. (2017). Understanding the motivational dynamics among unemployed individuals: Refreshing insights from the self-determination theory perspective.

Walker, C. M., & Hayton, J. W. (2017). Navigating austerity: Balancing 'desirability with viability' in a third sector disability sports organisation. *European Sport Management Quarterly*, 17(1), 98–116.

Walker, M., Hills, S., & Heere, B. (2017). Evaluating a socially responsible employment program: Beneficiary impacts and stakeholder perceptions. *Journal of Business Ethics*, 143(1), 53–70.

White, R. W. (1959). Motivation reconsidered: The concept of competence. *Psychological Review*, 66(5), 297–333.

Williams, D., Collingwood, L., Coles, J., & Schmeer, S. (2015). Evaluating a rugby sport intervention programme for young offenders. *Journal of Criminal Psychology*, 5(1), 51–64.

Sport development in challenging times: leverage of sport events for legacy in disadvantaged communities

Barbara Bell and John Daniels

ABSTRACT
This paper is focused on the legacy of 2016 BMX World SuperCross event held in Manchester. In the current social, political and economic climate, the consideration of wider impacts of major events has come under increasing scrutiny. An increasingly critical debate in a growing literature has addressed social benefits, sporting and community impacts of major events and the methods to achieve increases in sport participation. This paper considers the impacts on people, processes and practice, or "soft legacy" through the realistic evaluation of two BMX projects which were hosting. The impact of attempts to leverage social and sport development impacts in particularly challenging communities are examined, applying a Realistic Evaluation framework [Pawson, R., & Tilley, N. (1997). *Realistic evaluation*. London: Sage] to two programmes. Though the programme of Street BMX was successful in reaching over 500 participants and in the targeted event-based programme there were positive benefits to the participants, limited evidence of longer term impacts was found. Conclusions highlight implications for event-based sport development interventions attempting to engage hard-pressed communities.

Introduction

The emergence of a growing body of literature around events, legacy and impacts beyond sport has been one of the key features of the "golden decade" of sport in the UK, announced by Andy Burnham, as the then Secretary of State for the DCMS in 2009 (BBC, 2009) and reinforced in the post 2012 era in UK Sport policy (DCMS, 2012a, 2012b). The expected impacts both to hosting communities and the nation, of economic, social and sport participation benefits were highlighted as key to leveraging London 2012 legacy well beyond the Games. Despite the challenging public sector economic environment, and limited evidence of positive impacts on sport participation, Governmental expectations of sport and sporting events are arguably even greater, evidenced through the level of investments in major events since 2012.

However, expectations and projections around sport events have not been without criticism or debate. Grix and Carmichael (2012) highlighted the political and ideological processes in the leverage of events, based on the notion of a "virtuous cycle" link to mass participation. Several authors (Misener & Mason, 2009; Misener, Taks, Chalip, & Green, 2015; Taks, Chalip, & Green, 2015; Taks, Green, Misener, & Chalip, 2014) have also examined the often flawed approach to legacy building in sporting events aimed at the stimulation of sporting or other impacts in communities. The assumptions of the "trickle-down" of "inspirational" impacts of sporting events have also been widely criticised as often too optimistic and simplistic in the assumed impact on participation and Physical Activity (Weed et al., 2012; Weed et al., 2015).

Leverage of sporting or other benefits is based on the planned and focused work, strategies and tactics to increase the potential for outcomes beyond the event for hosts and organisers (Chalip, 2006). This is differentiated from the "legacy" of the event, which is the impact of this leverage approach, whether positive or negative (Preuss, 2007; 2015). Such legacy can be tangible and intangible, or "hard" or "soft". Many studies related to event leverage focus on the hard/economic or infrastructure impacts. However, other studies (Bell & Gallimore, 2015; Chalip, 2006; Misener & Mason, 2009; Taks et al., 2014) have considered the leverage of "soft legacy"; in people, processes and in communities hosting events, or linked to spreading benefits to wider communities.

This paper is based on a small-scale research project undertaken in 2016/17 around the Supercross BMX World Cup event, held for the third time in Manchester at the National Cycling Centre (NCC), early April 2016. It is focused on two specific projects, supported by Sport England, provided by the Eastland Leisure Trust [ELT], operators of the NCC to leverage a community sport legacy from the event.[1] The first project was a Street BMX outreach project, to stimulate participation and engagement in BMX. The second project was a targeted intervention using BMX training at the NCC track, in the lead up to the event, with a group of children attending a "Pupil Referral Unit".[2] Also part of the leverage approach was the provision of events and coaching programmes in Manchester Schools, but this was outside of the remit for the study. The research applied a "Realistic Evaluation" [RE] model (Pawson & Tilley, 1997) on very limited resources, to provide an independent evaluation of the programme impacts, and develop insight about the mechanisms and processes involved.

The paper firstly examines some of the literature around event legacy and leverage from major events, particularly around "sport for change" and social impacts. The paper then examines the background to the intervention and the potential for engagement of youth in urban cycling, particularly BMX, particularly with the "hard to reach" young people in this alternative, informal or lifestyle sport, as highlighted by Jeanes, Spaaij, Penney, and O'Connor (2018).

The main body of the paper examines the methods and key findings in the evaluation of the BMX projects. This was a mainly qualitative investigation, though there is also some registration data, to quantify the level of participation in the programmes and the "reach" into the targeted communities of South Manchester. Thus, we conducted within a RE framework, an investigation into the engagement of young people in the legacy projects, to examine whether the planned "legacy" was demonstrated.

Finally, there is an attempt to draw some conclusions about event legacy aspirations and the learning from the BMX-based projects, particularly in reaching hard to reach communities, in challenging circumstances and with a non-traditional sport. As noted above, sport has long been considered a vehicle for positive social impacts, but particularly since the origins

---

[1] Eastlands Leisure Trust was established in 2015, as the facilities operator of the NCC and other Manchester City Council sports facilities and services.
[2] More details of the 2 projects are provided in logic models. The original target was for young people Not in Education or Training [NEET] to be recruited, but this was changed to children in a Pupil Referral Unit [PRU] ie taught apart from mainstream school classes temporarily due to behavioural or educational issues.

of "sport development" in the 1980's (Collins, 2011). As highlighted by Brookes and Wiggan (2009) and Collins and Haudenhuyse (2015), through local policy implementation into urban environments, sport has been seen as a means to tackle social exclusion and address problems of young people in areas of disadvantage. As Gilchrist and Wheaton (2017) have identified there is a real potential for lifestyle or alternative sports to address the needs of young people who might be disengaged or excluded from mainstream sport, or traditional competitive structures and formal settings. Thus in the UK and elsewhere there has been a proliferation of "street" based projects – working in non-traditional settings and with hard to reach young people, more at risk of or subject to greater social exclusion (Collins & Haudenhuyse, 2015; Jeanes et al., 2018) and a growth in the area of "sport *for* development" (Schulenkorf, 2012). This movement has not without criticism, however, and the assumed "power" of sport to transform those in otherwise very challenging social circumstances has been subject to some fierce debate, particularly about the evidence of impacts and measurement of outcomes (Coalter, 2007, 2010; Collins, 2014). In the current austerity climate for public investment, with the inherent inequalities across communities under pressure (Widdop, King, Parnell, Cutts, & Millward, 2018) any public investment into major events for their sporting or other impacts into disadvantaged communities needs careful consideration.

Event legacies and non-mega events: communities and sport development impacts

Government policy in sport has increasingly supported the notion of sport for development and "addressing underrepresentation" (DDCMS, 2015, p. 20). Consequently, support for those deemed "hard to reach" such as women, girls, the disabled and those in low socio-economic groups has appeared high on recent government agendas (DCMS, 2002; DDCMS, 2015). Such policies have been criticised for a lack evidence of mechanisms and processes, particularly in tackling persistent social inequalities (Coalter, 2007). More recently, studies are recording positive outcomes to suggest that sport can develop social skills among youth from vulnerable backgrounds, improve social connectedness and enhance a sense of community (Sherry, 2016). Increasing levels of social participation have also been linked to a better quality of life and a "hook" back into education (Sherry, 2016). Alongside this trend of expected social impacts from sport, evidence has also been building to suggest that sports events may stimulate a developmental legacy by inspirational impacts on youth sport participation. This has prompted growth in the number of community sports projects linked to national and international sports events (Richards & de Brito, 2013; Taks et al., 2015). However, Chalip (2006) warned that rhetoric concerning legacy outcomes of sports events are generally hoped for and desired rather than planned for and delivered. Clearly, the political rhetoric around the "golden decade" of British sport (DCMS, 2012a, 2012b) emphasised this in the lead up to and immediately following the London 2012 Games and more recent policy announcements (DDCMS, 2015). Sport development policies have demonstrated a commitment to inclusive practices and have typically targeted specific populations, often with young people as the focus. Arguably since the very inception of sport development by the Wolfenden Report of 1960 (Bell, 2005; Collins, 2011), youth has been the focus of efforts to improve both the reach and impact of sport. More recently, young people have been the target of "Olympic legacy" projects based on a virtuous cycle theory (Grix & Carmichael, 2012) that explains increases in sport participation based on the inspiration of Olympic and Paralympic success. However, this assumed logic model of inspirational impacts has been criticised as being incomplete (Bloyce & Smith,

2012; Weed et al., 2015), particularly when looking at the translation into Physical Activity and "mass participation" related to national statistics for activity and sport engagement.

In theory, the sport of cycling should yield a good return on investment in terms of sport participation and impacts on youth engagement. British Cycling again demonstrating they are world leading, with 12 medals in Rio 2016, including 6 golds, building on London 2012 and previous successes. The city of Manchester has been home to the National Cycling Centre (NCC) from 1994 and since hosting the Commonwealth Games (CWG) in 2002, has been at the heart of the impressive medal factory for British Cycling for over two decades. While there were no GB medals for BMX events in Rio, Manchester has a rich history of BMX development, including hosting the UCI BMX Supercross World Cup events in 2013, 2015 and 2016 in the indoor track built in 2011. In South Manchester, an outdoor track at Platt Fields Park, built to national competition standards with a premise to be accessible to all, hosts regular national events as well as the competition and training for the Manchester BMX club, a leading club in national BMX leagues. However, rates of cycling in Manchester do not reflect a "trickle down" from this infrastructure and event hosting history.

The funding of projects for a legacy from international cycling events is part of investment in the sport at both national and city level, with Sport England supporting developmental programmes through partnership working across City Council, ELT (facility operators), schools and British Cycling. However, the partners are also acutely aware of the need to demonstrate programme impact and develop understanding of how their programmes work, hence the development of the research project with the local University.

In the Sport England Active People surveys (2005–2016) participation levels in the city have consistently been below that of regional comparators. Only 4.4% of the adult population did any cycling 3 times per week, compared with 6.1% in Liverpool and for those just occasionally cycling (once per month) the figure was 10.7% compared to 16.6% in Liverpool (Sport England, 2016). Liverpool has similar socio-economic indicators, but without the elite facilities, performance pathways or similar levels of schools based cycling programmes. Child health and wellbeing measures were also lower in Manchester compared with other regional profiles (Public Health England, 2018). A high proportion of children live in low-income families, and a relatively high proportion (9.4%) of young people 16–18 are classed as Not in Education Employment or Training or NEET, indicating the challenging circumstances faced by many young people in the city. Only 11.9% of children are active at the rate (one hour per day) advised as appropriate by the Chief Medical Officer, compared to the regional average of 13.2%.

BMX has also some issues with engagement and investment. In what has been described as "appropriation" of this alternative or lifestyle sport into the sport of cycling, there are criticisms of a commodification and "sportification" process (Edwards & Corte, 2010; Reinhart & Grenfell, 2002). This commodification might work against the growth of participation in young people in more difficult circumstances, due to increased costs and regulation of otherwise "free" activity in parks and streets (Gilchrist & Wheaton, 2017).

Legacy plans and SuperCross World Cup

Essentially the literature above highlights the assumptions underpinning the work of the City Council, that major events can potentially inspire youth to engage in sport for various reasons, but rates of activity shown in surveys and national health indicators shows this "trickle down" is far from clear. Manchester's designation as a "City of Sport" seems to have had limited impacts on activity or participation attributable to the elite sports based there. Accolades as the leading "city for sport" in the UK by ESPN (ESPN, 2015; Parker, Sarkar, Curran, & Williams, 2015), are mainly based on responses by sports fans to the opportunities for watching rather than playing sport. The City Council have supported over 216 major events hosted in the city since 2002, resulting in over £92 m of economic impact and additional investment of £37 m (Manchester City Council, 2015). Cycling was highlighted as key partner in this success, and one of the cities "Tier one" sports for investment.

In attempting to leverage the benefits from UCI BMX World Cup events at the NCC, Event organisers had previously incorporated into one of the final evening intervals a schools BMX race. This gave young and novice BMX riders a role in the major event, as a culmination of the schools coaching programme for the city. For 2016 this emphasis was changed, to develop two new programmes to create a "legacy" from the event.

The overarching aim of the evaluation research commissioned around the event in 2016 was to examine the impact of these legacy programmes. Specifically, a key objective was to establish and monitor the number of young people taking part in one or more Street BMX activity sessions and the transition of participants involved in the Street BMX activity to at least one formal session (Urban Expression) on the Platt Fields Park BMX track. The project was designed to investigate the impact of the two strands of the BMX legacy programme on the young people taking part, and analyse participant characteristics of the Street BMX legacy programme. Essentially the work was commissioned by the Eastlands Trust to evaluate the delivery, process and effectiveness of both programmes.

The ELT BMX Supercross legacy programmes:

(1) Street BMX – delivery of fun, taster, outreach sessions of BMX, coach, bikes and equipment provided across community sites across S/E Manchester. Coaches would offer one off sessions to clubs and community groups, in parks or open spaces, or at community events. The aim was to increase participation in BMX either informally (recreational cycling) or formally (e.g. at Urban Expressions, BMX club, track sessions)
(2) Event-based Development programme – A term time, weekly track based programme of training with a small group of local young people, in a pupil referral unit (PRU). This was taking place in the weeks prior to and following the BMX Supercross event. The young people were to train to "perform" in a race on the track during the event, and follow up with cycling coaching, volunteering or mechanics based training, depending on interest and progress.

Methods and challenges of the BMX programme legacy evaluation

This section overviews the evaluation methodology, data analysis techniques and ethical stance taken in the research. The evaluation took a multi – and mixed-method case study design (Yin, 2009), combining both qualitative and quantitative data in order to fully capture the process and outcomes of the BMX Legacy Projects. Pawson and Tilley's (1997) "Realistic Evaluation" approach, investigating the interactions between the context, mechanisms and outcomes achieved in the programmes, was developed in consultation with ELT during February/March 2016. During the evaluation (April-September), several meetings took place with programme management for the "theory of change", updating on progresses and to develop understanding of the mechanisms and processes during the programme. A logic model illustrating the connection between the programme mechanisms and its outcomes and to guide the evaluation design, was developed for each project, as shown in Figures 1 and 2.

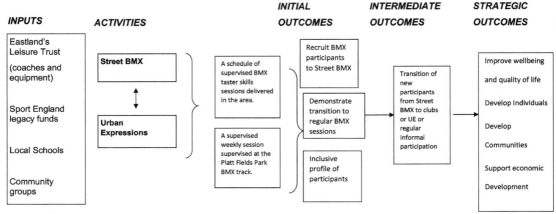

Figure 1. Street BMX initial logic model (developed from consultation with ELT).

Based on the assumed theories of change identified, each of the projects incorporated the perspectives of different stakeholders along with data from registrations provided by the coaches. Resources for extensive monitoring and data collection were limited. All participants were provided with information sheets about the research and individual informed

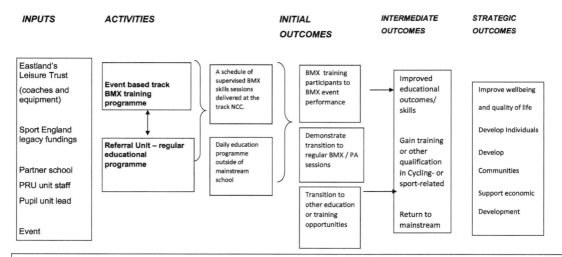

Figure 2. The Logic model for PRU-based BMX programme.

consent for interview, either face to face or via telephone was obtained. All methods and tools were approved via the University ethical approval process prior to data collection.

For the school-based referral group, in *loco-parentis* consent via the school and lead teacher of the group was obtained, and individual children also consented to interviews at the follow-up visit. Meetings with PRU participants took place at the track – during the BMX World cup and 1–1 interviews at their regular base out of school. Regular observations took place at the BMX track outdoors in Platt Fields park of the supervised BMX activity at the Friday night "Urban Expressions" session. This enabled an in-depth analysis of the interviews and informal conversations with participants, coaches, parents and volunteers involved and also contributed to recommendations about the communications around BMX. Thus, the range of methods used helped build a better understanding of the context of "BMX" in the formal and informal settings of the track, street or park.

The framework of "realistic" evaluation considered the interactions of the contexts, mechanism and possible outcomes achieved on both programmes – but it was also realistic in the sense of being constrained by "real world" issues of time and resource to complete a thorough and robust evaluation of the impacts at different levels. No economic analysis of costs or benefits was included – partly as this information was considered sensitive by ELT, but also that the cost of the data collection and analysis required to produce any evidence of social return on investment was considered prohibitive. Detailed questionnaires on activity and health indicators were deemed inappropriate for the Street BMX participants. The indicators of the achievement of intended outcomes at the PRU were based on teacher assessment of behavioural changes and educational status (i.e. back in mainstream school or having achieved a qualification) (Table 1).

Table 1. Methods used in the Realistic Evaluation of the BMX legacy projects.

Street BMX	BMX Event Track PRU
Stakeholder interviews (programme team, volunteers, youth workers), registration documents, observations at Platt Fields Park, informal conversations with participants and parents	Stakeholder interviews (coaches, teaching staff, participants), observations at indoor track, event and follow up visit to PRU, informal conversations with volunteers and young people at the event

Process and procedures in the evaluation

In the Street BMX programme, as indicated in the logic models, outcome measures were based on increases in or indications of PA level through BMX engagement in organised sessions, measured by analysis of names and addresses, matched with postcodes from the details obtained on outreach sessions.

Informal interviews and observations with participants and parents at track sessions and with the coaches and leaders aimed to get their perspective of any changes in the participation in open access or club sessions at Platt Fields track (where many of the outreach sessions were planned). These observations took place in monthly visits from April, to September to the track and "Street BMX" sessions in community venues.

Though the planned visits to the track took place, due to low numbers and late changes to arrangements for the community engagement sessions, there were no completed observations on the community "Street BMX" sessions. Follow up interviews (2) were undertaken with selected youth workers by telephone, to get feedback and indications of follow up actions. These discussions focused on the youth workers perceptions of the impact of the sessions on cycling engagement or attitudes to BMX, and how the sessions related to their wider objectives with the potential for any ongoing activity with the NCC or BMX track sessions.

Though focus groups were originally planned, less formal conversations were undertaken with parents and children at the regular observations at the track. These informal conversations provided useful insight into the attitudes of young people and their parents on the BMX projects. This also helped with the analysis of in-depth interviews with other stakeholders, as it identified the benefits and limitations of the BMX legacy programmes and the potential impact on wellbeing, health and personal development of the young people concerned. As young people did not complete any questionnaires regarding their Physical Activity, limited inference could be made about the health or activity status of the children taking part, except through indirect, qualitative methods. At *none* of the observed sessions were any children identified that had taken part in a "Street BMX" session or had been to the Supercross event at the NCC.

Stakeholder in-depth interviews

In depth, one-to-one interviews were carried out to capture the experiences of a range of stakeholders:

- the BMX legacy programme staff in the design and delivery of the programme
- the volunteers and coaches supporting the sessions and,
- Youth, education and community workers who had been involved with children attending organised StreetBMX sessions and Urban Expression NCC based Track sessions with PRU pupils.

Interviews with BMX Legacy Programme Staff explored staff working practices and service ethos plus issues concerning partnership working, with Programme Lead and several of the staff involved in delivery. The interviews took place at several intervals throughout the course of the BMX legacy project. Three staff members were interviewed informally on separate occasions to ensure progress and change in working practices was monitored and recorded. A formal interview with the lead coach on the legacy programme who had delivered the work with PRU and also many of the "Street BMX" sessions took place in July towards the end of the programme and in a follow-up interview sixth months later. Various emails were also exchanged with programme staff to check on arrangements and discuss the sessions during programme delivery.

Youth and community staff and teacher interviews over the phone or in person were undertaken with both the street BMX and PRU BMX event programme. An in-depth interview was undertaken with a lead teacher at the PRU in July after completion of the programme. A brief follow-up interview took place by phone in November, to follow up on 6-month outcomes and ongoing engagement with BMX. Due to changing arrangements with the PRU, school and the youth group involved, it was not possible to complete any further interviews in the 12-month follow up, as the schools contract had been terminated.

All formal interviews, with the exception of telephone interviews, were recorded with permission and informed consents obtained. Transcription of the interviews enabled thematic analysis (Braun and Clarke 2006) to take place. Field notes and observations from visits also assisted with interpretation. Detailed notes and memos from observations or telephone interviews were also coded then thematically analysed. The process of analysis involved various stages of reading and coding relevant sections of text, then grouping and sorting both inductively and deductively, into themes related to the Logic model, context, mechanism or outcome patterns. The sections below provide a narrative of the findings and interpretation from across all the qualitative data and include some selected quotes to illustrate the key themes identified.

The follow up, 1–1 Interviews with PRU pupils took place in July, towards the end of the school year, along with the leader of the unit, who had worked closely with the group. Unfortunately again a consequence of "real world" messiness in the evaluation process (Daniels, Bell, & Horrocks, 2018), these were deferred due to GCSE exams for the Yr 11 pupils involved and by then **all** of the (3) participants in the Supercross event had left the unit, for a variety of reasons not related to their BMX project engagement. Even though at least one had achieved their outcome measure of completing a skills-based course, only one of those involved with the event completed the cycle mechanics course with British Cycling at the NCC before the end of the academic year.

From Street to track? Street BMX programme impacts and mechanisms

Mechanisms in Street BMX

In the Street BMX, coaching was focused on giving the young people an introduction into the skills related to BMX riding, performing tricks and the potential to improve technique, safety, bike handling and therefore build confidence. The coach introduced activities like mini-races or skills competitions to maintain interest and add some elements that got young people more engaged. Based on the interviews with programme staff, the coaching was very successful, but there were concerns that in just one or possibly two sessions it was difficult to build up a rapport with the participants that might encourage young people to turn up independently to the urban expression or open track sessions at weekends.

In the main, these were one-off interactions as evidenced by the limited registers taken at the events. Based on the initial interviews and confirmed in the 12 month follow up, the lead coaches' confidence had grown over the course of the programme, so they were satisfied that the sessions provided a positive, active and engaging session – a point reinforced by the youth workers and leaders they worked with in the interviews notes above.

However, simply organising and planning the sessions in parks and with youth groups had been a considerable and unanticipated challenge. There were complications with staff at the centres, other Manchester City Council (MCC) staff regarding permissions to operate in parks and the weather. This meant that many sessions were planned and then changed, cancelled or had to re-locate at short notice. This unanticipated challenge was reflected in the interviews and interim reports by the programme manager. The sessions were subsequently targeted to existing community groups, rather than the original proposed approach to parks and open spaces, in a "pop up" session, an important contextual factor in their success.

Social media (Instagram and Facebook) had been incorporated into the efforts by the coaches to promote the sessions and show images of the BMX programmes, but there had not been any analysis of the impact of this. The interviews and informal discussions with the coaching team also reflected some frustration with the timing and form of marketing support the programme had. Despite this, the registers and feedback from community organisations showed that the Street BMX did engage children over 500 young people from across South Manchester, mainly focused on areas of deprivation, as discussed in the section below. The aims, in terms of the nature of the sessions provided and the target population, were clearly met. This appeared to be a result of the approach to target identified community groups and the use of community spaces close to their base.

Perspectives of youth workers – Street BMX impacts and transitions

Key themes identified from the interviews with Youth workers related to:

- Nature of the activity (related to enjoyment/thrills/novelty)
- Territoriality (in and out of area working)
- Group cohesion – (benefits of, tackling as a group, co-operation and competition)
- Gender – benefits to confidence for girls in girls-only sessions

- Staff and resources – (barriers to ongoing engagement with Platt Fields park sessions, limits and constraints, safe spaces to enjoy)

There were clearly positive evaluations of the Street BMX sessions by the youth workers. Once children had the chance to get onto bikes they were active, engaged fully and enthusiastic about their experiences afterwards. BMX appealed to both boys and girls in the mixed sessions but girls, in particular, welcomed their "girls only" sessions, particularly when they felt they were in a little more of a private area, even if this was a car park or open space by the community centre/park.

Both Youth workers commented on the way in which the coach managed to get young people working together. Girls were more likely to need more encouragement to visit again – but all groups would have more sessions of BMX at their club – not necessarily every week or formally for a set programme. The programmes of many existing youth groups were designed to include a range of activities but BMX was seen as part of wider programme. Taking the children to the track at Platt Fields (even for those who were relatively close) was unlikely or difficult to do, because of staffing – too few staff to spare someone to take a small group to the track; or due to concerns about working "out of their area".

The issue of territoriality for children and young people – getting to the NCC or Platt Fields was difficult from their club – travelling across the wrong postcodes. Either their parents would lack the resources (car) to take them, or the time/enthusiasm to make the journey, or children had concerns about safety in the parks or areas outside of their centres.[3]

Youth Staff were confident that all their children who had taken part could ride a bike, most had their own, though it was more likely they were into mountain bike type riding (not on organised trails but around local streets/open spaces). They considered the sessions would have contributed to more confidence and therefore more likely to do more cycling – but with dark evenings, they were unlikely to be doing this down at the track. There was no real assessment of the activity by children outside of their sessions but overall the youth workers felt this could be part of their overall programme in future, given sufficient staffing and some support for transporting children to the track.

The Urban Expression timing (6–8pm) on Fridays or Saturday evening at the NCC was seen to be an issue with several groups. This was in direct competition with their general youth sessions in the clubs – i.e. they could not spare people to take small groups and the whole group would only want to do BMX cycling occasionally unless it was on site.

"Better than hanging around" the views of parents and young people at Urban Expression sessions

Parents attending the Urban Expression were generally accompanying young people under 12 or small groups including some family groups. Many were mothers who were keen to express their approval of the format and availability of the sessions on the track. Several parents who had been involved with schools-based BMX sessions brought their children along to other track-based sessions, including the Friday night Urban Expression sessions. In all of the visits, insufficient numbers of young people were identified for any of the planned group-based discussions. Small numbers were attending, many of the children were reluctant to talk or they were perceived to be too young to approach without parental consent, or simply too busy riding the track or hanging about with their friends.

---

[3] The BBC filmed one of the training sessions and spoke to several participants posting the film onto the 'Get Inspired' website in the lead up to the April event – this was still available in 2017. Their views in the film were considered a good proxy for individual interviews as a 'baseline' of attitudes before the event.

Other parents had brought children to the park, without really understanding what the sessions were about. Often these were in large family groups with children taking part in a range of activities in the park (basketball, skateboarding, games of cricket, football, bike or scooter riding). Parents were enthusiastic to give the children the opportunity to ride the track for only £1.50 including the bike and all equipment. None of the parents spoken to had been aware of the sessions through any marketing, website or knew of any links to the Supercross event. They often lived relatively close to the park, having walked or taken a bus on evenings with good weather. Poor weather meant very few people in the park and very few riders on the track.

One mother who had brought her own 11-year-old and several friends on the bus, was making her first visit to the track, though her son had been before with school. She had plans to take the boys to the indoor track – provided it was going to be as cheap. Her main reason was to give her son a good experience of riding his bike which he did a lot of at home, but also to learn how to be safer on it. She talked about how the BMX session of 2-hours "really tired him out" all he did when he got back was go to bed and sleep – and how it "kept him from mischief". This was the sort of activity she preferred him to do i.e. better than just " … hanging around or going off with friends." This was something she said she would like to do more of and now she had seen the track, she would look out for details of when they could come as a family. Parents seemed to appreciate the emphasis on safety and use of protective equipment.

Most of the young people of 11 years or above seemed to come unaccompanied, or if younger, their parents were elsewhere in the park and just paid/booked the children in, then watched at a discrete distance. The lack of signage and clear instructions about what to do and what was happening at the sessions meant that some parents or children were unsure if sessions were open or not, or what the arrangements were, often hanging about at the gate observing before coming in. Volunteers were regularly sent out into the park to give out flyers to encourage people in the park to bring their children.

Programme staff and coaches'/volunteers' perspectives of the impact of Street BMX on regular BMX sessions

Based on the figures provided by ELT, there had been *lower* engagement in the UE summer sessions in 2016, compared to the previous year, when no additional legacy programme had taken place. Several weeks recorded only single figures of participants, particularly in the poor weather of April and May. Consequently, informal interviews with the staff coaching on Fridays focused on their view of the possible transitions from street style BMX engagement to the track sessions. The final interviews were conducted to reflect on the summers activity on the track. At the final session attended in early September, there were no participants, with poor weather and the park in darkness by 7.00 pm.

The programme staff and volunteers focused on their views on the reasons for poor numbers: They referred to a lack of support for marketing, problems with track signage and concerns of accessibility. Staff were clearly very committed to growing the sport, but felt some constraints at the track and its management. From early on in the summer, it was clear that the achievement of the stated KPIs in transitions to UE was going to be a challenge for the Street BMX, and it quickly became clear hitting the targets was extremely unlikely. On every visit before July, the research team was informed that the sessions would be much busier in the school holidays. However, this expected upturn never occurred. Also, with the delays and gaps in the Street BMX sessions, it was clear that any progression into regular BMX was unlikely to be picked up at the track. It was not possible, without clearer tracking of individuals, to do follow up investigations into the level of cycling or general activity as a consequence of taking part in one-off Street BMX sessions. The coaches certainly did not see this process working, except through schools visits, where they recognised some children as coming from their school's sessions.

The coaches and volunteers expressed concerns about the lack of clear marketing and promotion and general information about BMX and cycling at the track. Coaches felt under pressure to not only maintain a fun and safe session but also to act as a recruiter for the session by inviting people in from the park. This suggests that such community programmes require clear roles to allow for effective delivery of programme mechanism if outcomes are to be achieved. Volunteer Mike (pseudonym), when asked if he went to the BMX club sessions responded:

> ... no, not really my thing, I prefer to come to this' – the club was seen as about serious 'riders' and 'racers'... this Friday night is all about 'chilling and just relaxing on the bike', 'hanging out with mates.

An important aspect of the "context" was that the "closed" nature of the BMX track was seen as potentially off putting for informal cycling. Young people were likely to be using the track unofficially when it suited them, and had to be discouraged from riding with their own bikes – often without brakes and no safety equipment (e.g. helmets/gloves). On my final visit, John – (Coach) stated:

> I've had to just chuck 4 lads off.... they wouldn't stay and ride on our bikes with helmets so they had to go.... (Field Note: no other young people were out on the track that evening)

The coaches also pointed out that the reduced programme for the track meant that young people actually had very few sessions they could access by late September, so if any of the children attending Street BMX were interested in taking part, they might be going to open sessions at weekend. As far as they were aware, no one was going to club sessions having been in the Street Session, but they couldn't be sure. Overall, the coaches based at the track were concerned that young people were not aware of the sessions available to them, and the NCC website was not very helpful in promoting to young people or their parents.

This aspect of the evaluation, therefore, highlighted that the funding enabled an extensive programme of Street BMX sessions across the area of South Manchester, including in some of the most challenging communities for activity. There was some evidence that the Street BMX coaching and events might have raised awareness of BMX through positive experiences in sessions in clubs, groups and events. There was evidence of the successful and positive approach in the less formal Street BMX sessions provided. Despite this engagement in extensive sessions, there was no clear evidence of transitions into regular Urban Expression or other BMX activity from those who participated in the Street Sessions or taster events – i.e. a failure in the logic model proposed, and no achievement of the planned KPI measures in transition to regular BMX sessions.

Progression in Street BMX and the achievement of the legacy objectives

Quantitative data on engagement was recorded at a number of Street BMX activities/ venues, via registers completed by NCC staff. These included: Indoor track at NNC Sessions, Parks, church and youth groups and schools sessions. Registers recorded 285 participants across 10 events and sessions. These indicted in summary:

- A significant proportion of female participants, important given the current efforts to make sport more accessible for women and girls.
- A significant proportion of BME children reported by coaches

- A purposeful reach in terms of socio-demographic area, based on postcodes (high BME populations).

A further 298 participants were recorded at various community and education events such as "Schools Together" days and activities at local voluntary organisations or community events – though individual registration data was not taken. Thus, 583 participants engaged with the project representing 97% of the agreed target of 600 participants.

The registrations for these sessions by gender (where recorded) can be found in Figure 3 and clearly indicated the NCC, Schools Together and the "BiggaFish" group from Trinity House as the most popular sessions in terms of participation. The NCC and the Ladybarn Community Centre sessions were particularly successful in engaging females for the mixed sessions. The participants also reflected the ethnic diversity of the areas targeted, though details of ethnicity were not captured on registrations.

The "reach" of the project into local communities

Of the 285 participants, 99 recorded post codes were obtained. Postcodes were concentrated around the Southeast of Manchester, including Hulme, Withington, Burnage, Rusholme and Levenshulme. These districts are acknowledged as some of Manchester's most deprived areas according to the 2015 Indices of Deprivation published by Manchester Council (2015). According to Sport England, it is in these areas that participants are "hardest to reach" or engage in sport (Sport England, 2015). These are also the areas hit hard with austerity climate issues. – who suffer from low participation rates in PA in general, and organised sports in particular (Public Health England, 2018). Given the locations of the Street BMX sessions, reflected in the postcodes of participants, the programmes successfully reached the populations of young people in the areas around the NCC and Platt Fields Park and made some contribution to the sporting capital of young people there, albeit over a short engagement period.

From event to engagement? the impacts of BMX event-based programme with PRU based young people

A BBC "Get Inspired" film made with the PRU group at their training event, suggests that the sport of BMX has potential to have an impact on children who are struggling with mainstream school, who have significant issues to deal with and who may be at risk of permanent exclusion. There were clear disciplinary, behavioural and physical challenges involved in the intensive training at the track, which were recognised by the coach as presenting a clear challenge to him also: "it was by far the hardest thing I've done" – BMX Coach of the PRU group.

The impact of the event at the supercross World Cup

The first author met the children, coach and teacher at the 2016 UCI BMX SuperCross World Cup event in April, at the culmination of their training, where the young people "competed" in a race during the interval of the elite event. They were kitted out in specially designed shirts (designed by one of the group riding) in honour of their successful completion of the programme. Unfortunately, only 3 out of 14 young people who had gone through the training took part, despite the clear enthusiasm. As the event was in the Easter holidays, several were on holiday with families or simply failed to turn up at the collection point, with one pupil injured on the track in the final training session and unable to take part. It was clear that this small group were nervous and found this experience to be a great challenge, despite the excellent and calming support from their coach and teacher. However, it was also clear that the successful completion of the race and the rest of the experience

Figure 3. Attendances at Street BMX sessions by gender.

surrounding the event was seen as quite an achievement and something they had pride in completing.

This was quite clearly expressed in the BBC "Get Inspired" clip (BBC 2016, see link below)[4] – where the only female taking part, expressed her views on how she was looking forward to the event. At the event they were supported by volunteers from the BMX club, and accompanied round the track. However it was clear, in front of a large and vociferous crowd of real BMX enthusiasts, this was a significant challenge to the young people.

Despite the great experience for the three riders, non-attendance by other members of the group was noted as a key disappointment, particularly given the extra time put in by coach, volunteers and the accompanying teacher. Unfortunately, by July when the follow-up visit took place, **none** of the three young people who had taken part in the event were still attending the PRU, so no first-hand accounts of their reflections on this experience could be obtained. The reasons for their problems in mainstream education had not been addressed despite their successful engagement with the BMX project. The teacher concerned was careful to point out that their behaviour while at the unit had definitely improved during and after the BMX programme, and their ongoing personal issues were external to their positive improvements whilst at the unit and taking part with BMX and other activities.

Other students who took part in the pre-event training and some subsequent sessions at the track, (including the mechanics course) were no longer at the unit having returned to mainstream school. This could be seen as a positive outcome, related to the indicators for the legacy programme, but clearly, the BMX sessions alone could not account for the relevant educational outcomes achieved by the young people, something their teacher/youth worker had worked intensively on an individual basis with young people involved for many months.

Young participants perspectives on their BMX experience

There were 4 young people still attending the unit in July who agreed to be involved in short interviews to discuss their experience and the value of their BMX programme. They had gone to most if not all of the sessions available and were all very positive about the sessions. Some expressed regret at not having

---

[4] http://www.bbc.co.uk/sport/get-inspired/35947269 – Film by BBC of the group training (8 April 2016)

taken part in the event. Either due to problems with being "sent back" to school in the week before end of term (thus missing final training session), or the event being in the Easter break, they had simply "forgot" about it. All the young people interviewed referred to the importance of their enjoyment of riding the track for achieving something positive from the sessions.

After analysis, the following themes were identified in the pupil interviews:

- Enjoyment of BMX
- Personal development and growth – skills and confidence
- Impacts on future and or school
- Role of the coach

All the pupils highlighted fun, enjoyment and excitement of the sessions on the track as an important contextual element of the programme:

> It's just more fun to do, you just learn different things you learn something new every day. Pupil1

> I wanted to do it because it sounded fun- and it was good. Pupil 2

The benefits of the BMX based programme at the track to personal development and growth was clearly highlighted in the interviews. They identified important contexts such as a positive coaching environment, which was clearly important to the children, it facilitated significant outcomes, interacting as a group, talking and supporting each other, they were treated with respect and had to listen (for safety and to learn new skills).

> It just like gets us away from like doing bad things and gets us all interacting with each other. Pupil 3

BMX riding wasn't seen as a serious activity, but it was something new and different, something they could do with their mates – but not get into trouble doing (i.e. it kept them out of trouble):

> It's just like because you can interact more with people and it's not as its serious but not as serious as the others. So yeah, its good fun, but at the same time you're having fun with your mates, so like, you're not about on the streets getting into trouble and stuff. (Pupil 3)

It was useful to be trained to ride properly, children appreciated the opportunity to get these skills in riding such as learning new tricks, going faster on their bikes, experiencing the track and learning how to look after their bikes. This reinforced how young people perceived developing new competencies as contributing to their sense of achievement.

> They taught us like different ways and like, how to do tricks and stuff and how to move quicker on the track. (Pupil 3)

The experiences itself was both fun yet challenging (scary/exciting/fun) but also about learning (skills, how to get on, being more safe/ more independent / save money (on bike repairs):

> It's good they teach you because, like it could save you money and stuff. (Pupil 3)

Children referred to how this course was going to help them – seen as a diversion from trouble, and an opportunity to learn new skills with possible career benefits, vocational training routes, or getting them back into school. They noted it had improved their attitude:

> Because with good behaviour and stuff and like interacting with things ... I used to have an attitude ... I could go back to school. (Pupil 3)

And having taken part in the whole programme (despite missing the event), something they were proud to have completed. Asked about how he felt about going on the track:

> It was scary at first, but then I did it ... I still got a lot out of it. (Pupil 1) (only missed the event)

Some children were clearly engaged with other sports out of school – all had the ability to ride a bike and were active outdoors. They indicated that BMX was better than some more traditional sporting experiences (e.g. with Rugby) which seemed to have put them off from engaging in activity – as it wasn't all about being in a team or competition – they enjoyed being faster and competing, learning new things together as a group and were happy to work together.

The teacher of the unit reinforced that the work on the track clearly complemented their approach to using purposeful activity to develop concentration, improve attitudes to learning and experience new physical skills:

> I was really impressed with the whole thing, the fact that health and safety, the way they took to it, the fact there was a team spirit within it, the skills that were involved and the behaviour on the track. (Teacher at Pupil Referral unit)

The teacher's perspective echoed those of the children regarding the challenges in BMX. They enjoyed the sessions so much he was able to incentivise good behaviour with the potential of attending or stopping the sessions if they misbehaved. The positive management of the sessions by the coach clearly reinforced his approaches – a positive mechanism of the programme. There were clear impacts on the behaviour of the group as they got to know the coach and were more confident and respectful of him. From the teacher's perspective, BMX and cycling centred approaches had good vocational and practical potential for this group of boys (and the one girl who had taken part) over and above the physical aspect. Learning about bike maintenance was clearly linked to the aspirations for jobs in engineering or other practical aspects, such as working at sport facilities.

The teacher, experienced in this type of work, considered the engaging, active sessions kept the interest of this notoriously difficult group – and reinforced teamwork, better interactions between the group and with the leaders, which would stand them in good stead on return to school.

> These kids have got a problem with authority and following instructions. We've been there an hour two hours, and Rob's really retained their enthusiasm and interest. (Teacher Pupil Unit)

In conclusion, and after the follow-up interview, in particular, he reinforced he was still taking other children and some from this first group back to the NCC for more sessions, in order to build on this work. The only aspect he might have improved would be to have a much clearer exit route into mechanics or work at the NCC clearly set out at the start. It wasn't really necessary, from his perspective, to be part of the big event to achieve the most benefits for the young people. If the event had taken place in term time rather than in the Easter break, it would have been easier manage attendance.

Working with more challenging groups – the coaches perspective

The style of this work was very different to that the coach had experienced before. Though he had some training in dealing with challenging behaviour, the work with the PRU was the first prolonged engagement with anyone other than the BMX club participants or enthusiasts at the track. There were clear developmental gains for the coach as well as the children in a possibly an unintended consequence of this and the Street-based work.

In this session, the key contextual issues from the coach's perspective were to do with the importance of building relationships with the young people over time, to establish their trust and also gain their respect. He was able to gain some understanding of their difficulties and rather complex lives and see things from their point of view – something that the teacher working with them had more experience with. Clearly, that only 3 of the group took part in the event was a disappointment. However, all made significant progress in their BMX work, and the progression onto bike mechanics was seen as clear "added value", as was the ongoing relationship with the PRU and the potential for new groups to go the NCC.

Another unforeseen outcome related to the event was highlighted in the engagement of young volunteers from the BMX club (who he normally coached) who were able to gain experience of leadership and support to the inexperienced riders, and also the background working of the event itself. This helped to deliver some "legacy" in terms of their ongoing qualification as event volunteers with BMX youth ambassador programme.

Therefore, while the programme of BMX training, event and post-event engagement was followed as planned (eventually), this was not without its problems. Those children who engaged fully with event and training had positive experiences and showed improvements in behaviour back at the unit. However, very few impacts were solely due to this programme and even so, no clear evidence of any improved educational outcomes was obtained. The one pupil who had gone on to college was arguably positively influenced by the individual level of attention afforded in the programme and support he had received as a result of this engagement with additional training in cycle maintenance. BMX cycling had retained his interest and enthusiasm and provided an interesting programme of activity for him, helping to keep him engaged with the unit, back to school and linked to his vocational aspirations, successfully get a place at a college.

Mechanisms, contexts and outcomes: the leverage process in the BMX programmes

Though KPIs might have been missed in both strands, there was clear and positive learning at both individual and organisational level, to show how the leverage of a BMX programme was able to contribute to the sporting capital of Manchester and achieve worthwhile outcomes for participants involved. The different contexts in which the programme mechanisms operated clearly had some different impacts on outcomes achieved. The Coaches, Leaders/volunteers /Teachers/Youth workers – all clearly gained in knowledge and experience through this programme, contributing to the sporting infrastructure and personnel involved in BMX/Cycling – a perhaps unforeseen outcome in "soft legacy". For young people – there were clear benefits to behaviour and attitude for example, in the PRU group children who took part, even if they did not attend or race at the BMX SuperCross event. In the Street BMX programme, delivered across appropriate communities in Manchester, to a good range and number of young people – achieved the planned impact through a mixture of community events and targeted sessions, rather than the original planned context of "pop-up" delivery. BMX sessions clearly reached the targeted areas and populations and provided positive and engaging experiences for those who took part. The outreach work contributed to the overall programmes of established youth groups, providing important contexts for the programme mechanisms to work more effectively.

Though the awareness of the BMX offer in Platt Fields and NCC was raised, due to territorial or other issues for young people the regular organised sessions (where registers were made available) could not show any transition by participants. Any ongoing participation or engagement by young people was likely to be of very informal or related to ongoing street-based activity in cycling, rather than BMX specifically, hence almost impossible to verify.

Process outcomes and consequences – reaching the "hard to reach" with BMX

Despite the lack of progression for some children with very positive experiences at the track this wasn't necessarily a reflection of a lack of success of the programme. Their complex lives and wider influences on behaviour and progression intervened and their improved behaviour did not necessarily result in longer-term changes the programme was aiming for. However, there was some evidence of the potential for a BMX intervention with "hard to engage" pupils, with the coaches working in an appropriate way, in small groups under supervision from their regular unit leader, or specialised worker.

This programme seemed to work best where there was a good match with the ethos of the unit and staff involved. Based on the follow-up reflections with staff at the track and unit, the targeted sessions would not need a major event involvement, except perhaps for celebration of completion, or with tickets to watch the event as incentive. A longer programme of work, over a full term rather than 6 weeks, a planned exit route into mechanics and or other vocational training, or other work-related experience at the NCC could potentially produce the outcomes sought.

The research processes thus developed some insight into the relationships in the BMX projects, though there appeared to be some lack of clear "process" as expected in the logic model. There was some evidence of what Rossi, Freeman, and Lipsey (2003) suggest is "process failure" – i.e. the programme was not delivered or received as originally intended. Consequently this limited any possible impacts and subsequent outcomes – there was insufficient engagement in the taster sessions provided to do much more than provide a one-off experience, only small number of the referral group actually took part in the full process of pre- event and follow up training.

Youth groups were reluctant to re-locate their own work to the NCC or BMX track as it was felt to be "out of their area". The planned outcomes were arguably too ambitious and or difficult to measure to provide any real evidence of impact – some "theory failure" therefore contributed to lack of evidence and impact, an issue recognised by the ELT programme staff later. Despite this, the main coach involved clearly developed new skills and competencies in relation to the non-traditional settings of the youth projects or community spaces and halls, and working with the "hard to engage", which was perhaps an unintended but important part of the "soft legacy" of the event-funded programmes.

There were other unintended consequences other legacies, for example, the involvement of the volunteers from the BMX club, the increased engagement of youth groups and youth workers in South Manchester and the clear ethnic diversity represented in community engagement sessions. The BMX club and their participants represent a range of Manchester and beyond postcodes, reflecting its status as a major hub for the sport, attracting participants from a wide catchment. In contrast, the youth groups came from very targeted areas of South Manchester and despite the low numbers in Friday night sessions, the diversity and inclusion of different ethnic groups was clearly observed.

Therefore the Street BMX programmes have helped to raise the awareness of the sport in local communities, even if the formal sessions were not well supported. Through their engagement with the event in April, the BMX club young members supporting the novice riders had been able to develop their leadership skills and through engagement with the event, had gained significantly in their own development, as this had contributed to their leadership and event training in BMX.

The lead coach highlighted that the coaching he had done on the Street and PRU-based sessions was a real challenge and clearly developmental for him, as he was supported by a manager with some genuine empathy and understanding of the challenges an important context or condition for success. There was clearly an impact on his confidence and the recognition that he was now much better equipped to do this work in the future.

Learning about legacy, leverage and impacts from BMX projects

There are clearly inherent challenges for Sport Development from major events – particularly in challenging environments and difficult groups – as this albeit limited study shows. For robust research "evidence" this project lacks definitive before and after measures on individuals or groups, controls, for observable "changes" attributable to the event. The study is reliant on qualitative/observational data, with problems of missing data in registrations and details of participants at Street sessions, a lack of access to participants and longitudinal outcome tracking. There were also practical and logistical difficulties with the time frame of the study, intervening school holidays and even the weather. However, this project has clearly illuminated some problematic aspects of event-led sport development research, particularly working with disadvantaged communities or difficult to reach groups, in the messy reality of community sport. Presumed or planned for outcomes remain elusive and perhaps overstated in the original logic model and plans. The original research design was based on assumptions, which proved to be inappropriate, overoptimistic or inaccurate.

Through the qualitative approach within the Realistic Evaluation framework, it was possible to identify the interactions of mechanisms (M) and contexts (C) through interviews and observations. The outcome (O) of positive impact of short term engagements on the competency of young people (O), was achieved through the skills and fun emphasis of sessions (M), in keeping with freedom and self-expression of the informal activity (C), rather than on a competition focus. It was also possible to determine, through the interviews with practitioners and managers, a "soft legacy" in changes in approaches and in skills related to practice with targeted groups and the so called "hard to reach" groups. This identified the need for close collaborations with relevant groups and agencies already working with the communities, for example other charities and established PRU units, which provided the important context (C) for the mechanisms of good coaching to be effective.

Building a legacy for BMX?
Suggestions for action by ELT and Cycling programme management included the need to establish some ongoing/additional engagement with research and evaluation of impacts on young people in PRU settings, looking at the link from BMX or other cycling activity and educational benefits in more depth. This "Realistic Evaluation" of the event-based PRU-based approach was too limited to be able to draw specific conclusions, based on the relatively small group who completed the relevant training. Clearly, there is potential for more research into educational impacts on young people, using more refined before and after measures of selected attitudes or behaviours, and the impacts on physical activity levels of participants, with more focused evaluations, including more outcome tracking. However, this was beyond the scope of this limited project and the resources available. The evaluation approach had demonstrated the potential for BMX-based training programme of sessions to specialised units, but not fully evidenced the impacts.

To enhance the potential impacts of Street BMX, there was a clear need to develop more effective marketing and promotional material for distribution at Street or Outreach Sessions to established youth groups. Also, to monitor impacts on future users of the track and in informal BMX through more individualised tracking via a form of "passport" for riders to flag (through the database of registered users) any later engagement with NCC or ET facilities. This required closer liaison with established youth groups, the existing Cycle Hub at Platt Fields Park and other potential stakeholders, for example, the local Universities, for increased access to the open track when not in use by clubs.

It was also possible to see the potential for BMX work to link with other related projects in the city, and in the development of more "open access" tracks across Greater Manchester.[5] Without some appreciation of the different

---

[5] At the time of the research the issue of gang and related violence in South Manchester was a real and genuine concern.

motivations and perceptions of the sport of BMX from the local communities, any similar project was likely to struggle to appeal to those young people who prefer the "chilling" and hanging out with friends to the regulated, commodified and competitive sport of BMX.[6]

Throughout the whole process, it was clear that the event, the BMXSuperCross World Cup, had a very limited impact into local communities, unless they were already engaged with the sport, a criticism highlighted in many studies of events above (Misener et al., 2015; Misener & Mason, 2009; Taks et al., 2014). There was clear tension in the perception of the sport of BMX, compared to the "street" activity – based on the strictly regulated access to the track, as shown in previous research into the development of the sport away from its informal roots (Reinhart & Grenfell, 2002). There were still unresolved issues regarding the "open" track sessions and the level of access to local young people, in the management and operation of Platt Fields Park track.

Though relatively small scale this study has demonstrated the complex nature of the legacy debates around sports and city-wide investments. This is particularly topical with the announcement in 2017 of the Commonwealth Games returning to Britain in 2022, following Glasgow 2014 and Manchester in 2002. The assumption of achieving positive outcomes for local communities around major events remains a powerful political argument, even if evidence of actual benefits is difficult to find. The communities in and around our major cities provide significant challenges for sport development – both in ensuring that the communities benefit from these events, and also that inclusive and accessible services can be sustained in the longer term.

Acknowledgements

The authors acknowledge the support of the ELT Cycling Programmes Manager and staff on the projects for their co-operation and contribution to the research project. The research was conducted on behalf of the Eastlands Leisure Trust, funded with the support of Sport England. Our findings and conclusions are independent, though we have drawn upon reports submitted to ELT and by ELT to Sport England. No individuals are identified in the paper, unless with official title/role and their prior consent.

Disclosure statement

No potential conflict of interest was reported by the authors.

ORCID

Barbara Bell http://orcid.org/0000-0001-6436-2041

References

BBC News. (2009, January 1). *Minister promises sporting decade.* http://news.bbc.co.uk/1/hi/uk/7807169.stm

Bell, B. (2005). Evaluating programme impacts: Champion coaching on Merseyside – pathways to opportunities? In K. Hylton, A. Flintoff, & J. Long (Eds.), *Evaluating sport and active Leisure for young people* (pp. 75–108). Brighton: LSA.

Bell, B., & Gallimore, K. (2015). Embracing the games? Leverage and legacy of London 2012 Olympics at the sub-regional level by means of strategic partnerships. *Leisure Studies*, 34(6), 720–741. doi:10.1080/02614367.2014.994553

Bloyce, D., & Smith, A. (2012). The "olympic and Paralympic effect" on public policy: Use and misuse. *International Journal of Sport Policy and Politics*, 4(3), 301–305. doi:10.1080/19406940.2012.746236

Braun, V., & Clarke, V. (2006). Using thematic analysis in psychology. *Qualitative Research in Psychology*, 2(3), 77–101.

Brookes, S., & Wiggan, J. (2009). Reflecting the public value of sport – A game of two halves? *Public Management Review*, 11(4), 401–420.

Chalip, L. (2006). Towards social leverage of sport events. *Journal of Sport & Tourism*, 11(2), 109–127. doi:10.1080/14775080601155126

---

[6]The City of Manchester and other Local Authorities have plans for increasing open access BMX parks across the region, as seen in London after 2012, as identified by representative of Access Sports – a national charity contributing to BMX plans in Manchester, as they had in London.

Coalter, F. (2007). Sports clubs, social capital and social Regeneration: Ill-defined interventions with hard to follow outcomes? *Sport in Society: Cultures, Commerce, Media, Politics, 10*(4), 537–559.

Coalter, F. (2010). The politics of sport-for-development: Limited focus programmes and broad gauge problems? *International Review for the Sociology of Sport, 45*(3), 295–314. doi:10.1177/1012690210366791

Collins, M. (2011). Children's sport in policy contexts. In I. Stafford (Ed.), *Coaching children in sport* (pp. 276–277). London: Routledge.

Collins, M. (2014). *Sport and social exclusion* (2nd ed.). Oxon: Routledge.

Collins, M., & Haudenhuyse, R. (2015). Social exclusion and austerity policies in England: The role of sports in a new area of social polarisation and inequality? *Social Inclusion, 3*(3), doi:10.17645/si.v3i3.5

Daniels, J. E., Bell, B., & Horrocks, C. (2018). Capturing the realities of sports programmes: Systematic "messiness"? *International Journal of Sport Policy and Politics, 10*(4)), 779–794. doi:10.1080/19406940.2018.1513414

Department for Culture Media and Sport. (2002). *Game plan: A strategy for delivering government's sport and physical activity objectives*. London: Strategy Unit.

Department for Culture Media and Sport. (2012a). *Creating a sporting habit for life*. London: DCMS.

Department for Culture Media and Sport. (2012b). *Beyond 2012: The London 2012 Legacy story*. DCMS. https://assets.publishing.service.gov.uk/government/uploads/system/uploads/attachment_data/file/77993/DCMS_Beyond_2012_Legacy_Story.pdf

Department for Digital Culture Media and Sport. (2015). *Sporting future: A new strategy for an active nation*. London: DDCMS.

Edwards, B., & Corte, U. (2010). Commercialization and lifestyle sport: Lessons from 20 years of freestyle BMX in "Pro-Town" USA. *Sport in Society, 13*(7/8), 1135–1151.

ESPN. (2015). *Manchester beats London as Top UK sporting city*. http://www.espn.co.uk/espn/story/_/id/13368888/manchester-beats-london-top-espn-uk-greatest-sporting-cities-2015-study

Gilchrist, P., & Wheaton, B. (2017). The social benefits of informal and lifestyle sports: A research agenda. *International Journal of Sport Policy and Politics, 9*(1), 1–10. doi:10.1080/19406940.2017.1293132

Grix, J., & Carmichael, F. (2012). Why do governments invest in elite sport? A polemic. *International Journal of Sport Policy and Politics, 4*(1), 73–90.

Jeanes, R., Spaaij, R., Penney, D., & O'Connor, J. (2018). Managing informal sport participation: Tensions and opportunities. *International Journal of Sport Policy and Politics*, 1–17. doi:10.1080/19406940.2018.1479285

Manchester City Council. (2015). *Indices of deprivation 2015*. Manchester: Chief Executive Department.

Misener, L., & Mason, D. S. (2009). Fostering community development through sporting events strategies: An Examination of Urban Regime Perceptions1,2. *Journal of Sport Management, 23*, 770–794.

Misener, L., Taks, M., Chalip, L., & Green, C. B. (2015). The elusive "trickle-down effect" of sports events: Assumptions and missed opportunities. *Managing Sport and Leisure, 20*(2), 135–156.

Parker, A., Sarkar, M., Curran, T., & Williams, S. (2015). *Greatest sporting cities 2015 research Report*: A report prepared for ESPN University of Gloucester. Gloucester: University of Bath.

Pawson, R., & Tilley, N. (1997). *Realistic evaluation*. London: Sage.

Preuss, H. (2007). The conceptualisation and measurement of mega sport event legacies. *Journal of Sport & Tourism, 12*(3–4), 207–228.

Preuss, H. (2015). A framework for identifying the legacies of a mega sport event. *Leisure Studies, 34*(6), 643–664.

Public Health England. (2018). *Physical activity profile north west region*. https://fingertips.phe.org.uk/physical-activity#gid/1938132899/ati/102

Reinhart, R., & Grenfell, C. (2002). BMX spaces: Children's Grass roots' courses and Corporate-Sponsored tracks. *Sociology of Sport Journal, 19*, 302–314.

Richards, G., & de Brito, M. P. (2013). *The future of events as a social phenomenon: Exploring the social impact of events*. London: Routledge.

Rossi, P. H., Freeman, H. E., & Lipsey, M. W. (2003). *Evaluation: A systematic approach* (7th ed.). London: Sage.

Schulenkorf, N. (2012). Sustainable community development through sport and events: A conceptual framework for sport-for-development projects. *Sport Management Review, 15*(1), 1–12. doi:10.1016/j.smr.2011.06.001

Sherry, E. (2016). The community Street Soccer Program. In D. Conrad & A. White (Eds.), *Sports-Based health interventions* (pp. 181–188). New York: Springer.

Sport England. (2016). *Local area statistics (16+) active people survey 10*. Retrieved from December 2016, https://www.sportengland.org/research/about-ourresearch/active-people-survey/

Taks, M., Chalip, L., & Green, B. C. (2015). Impacts and strategic outcomes from non-mega sport events for local communities. *European Sport Management Quarterly, 15*(1), 1–6.

Taks, M., Green, B. C., Misener, L., & Chalip, L. (2014). Evaluating sport development outcomes: The case of a medium-sized international sport event. *European Sport Management Quarterly*, *14*(3), 213–237. doi:10.1080/16184742.2014.882370

Weed, M., Coren, E., Fiore, J., Wellard, I., Chatziefstathiou, D., Mansfield, L., & Dowse, S. (2015). The Olympic Games and raising sport participation: A systematic review of evidence and an interrogation of policy for a demonstration effect. *European Sport Management Quarterly*, *15*(2), 195–226. doi:10.1080/16184742.2014.998695

Weed, M., Coren, E., Fiore, J., Wellard, I., Mansfield, L., Chatziefstathiou, D., & Dowse, S. (2012). Developing a physical activity legacy from the London 2012 Olympic and Paralympic Games: A policy-led systematic review. *Perspectives in Public Health*, *132*(2), 75–80.

Widdop, P., King, N., Parnell, D., Cutts, D., & Millward, P. (2018). Austerity, policy and sport participation in England. *International Journal of Sport Policy and Politics*, *10*(1), 7–24. doi:10.1080/19406940.2017.1348964

Yin, R. K. (2009). *Case study research: Design and methods* (4th ed.). London: Sage.

Inspiring a generation: an examination of stakeholder relations in the context of London 2012 Olympics and Paralympics educational programmes

Verity Postlethwaite, Geoffery Z. Kohe and Gyozo Molnar

ABSTRACT

The London 2012 Olympic and Paralympic Games (London 2012) inspire a generation legacy aim targeted young people in the United Kingdom (UK) and internationally. This article explores how the London 2012 education-based legacy programmes aimed at young people, such as the Get Set initiative, affected relations between stakeholders connected to the Games. Utilising a stakeholder relations theoretical perspective we analysed documentary-based dialogue from a UK parliament Education Committee inquiry through a critical discourse analysis. From the analysis two discourses emerged. Firstly, around clarity of the purpose of the London 2012 educational programmes. Secondly, varying stakeholders' understanding during the inquiry of the inspire a generation legacy aim was articulated around the notion of a "missed opportunity," in particular, when translated into the domestic policy context around education and sport. The findings encourage stakeholders to reflect on potential fragmented accountability between sport mega event and domestic sectors; and achieving greater clarity to the purpose of legacy-based educational programme within a broader policy context.

Introduction

In 2013 the former London Organising Committee of the Olympic and Paralympic Games (LOCOG) chairman, Lord Sebastian Coe, spoke of "his regret that school sport became a political football during the Olympic Games" (*The Guardian*, 2013). The regretful sentiment about the politicisation of sport within the education system is an example of the wider public and political discourses surrounding the London 2012 legacy aim of "inspiring a new generation of young people" (DCMS, 2008, p. 6). The origins of the inspire a generation legacy aim had been influenced by the key governing stakeholder of the Olympic movement the International Olympic Committee (IOC). In the era of the modern Olympiad the IOC have developed a philosophy referred to as Olympism and the principles explicitly connect sport and education, whereby:

> blending sport with culture and education, Olympism seeks to create a way of life based on the joy of effort, the educational value of good example, social responsibility and respect for universal fundamental ethical principles. (IOC, 2013a, p. 15)

In recent decades Olympic and Paralympic Games bidding cities have systematically included the pillars of Olympism within tangible and intangible legacy aims (Tomlinson, 2014). Including a more pronounced emphasis and influence on the Paralympics and the international federation the International Paralympic Committee (IPC) (Kerr, 2018). In the context of London 2012, this use of Olympism was evident in the early stages of the bid by including young people and the emotive, mythic power of Olympism in the supporting narrative for the London bid (Girginov, 2016; Kohe & Chatziefstathiou, 2017; Lee, 2006). The pinnacle of this was in 2005 at the 112th IOC Session where the London bid delegation included a third of "East London school children from twenty-eight different ethnic backgrounds" (Lee, 2006, p. 178). The London bid led by Lord Coe and other strategic figures, such as, the Prime Minister at the time Tony Blair strategically placed youth engagement and participation front and centre to convince IOC committee members to vote for London (Girginov, 2013).

Coe's and his team's efforts were successful, and the win precipitated Games delivery efforts that interacted with the UK's domestic policy environment[1] around youth and sport. In the area of domestic policies related to young people and sport the dominant site of delivery has been school sport and physical education (Houlihan & Green, 2006; Phillpots, 2013). The London 2012 legacy aim to inspire a generation directly engaged with school sport through the main programme, Get Set, where a series of resources were made available to schools around Olympic and Paralympic values (Chen & Henry, 2019; Kohe, 2017; Kohe & Bowen-Jones, 2016). Post London 2012 the organising committee LOCOG and the key international federation the IOC deemed the Get Set programme a success, illustrating this claim with quantifiable figures, such as, the programme engaged "25,000 schools and 6.5million young people" (IOC, 2013b, p. 6). The statistics juxtaposed with the opening quote from Coe and his regretful sentiment around the politicisation of the school sport during London 2012 demonstrate differing views on the success and legacy potential of the London 2012 educational programmes. As noted in various academic studies around sport mega events and education programme contexts, such as Binder (2012) in the Olympic values education programmes context and Chen and Henry (2019) in the delivery of Get Set in a non-host city context, statistics do not show in full the intricacies, impacts or processes of a programme. The contribution of this article, therefore, is to examine differing views of stakeholders and go beyond quantified evaluations to provide a new critical evaluation of London 2012 educational programmes.

In order to develop the article's contribution the aim is to use London 2012 and the Get Set programme as a case study to engage with the wider academic debate around sport mega events, Olympic and Paralympic education programmes, and policies based on sport and education. The research objective is to illuminate how conceiving and enacting educational legacy programmes, such as the Get Set, affected relations between stakeholders in the Olympic and Paralympic movement, and UK sport and education sectors. Theoretically, the article draws upon stakeholder relation scholarship (e.g. Friedman & Miles, 2002; Jensen, 2010; Viollet, Minikin, Scelles, & Ferrand, 2016), and, specifically relevant to the paper, the use of a stakeholder approach within sport mega event literature (e.g. Leopkey & Parent, 2015; Parent, 2008) and sport policy literature (e.g. Lindsey, 2010; Lindsey, 2018). Furthering this academic work and engaging with both sport mega event and sport policy debates, this paper contributes theoretically to understanding

---

[1] It is acknowledged that the UK consists of devolved policy areas to the home nations, where appropriate reference will be made to English, Scottish, Welsh or Northern Irish differentiation in policy. However, for the purpose of this article and the UK sentiment around London 2012, policy is referred to as UK based.

stakeholder relations when connected by policy and legacy aims around young people and sport.

In examining stakeholder relations around the London 2012 educational programmes the paper is structured as follows. The next section introduces the theoretical framework adopted, drawing on stakeholder relations approaches, then sport mega event and policy literature. To complement the theoretical framework further contextual detail will be outlined in terms of the UK policy and education space. A brief review of the research methods will then be provided, including, document analysis and a critical discourse analytical framework. The findings and discussion section subsequently examine documentary materials from a UK parliament, House of Commons Education Committee inquiry (2013a, 2013b, 2013c, 2013d) titled "School sport following London 2012: No more political football." Two prominent discourses emerged. Firstly, around the clarity of the purpose of the London 2012 educational programmes. Secondly, varying stakeholders' understanding during the inquiry of the inspire a generation legacy aim was articulated around the notion of a "missed opportunity," in particular, when translated into the domestic policy context around education and sport. Finally, conclusions are drawn for future academic research and education related sport policy, in particular, the findings encourage stakeholders to reflect on potential fragmented accountability between sport mega event and domestic sectors; and achieving greater clarity to the purpose of legacy based educational programme within a broader policy context.

Theoretical standpoint

The bidding and hosting of London 2012 cost around nine billion pounds of public sector funds and became a source of significant public and media based scrutiny (DCMS, 2010; Girginov, 2013). From formally bidding in 2002 to hosting in 2012, the preparation involved multiple governmental departments across numerous government terms and intersected with a variety of non-governmental stakeholders. Consequently, to capture this complex landscape of actors our considerations are underscored, in the first instance, by a theoretical interrogation of stakeholder relations (Friedman & Miles, 2002; Jensen, 2010; Viollet et al., 2016) in connection to sport mega event specific research (Leopkey & Parent, 2015; Parent, 2008).

Stakeholder critique, in essence, requires an examination of the interactions of entities and relationships in and across sectors, including, power relations, shared agenda setting and value creation. Friedman and Miles (2002) emphasise the range of stakeholder relations that can occur, and note that previous research has frequently ignored negative relations between stakeholders. Parent (2008) and Leopkey and Parent (2015) isolate sport mega event stakeholders to those connected to the local organising committee: staff and volunteers, host governments, the community, sport organisations, delegations, media, sponsors and other stakeholders (e.g. consultants). The authors emphasise the role of governance for an organising committee to manage the multitude of stakeholders, however, do not explicitly consider this beyond the hosting period or into a domestic policy space around youth, sport and education. A useful discussion point from Leopkey and Parent (2015, p. 542) is developed around the Rhodes (2000)

> accountability fragmentation, that is, when being accountable to many entities, it can potentially provide the opportunity to play one or some stakeholders against others, creating ambiguities, and thereby reducing overall accountability with regard to the resulting legacy of the event.

In this paper, we advance this body of research by considering stakeholder relations beyond the sport mega event hosting period, and question whether London 2012 educational programmes demonstrated characteristics of negative stakeholder relations or accountability fragmentation.

In the context of London 2012 educational programmes the element of shared value creation among stakeholders is important. Namely, because of the Olympic and Paralympic values included in the main educational programme, Get Set, the main London 2012 education programme delivered through primary and secondary schools across the UK. Jensen (2010) suggested that adding the process of creating value to the framework of stakeholder relations is useful, as it involves balancing varying constituencies with a vision that can unite stakeholders. While connectivity of thought can create, consolidate and enhance stakeholder relations within the sport-education sector (Kohe & Collison, 2019), there can be no guarantees that collaborative efforts may be mutually beneficial, sustainable, or, least of all, meaningful (both in an ideological or practical sense). Regarding London 2012, two significant actors simultaneously, but not necessarily collaboratively, were creating value and relations around the inspire a generation legacy aim. Firstly, LOCOG, who drove the delivery of the London 2012 Games and were accountable to the IOC and UK government, plus worked alongside a range of other stakeholders, such as, schools and sponsors. The role of LOCOG is not permanent. As Agha, Fairley, and Gibson (2011) illustrated the organising committee often commit and construct legacy aims yet disband when the event is over and have limited accountability to fulfilling long term legacy. The host city and national government, therefore, are often drivers of the long term value creation and sustainable legacy.

The other significant actor, therefore, is the UK government and parliament. The UK political landscape changed significantly in leadership over the life of bidding and hosting London 2012, due to changes through general elections (from a Labour majority during the bidding and early preparations, to a Conservative-Liberal Democrat coalition between the preparation and hosting up to 2012). In the post Games epoch, the UK parliament changed again to a Conservative majority and at this time the Secretary of State for Education, Secretary of State for Culture, Media and Sport (plus, more minor ministerial roles), also, changed. Consequently, the UK government in the context of London 2012 and legacy is, also, not a fixed long term driver of legacy aims. Rather, government based stakeholdership passed between the major political parties and changes in leadership position across departments connected to sport and education. It is an important element of the paper, therefore, to detail the UK policy in regard to sport and education space, furthermore, how this intersects with the Olympic and Paralympics values on education and sport. The section below builds on policy focused scholarship, such as, Viollet et al. (2016, p. 322) who have used stakeholder relations to explore sport policy "through an understanding of the dynamics of the relationships between the actors and their perceptions." To articulate actors and known perceptions, the following section details the roles of stakeholders who in the context of 2012 engaged with the Olympic and Paralympic movement, and UK sport and education sectors.

UK policy and education space

Academic interest in UK sport policy has frequently obeserved the intricate nature of stakeholder relations and a sustained critique of sport being a crowded and fragmented policy space (Coalter, 2010; Houlihan, 2016; Lindsey, 2010). As Lindsey (2010) contends, moments, such as the creation of the National Lottery in 1994, have raised questions and debates around the governance of local partnerships by national programmes (i.e. the New Opportunities for PE and Sport programme). Drawing on Rhodes (2000), Lindsey (2010, p. 200) demonstrates the breadth of interpretations around governance at macro policy level concluding that the changes in public policy contexts within the UK showed "fragmented" sport policy and sector governance in a "crowded policy space." The use of broader governance literature by Lindsey links to aspects of sport mega event scholarship that consider governance issues. For instance, Leopkey and Parent (2015) utilise Rhodes (2000) to highlight potential accountability fragmentation when a local organising committee attempts to manage a complex web of stakeholders connected to legacy. However, what has not been extensively considered previously are governance and accountability between an organising committee and a national government around the sport and education space explored in this article. The connection here bridges into the policy space of education and its connection to education based legacy aims from sport mega events.

Focusing specifically on the education sector in the UK, seminal work by Houlihan and Green (2006) highlighted the importance of advocates and coalitions for increasing and sustaining national political interest in the UK around physical education. Yet, while adopting a multiple streams policy analysis was of value in articulating policy complexities, the evaluation did not explicitly take into consideration the role of London 2012 and the concurrent efforts around legacy programmes. Rather, the authors' attention was on domestic policy space and actors, such as the Youth Sport Trust[2] and the Department for Education. Accordingly, to build on this work, this paper bridges and adds to articulating stakeholder relations around the Olympic and Paralympic movement and the role of LOCOG in developing educational programmes during preparing and hosting London 2012. In regards to the education sector and connections to London 2012 a number of scholars have considered the intersections, such as, Jung, Pope, and Kirk (2016) and Lindsey (2018). Jung et al. (2016) contend that an emerging Olympic discourse influenced the physical education space and National Curriculum, but nominally in comparison to the dominant discourse around competitive sport. Physical education during the 2000's had been dominated by the traditional curriculum and community aims of increasing opportunities for young people to access and participate in competitive sport, through high quality physical education and school sport partnerships (Jung et al., 2016; Mackintosh, 2014). Lindsey (2018, p.14) considers the physical education and policy landscape beyond London 2012 and into the current Conservative government and describes London 2012 as an example of a "policy window [that] can 'open' at both unpredictbable and predictable times." The analysis from Lindsey (2018) and Jung et al. (2016) is also reflected by Chen and Henry (2019) and Griggs and Ward (2013) who have respectively noted that the inspire a generation legacy aim was not substantively embraced alongside changes to domestic policy or the historical functioning of actors (e.g. schools) who delivered the programmes. It is, therefore, timely to coalesce discussions over educational spaces with sport mega event based literature to fully understand whether London 2012 and the inspire a generationa legacy aim impacted on stakeholder relations between stakeholders engaging with the London 2012 educational programmes and the policies connected to UK sport and education sectors.

The prominent domestic policy changes around sport, education and young people during the preparation and hosting of London 2012 is the dramatic funding change in 2010 (Mackintosh, 2014). The Secretary for Education in 2010, Michael Gove, announced the end to "the £162 million PE and sports strategy of the previous administration, to give schools the time and freedom to focus on providing competitive sport" (UK Government, 2010). This decision two years before London 2012 called into question publicly the unity between the inspire a generation legacy aim of London 2012 and the UK government, for example, in

---

[2] A British charity which aims to support education and development of young people through physical education, established in 1994.

the media headlines highlighted the reactions "Teachers stunned after Michael Gove scraps "sport for all" funding" (*The Guardian*, 2010) and "Michael Gove forced into about-turn over scrapping School Sports Partnerships after outrage over cuts" (*Telegraph*, 2010). Prior to 2010 the school sport partnerships were the focal point of the Labour led national structure that had evolved over 13 years into a wider 'Physical Education, School Sport and Club Links' (PESSCL) structure (Phillpots, 2013). The Labour PESSCL strategy had contributed to wider agendas of social inclusion, health promotion and education attainment (Houlihan & Green, 2006). The governmental change is not mentioned in the planning or evaluation of the London 2012 educational legacy programmes as LOCOG, IOC and IPC do not explicitly identify or function as policy actors. Yet, for the domestic stakeholders, such as, the Youth Sport Trust who prior to and beyond London 2012 contributed to the long term structures of sport and education, the 2010 policy changes had a significant impact. Stakeholder relations theory is useful here as it goes beyond traditional policy actors, instead considers a greater range of stakeholders connected to London 2012 that intersected with the domestic policy space and education legacy programmes.

In terms of the Olympic and Paralympic movement, London 2012 and education programmes. The influence of the IOC and IPC is evident in the London 2012, Get Set programme, with the aim to: give all young people the chance to learn about and live the Olympic Values of friendship, excellence and respect and the Paralympic Values of inspiration, determination, courage and equality (LOCOG, 2012, p. 1). The Get Set programme is still an active resource under the remit of the British Olympic Association and British Paralympic Association (Get Set, 2018). While the resources enable schools and practitioners to draw down potentially useful content, a number of scholars have questioned the programme's effectiveness. Kohe (2017), for example, uses memory techniques to explore how young people understood hosting London 2012. Both sets of studies highlight the complex circumstances around trying to educate young people and reach a national audience. Such findings relate to the broader sport policy and sport mega event stakeholder studies that discuss fragmentation and crowded spaces as hindering stakeholder relations and potential outcomes of policy or legacy programmes. Yet, unsurprisingly, IOC and IPC evaluations have not discussed such intricacies, instead have been wholly positive towards the Get Set programme, reporting that "an impressive 85 per cent of UK schools signed up to this programme" (IOC, 2013b, p. 6). Going beyond the quantifiable reach of the programme to assess its actual efficacy for young people remains difficult and, in part, may explain why the effectiveness of the inspire a generation legacy aim was not systematically tracked by the IOC, IPC or LOCOG. The gap in knowledge of understanding and measuring the success of the legacy aim has been placed largely on local, regional and national domestic stakeholders.

As noted the key organisation is the IOC who use values based principles to promote Olympism. Such was evident in the London 2012 main education programme Get Set where the Olympic values were at the centre of the content. LOCOG, also, integrated Paralympic values into the Get Set programme show casing the Paralympic Games that is governed separately to the Olympic Games through the International Paralympic Committee (IPC). The values approach taken by LOCOG, IOC and IPC contrasted to the UK's pedagogic approach to physical education, which, as shown above, had been largely dominated by the discourse of competitive sport (Jung et al., 2016; Mackintosh, 2014). The vested interest in promoting the IOC and IPC movement to young people aligns to a broader aim from the international federations of making "young people... a key priority" in terms of audience and brand

Table 1. Description of data.

Title of Document	Description of Data	Contributing Stakeholders
Volume I	Report, together with formal minutes	House of Commons, the Education Committee (membership includes Conservative, Labour and Liberal Democrat Members of Parliament).
Volume II	Oral and written evidence	Representatives from national sporting bodies, representatives of regional sporting bodies, former Olympic competitors, representatives of a range of schools, Olympic and Paralympic legacy "visionaries" and, the responsible Minister (Edward Timpson MP, Parliamentary Under Secretary of State for Children and Families).
Volume III	Additional written evidence	Schools, school sport co-ordinators, National Governing Bodies of various sports, national sport delivery bodies, local government, academics in the field, and the Departments of Health and for Education.
Appendix	Government Response	Central government representatives.

(Chatziefstathiou, 2012, p. 31; for more on the IPC see Kerr, 2018).

The use of education and youth by the IOC (more so that the IPC) has come under significant academic scrutiny (e.g. Chatziefstathiou, 2012; Coburn & McCafferty, 2016; Lenskyj, 2012). Chatziefstathiou (2012) considers the evolution of Olympism in light of challenges around gender discrimination, commercialisation and Euro-centrism and notes that host cities continue to embrace the principles and this links to the increased (Western) governments' domestic interest for youth and sport. The commercialisation and Western-centric critiques have been extensive around the role of the IOC and its educational programmes. Lenskyj (2012), for example, claims the idealistic tones of the resources overtly celebrate the Olympic movement and offer scant space for critique from other stakeholders, such as, schools. The role of the IOC, therefore, has been seen as an oppressive and problematic stakeholder controlling the content and ethos of Olympic educational programmes. The London 2012 educational programmes, therefore, offer a useful case study for examining how UK based stakeholders engaged with the IOC influenced agenda and the impact on stakeholder relations domestically around sport and education policies.

Beyond the IOC, critique has also extended towards sponsors and issues of corporate social responsibility. For example, Coburn and McCafferty (2016) problematise the role of Coca Cola in the sponsorship of the IOC activities around schools and broader discourse around health and childhood obesity. An under-researched element of this debate is the role of the IPC and the growing Paralympic influence on Olympic education programmes. London 2012 combined systematically the Olympics and Paralympics. This combined approach encouraged the conflation of the two movements in the delivery of "one" Games (Brittain & Beacom, 2016; Kerr, 2018). Consequently, in relation to the Get Set programme, the Paralympic aims and brand were given equal weighting to the elements of Olympism. A benefit of using stakeholder relations as the grounding concept for the paper is to allow for the inclusion of disability and Paralympic discourses as an influence on stakeholder relations during London 2012 and the educational legacy programmes, rather than simply focusing on the IOC – Olympism connections.

Moving into the post London 2012 landscape and beyond IOC, IPC and LOCOG evaluations, the political framing of measuring the success of the inspire a generation legacy aim was reduced to the domestic structures of school sport (not the Get Set programme). Lord Coe, stated in a national newspaper, "I'm sorry school sport became tribal, that's probably the only thing we did not deliver in the same spirit as everything else was delivered" (*The Guardian*, 2013). This quote was captured around the same time that the UK Parliament

Education Committee (2013a, 2013b, 2013c, 2013d) launched an inquiry "School sport following London 2012: No more political football." The quote from Coe and title of the committee inquiry counter the positive narrative from LOCOG, the IOC and IPC around the success of the Get Set programme. Plus, as shown below in detail, offer a great deal of stakeholder repsonses and understanding to the diaglogue around London 2012 inspire a generation legacy aim, educational programmes, and wider sport and education policies.

Materials and methodology

A qualitative case study design for this project was adopted as it is "useful for exploring and describing elements of a problem in depth and detail, by examining situations with characteristics that may not be easily represented in numerical format" (Viollet et al., 2016, p. 324). As noted, there have been statistical evaluations of London 2012 however, these do not outline the depth of stakeholder relations. The approach taken here is in line with the methodological articulations of Yin (2003) and Bryman (2016) who advocate using a case study to comprehend phenomena as a whole, whilst detecting particular dynamics and changes. The methodological decisions of this paper are underpinned philosophically by an interpretive approach guided by a critical ontology. This philosophical standpoint is appropriate because the paper does not seek to identify stakeholders or their actions per se, but rather consider stakeholders' relations in the context of London 2012 educational programmes.

To complement the aim of the paper and methodological approach, the materials selected capture a broad range of stakeholders in direct dialogue around London 2012 and school sport. The materials for this paper were official documents deriving from the state. Specifically, documents connected to the House of Commons Education Committee inquiry (2013a, 2013b, 2013c, 2013d) "School sport following London 2012: No more political football" and the submissions of evidence (outlined in Table 1). The use of documents in this paper was affective because of the relevance and extensive nature of the documents connected to the House of Commons Education Committee inquiry (2013a, 2013b, 2013c, 2013d) this can be illustrated by the terms of reference of the inquiry:

> The impact and effectiveness of current Government policy and expenditure on increasing sport in schools;
>
> The scope, appropriateness and likelihood of success of the Government's plans for a school sport legacy from London 2012;
>
> The impact so far of London 2012 on the take-up of competitive sport in schools; and
>
> What further measures should be taken to ensure a sustainable and effective legacy in school sport following London 2012. (HoC Vol 2013b, p. 5)

The extensive range of evidence submitted to the inquiry that is publicly accessible created a substantive set of documents which included transcribed dialogues, formal reports, and voices from stakeholders with a vested interest in the terms of reference quoted above (totalling 253 pages comprising of: 49 written submissions, three formal evidence sessions and engagement with visit/survey data from schools). Macdonald (2008) describes the advantages of using documents as data to have the opportunity to study something where access to people or observation is not possible. Of value to this paper, the inquiry represents voices from government, delivery agents, Olympic and Paralympic stakeholders and varying sport policy actors, who otherwise may not have been willing to contribute evidence.

The analytical approach taken to synthesise the data was based on Critical Discourse Analysis (CDA), as advocated by a variety of scholars when considering political or policy based case studies, for example, van Dijk (1996), Bryman (2016), and Whigham and Bairner

(2018). CDA allows the researcher to account for dominant ideas (discourses) and social relations. As quoted in Whigham and Bairner (2018), van Dijk (1996, p. 84) highlights that:

> one of the crucial tasks of Critical Discourse Analysis is to account for the relationships between discourse and social power. More specifically, such an analysis should describe and explain how power abuse is enacted, reproduced or legitimised by the text and talk of dominant groups or institutions.

CDA offered an appropriate framework of analysis for this paper as the dialogue documented in the inquiry could be understood in terms of discourse and assumptions formed by dominant groups around London 2012 education programmes. Moreover, CDA emphasises going beyond identification and developing a critical stance on findings. In this paper, where dominant understandings between different stakeholders in the inquiry created points of tension or opportunity, CDA allowed for this to be connected to a critical discussion of broader debates around the Olympic and Paralympic movement, and UK sport and education sectors. CDA goes beyond identifying the stakeholder and process of interaction by using evidence to critically examine relations based on dominant discourses, such as competitive sport, health and funding, and identifying further discourses.

Limitations of this approach are linked to the use of publicly accessible and official documents that reflect a particular type of conversation where stakeholders could be speaking in a performative manner (Bryman, 2016). Moreover, the inquiry submissions are a snapshot of all national stakeholder voices, for example, the schools that submitted evidence could not be seen to be representative of the thousands of primary and secondary schools across the UK. However, for the purposes of this paper the inquiry offered a substantive insight into the context of London 2012 educational programmes, this was understood based on the range of stakeholders Parent (2008) identified as relevant to an organising committee and legacy, such as host governments and sport organisations. Furthermore, in contrast to studies that use privately collected data (e.g. interviews), the data set for this paper is publicly accessible, encouraging further scholarly scrutiny of it.

The steps taken in the analytical element of the paper involved data identification (inquiry documents, outlined in Table 1). Then an initial reading and grouping was based on any specific dialogue pertaining to the Get Set programme and the Olympic and Paralympic educational values within the inquiry documents. Then a grouping of dominant discourse (as noted in previous literature above, such as, competitive sport) and reinterpretation of the data (in terms of the objective of this paper and the theoretical framework around stakeholder relations). The grouping and reinterpretation of the data produced two overarching discourses around the stakeholder relations – purpose and missed opportunity. These discourses, supplemented by selected verbatim quotes from the inquiry, we discuss, below.

Findings and discussion

Purpose

In the inquiry, a number of stakeholders made the direct connection between London 2012 educational legacy programmes and the traditional domestic platform of school sport and related policies. The Department for Education, for instance, evidenced that "in 2012–13 the Department provided £500,000 to Get Set to support schools to develop and deliver activities to capitalise on the learning opportunities arising from the Games (with particular emphasis on the Paralympic Games)" (HoC Vol II, 2013c, Ev 83). The use of the phrase "learning opportunities" is vague and does not directly indicate whether this is through sport, wider curriculum, values, etc. Although it does state in brackets that there was an emphasis on the Paralympic Games, this is a learning opportunity that is not fully discussed in wider academic literature as the dominant discourse has been around the Olympics and Olympism. As noted by Binder (2012) and Chatziefstathiou (2012), the values based education is commonly understood as Olympic values and IOC based principles. The UK government decision to emphasise the Paralympics, however, was not explicitly based on the values or engaging the IPC in substantive partnership. It was understood, instead, in the inquiry report that "one of the most outstanding successes of London 2012 was in raising the profile of Paralympic sports" (HoC Vol I, 2013b, p. 27). This implies that the purpose of Get Set was about profile, not values which differs from the LOCOG, Olympic and Paralympic values-based understanding of the purpose of the programme.

Jackie Brock Doyle, Director of Communications and Public Affairs at the LOCOG submitted written evidence outlining that "the education strategy was built around the Get Set programme, which gave schools the tools to integrate the Games and the Olympic and Paralympic Values into their own activities" (HoC Vol III, 2013d, Ev w10). The "Values" that Doyle refers to were not explicitly what the government or other stakeholders contributing to the inquiry saw as the purpose or outcome of Get Set and more broadly the inspire a generation legacy aim. The dominant conversation by non-LOCOG stakeholders was around competitive sport and the continued focus of domestic sport policy on the elements of winning and losing. Mike Diaper, then Director of Community Sport, Sport England commented: "School sport and also competition in schools can be about fun. It is definitely about winning and losing. It helps us to build team and leadership skills" (HoC Vol II, 2013c, Ev 2). Beyond the national policy perspective, Linda Cairns (HoC Vol II, 2013c, Ev 14), School Sport Co-ordinator, George Abbot School stated:

> ... if we put too much focus on competition, we are missing out on delivering sport, PE and physical activity to the large majority of our children and students. When you offer more and more competition, you are offering it to the same select, top, able athletes, so you have the same players in your hockey team, football team, rugby team and athletics.

The variation on the understanding of the purpose of school sport and the role of London 2012 is supported by Jung et al. (2016) noting competitive sport as being the dominant discourse in 2000s. The authors found that "sport discourse appeared to be the largest set of practices in the primary field of knowledge production and provided resources upon which other discourses such as health, citizenship and Olympic legacy drew" (Jung et al., 2016, p. 508). The role of LOCOG as a stakeholder and Get Set here and elsewhere is a minor relation in the broader discourse around sport and competition. Yet, this minor role in the broader set of relations is not explicitly acknowledged by the LOCOG or Olympic and Paralympic based stakeholders implying a significant tension in the understanding of the relations and ability to build a values based outcome from a specific programme or legacy aim.

Stakeholders who have a knowledge of the Olympic movement and Olympism evidenced the tension between the dominant domestic discourse of competitive sport and the London 2012 values-based discourse in the inquiry. For example, Jonathan Edwards former Olympic Gold medalist noted:

> There is a real irony, in that the modern Olympic movement started because Pierre de Coubertin came over to this country to look at the education system and how it integrated sport – a healthy mind in a healthy body. Here we are, having just celebrated London 2012, and we still face this question about where sport fits in and how important it is. (HoC Vol II, 2013c, Ev 17)

In contrast to the stakeholders who engaged from a national organisation or school setting and focused on sport and competition,

Edwards connects the principle of Olympism to the IOC (not explicitly including the IPC). He speaks to the purpose and value of a "healthy mind in a healthy body" rather than winning or losing, or specific sporting endeavours.

The dialogue between LOCOG, Department for Education, Sport England, school based and ex-Olympians demonstrate tension around the agenda of London 2012 education programmes and the inspire a generation legacy aim more broadly. It aligns with the points raised by Lindsey (2010) and Leopkey and Parent (2015) where an organising committee and, in this case, the educational programme have too many constituent stakeholders to manage in a short space of programme implementation, leading to accountability fragmentation. This is particularly evident in the tension between the Olympic and Paralympic discourse of values based education with the domestic stakeholders' dominant discourse of competitive school sport education. Get Set and LOCOG could have facilitated a higher level of understanding around who was accountable for the content of the Get Set in the context of domestic school structures and long term legacy outcomes beyond London 2012. In reality, however, this case study supports Agha et al.'s (2011) observation that the local organising committee is void of long term accountability as it does not engage in stakeholder discussion beyond hosting an event.

Missed opportunity

In connection to tensions around purpose, another discourse manifested around London 2012 being a missed opportunity and implying from a variety of stakeholders that legacy outcomes within school sport were not immediately successful. This discourse predominantely focused on dialogue about domestic policy changes, especially, funding and power structures. For example, Andy Reed, then Chairman of the Sport and Recreation Alliance, commented that:

> Part of the problem is that there has not been a definition of strategically who is leading all these things, and of course when there are new moneys around, there is a tendency to try to find out which part in which slice of the cake is relevant to each. (HoC Vol II, 2013c, Ev 2)

As discussed by Mackintosh (2014) the decision by the Coalition government to bring a direct investment tool to "primary school sport premium" in 2010 was a focus of debate. The prevalence of this discourse reduced the amount of dialogue around the significant investment made through London 2012 and Get Set programme by various stakeholders. Instead the focus was more on the domestic policy and political changes. For example, Dame Tessa Jowell, former Olympic Minister in the Labour Government stated:

> policy has suffered to some degree through fragmentation across Government. That was a struggle that we had when we were in government—to achieve proper lockstep between DCMS [Department for Culture, Media and Sport] and DFE [Department of Education]. Also … there is an important role for the Department of Health. (HoC Vol II, 2013c, Ev 35)

The comment here illustrates the tension within central government regarding who is the dominant governmental stakeholder in school sport and what that means for relations around London 2012 legacy and school sport. This supports wider scholarly discussion, in particular, from Houlihan and Green (2006) and Lindsey (2010, 2018) that fragmentation within government hinders other stakeholder relations around broader sport policy and into the education and sport landscape.

The evidence of continued fragmented governmental approaches during the preparation and hosting of London 2012 contributes to understanding that stakeholders utilising the inspire a generation legacy aim and/or the Get Set educational programme independently interpreted the use and role in their own context. Derek Peale, Head teacher Park House

School, explicitly aligned the need for bottom-up and local stakeholders understandings of the "wider impact on school improvement, including positive outcomes in relation to Social, Moral, Spiritual and Cultural Development … reflect creative approaches to the integration of sports-themed programmes such as Get Set" (HoC Vol II, 2013c, Ev 62). The understanding from a Head Teacher and school perspective here goes some way to being an opportunity discussed by Binder (2012) that the IOC and IPC brand can galvanize a stakeholder to create educational outcomes in their own setting. Such evidence supports Jensen (2010) suggestion that values based framework can be a useful way to enact a vision amongst stakeholders. However, Peale and Park House School appear to be the exception not the norm as the majority of school based evidence reported passive engagement rather than opportunity to translate it into the local context (HoC Vol I, 2013a). In a non-school perspective, the Wellcome Trust contributed evidence from their "In the Zone" initiative that used sport and physiology content in a touring exhibition and experiment kits for school. In terms of London 2012 the Trust summarised their contribution as:

> Part of the practical learning strand of Get Set – the official London 2012 reward and recognition scheme for schools and colleges demonstrating a commitment to living the Olympic and Paralympic values – and was awarded the Inspire Mark by the London Organising Committee of the Olympic Games. (HoC Vol III, 2013d, Ev w34)

The dialogue from the Wellcome Trust, similarly to the Head Teacher perspective, demonstrates a more independent interpretation of the London 2012 educational agenda. Moreover, the ability to gain reward and recognition as an outcome for their own ends. The Inspire Mark referenced in the quote from the Wellcome Trust is a separate scheme to the Get Set programme. To date there has not been a significant amount of scholarship to how LOCOG brokered a deal with the IOC and IPC to use the London 2012 brand beyond hosting the Games' as an incentive to "attract private sector finance … and reward other organisations" (DCMS, 2008, p. 15). The aim of Inspire Mark scheme and the interpretation of the Get Set programme links to the critique by Lenskyj (2012) and Coburn and McCafferty (2016) where further critical interrogation of the commercialised element of the Olympic and Paralympic Games approach to education and targeting young people is needed.

Finally, the independent interpretations of the Get Set programme and evidence of governmental fragmentation raises the question about the role of LOCOG and an organising committee beyond a Games to facilitate long term legacy. As noted, current sport mega event literature views an organising committee (Agha et al., 2011) and legacy outcomes (Leopkey & Parent, 2015; Tomlinson, 2014) to be time-limited to hosting and the disbanding of the organising committee. In this inquiry dialogue, the use and effectiveness of a programme to contribute to long term outcomes is facilitated by individual stakeholder interpretation and their ability to translate it into their own circumstances. The discourse of missed opportunity, therefore, can be isolated to those stakeholders that based their relations on the fragmented governmental approach to London 2012 educational programmes, rather than a more nuanced reimagining of the programmes from a more bottom up approach.

The ability of LOCOG to recognise or articulate the nuances of political changes and varying stakeholder interpretations of legacy or educational programmes was not evident in the inquiry. In contrast, Jackie Brock Doyle, Director of Communications and Public Affairs at the LOCOG commented about London 2012 educational programmes and political changes:

> Thanks to the structure put in place and for the strong support of both the previous Labour

Government and the incoming Coalition Government, our work was not hindered by the change in administration in 2010, and in a way that will continue to inspire change and enhance lives for years to come. (HoC Vol III, 2013d, Ev w11)

Yet, as noted, LOCOG and the IOC based a significant amount of their evaluation on numerical data and statistics that culminated in 2013 and did not measure beyond. Consequently, although LOCOG delivered a programme and could report on what success was, this could not be extended to long term outcomes without a more nuanced understanding of what other stakeholders deemed successful. An example of this comes from the written evidence submitted by the Association for School and College Leaders:

> For many schools the notion of a London 2012 legacy has been an aspirational one rather than seeing evidence of a strategic plan for take-up of competitive sports in schools or developing links with local sports clubs and national governing bodies. It appears to depend on the enthusiasm and commitment of local teachers and coaches, rather than on a legacy strategy from government. (HoC Vol III, 2013d, Ev w46)

Notably in this quote is the erasure of the role of stakeholders connected to the Olympic or Paralympic movement around London 2012. The ongoing national stakeholders of the British Olympic Association and the British Paralympic Association (although maintaining the Get Set website beyond London 2012) did not participate in the inquiry or submit evidence. The abstention is based on the self-identified role of the organisations as being "independent, privately funded and receives no annual funding from the lottery or government and has no political interests" (BOA, 2018). In terms of stakeholder relations, this poses tensions rather than opportunities to connect with stakeholders in the domestic education sector as the Olympic and Paralympic organisations are functioning in a self-regulating space. The missed opportunity discourse, therefore, is perpetuated by Olympic and Paralympic based stakeholders. Who beyond hosting do not proactively engage with policy in a way that fosters sustained understanding of the role the Get Set programme and inspire a generation legacy aim can play within the exisiting and evolving domestic policy around sport, young people and education.

Conclusion

The aim of this article was to use London 2012 and the Get Set as a case study to engage with wider academic debates around stakeholder relations in the context of sport mega events, Olympic and Paralympic education programmes, and ongoing policy based on school sport and physical education. It is noted that as a qualitative case study this article does not seek to achieve generalisable principles that are representative of other sport mega events or hosts (Bryman, 2016). Rather the concluding points demonstrate implications and lessons for future organising committee members, policy makers and then academics that engage in legacy, policy or sport educational based debates. The objective of this article, specifically, was to illuminate how conceiving and enacting educational legacy programmes, such as the Get Set programme, impacted on stakeholder relations during the preparation, delivery and post-Games epoch. To articulate stakeholder tensions and incongruity (Friedman & Miles, 2002; Jensen, 2010), the paper's focus considered both negative and positive elements of the relations between stakeholders. Drawing on the inquiry data, the paper advances current London 2012 legacy debates by illuminating policy developments and stakeholder relations in the post Games landscape.

From a CDA framework, two main discourses emerged. Firstly, the purpose of the London 2012 educational programmes lacked clarity and clear relations between key stakeholders, such as, LOCOG and the UK government. The implication of such on wider stakeholder relations was demonstrated in the contrasting dialogue in the inquiry. Domestic influenced stakeholders were largely influenced by the outcomes of school sport and the Get Set programme based on competitive sport; whereas stakeholders influenced by the international perspective of the IOC and IPC, in contradistinction, focused on the values element of education, sport and the London 2012 opportunity. The different understanding of the purpose of the London 2012 educational programmes and how they could complement to existing relations in the competitive sport driven domestic space is a source of tension between how the different stakeholders related to each other. This supports broader scholarship around school sport and sport policy in the UK where the sectors demonstrate fragmented and contested spaces (Houlihan & Green, 2006; Lindsey, 2010; Mackintosh, 2014). Moreover, supports broader scholarship around sport mega events and policy where there is the a vulnerability to fragmented accountability when a number of time based or changing stakeholders are gatekeepers to the long term vision (Leopkey and Parent, 2015; Lindsey, 2010; Rhodes, 2000).

Secondly, the discourse of 'missed opportunity' dominated the inquiry dialogue around the educational programmes and broader legacy aim to inspire a generation. Tension was evident between stakeholders who included domestic policy and funding changes as part of the landscape of London 2012 legacy and school sport; whereas representatives of LOCOG contributed overtly positive dialogue to government support (largely as a consequence of not being impacted by changes in domestic policy and funding). The British Olympic Association and British Paralympic Association did not contribute evidence to the inquiry and sustained this viewpoint from LOCOG further, as there was no explicit engagement at a policy level with domestic circumstances. The findings here contribute to the wider debate around the Olympic and Paralympic value based education programmes (Binder, 2012; Chatziefstathiou, 2012; Coburn & McCaffery, 2016; Lenskyj, 2012), and support that although the programmes provide opportunities in the domestic setting, for sustainable legacy outcomes these must translated to the messy context of existing school sport policies. Future hosts of the Olympics and Paralympics, plus future UK sport mega event organising committees would need to be more effective if the relations with stakeholders were to go beyond accessing the programme, and instead resulted in translating the vision and programme into their local context for sustainable long term outcomes. However, linking to the first discourse, this would involve enacting a clear accountability structure, furthermore, the ability to agree on the overall purpose of a programme and policy. In this case study, the contested nature of sport and education policy during London 2012 did not facilitate an environment where it was completley possible to unite Olympic, Paralympic and domestic stakeholders. Consequently, further research around international, national and local stakeholders involved in sport mega events and policy around young people and education would be useful.

Finally, in the case of London 2012 and from the inquiry dialogue the position of Olympic and Paralympic (e.g. the British Olympic Association) based stakeholders to not publicly comment on or relate to domestic policy around school sport hindered the relations to stakeholders who actively had to consider the domestic policy landscape (e.g. the Youth Sport Trust). A contrast to this was stakeholders who connected the value of the Olympic and Paralympic brand/values to develop their own independent outcomes (e.g. the Wellcome Trust). In this dialogue, there was recognition of the opportunity London 2012 presented and how in their localised setting the educational programmes could contribute via a bottom-up approach. Here the stakeholders did not actively seek relations with the Olympic and Paralympic stakeholders, but utilised the value based outputs from such sources to further their own means and ends, which was not necessarily to inspire a generation. In line with the value creation component of stakeholder relations highlighted by Jensen (2010), the inspire a generation legacy did not unite stakeholders but galvanised opportunities for some who built the values into their existing visions. Moving forward, if an organising committee aims to impact the values of a host city or nation, in particular, around educational programmes they must consider how they can unite or empower the constituent stakeholders. The inquiry based evidence presented in this article shows this could be successful through a more bottom-up stakeholder approach, however, more needs to be understood how this can be enacted effectively in future sport mega event contexts. As sustainable legacy and targeting young people is a continued endeavour for policymakers, sport organisations and organising committees, academically, further study is encouraged to reflect on and bridge sport mega event literature and literature around domestic policy and young people.

Acknowledgements

The data for this paper was largely collected as part of the PhD studentship commissioned by the University of Worcester and ongoing collaboration with the Sport and Recreation Alliance. The authors would like to thank Dr. Aaron Beacom and Dr. Vassilios Ziakas for putting this valuable Special Issue together as well as the referees for providing comments on the paper.

Disclosure statement

No potential conflict of interest was reported by the authors.

ORCID

Verity Postlethwaite http://orcid.org/0000-0003-3246-4611
Geoffery Z. Kohe http://orcid.org/0000-0001-6683-6669
Gyozo Molnar http://orcid.org/0000-0003-1732-5672

References

Agha, N., Fairley, S., & Gibson, H. (2011). Considering legacy as a multi-dimensional construct: The legacy of the Olympic games. *Sport Management Review*, *15*(1), 125–139.
Binder, D. (2012). Olympic values education: Evolution of a pedagogy. *Educational Review*, *64*(3), 275–302.
British Olympic Association. (2018). About us. Retrieved from https://www.teamgb.com/about-boa
Brittain, I., & Beacom, A. (2016). Leveraging the London 2012 Paralympic Games: What legacy for disabled people? *Journal of Sport and Social Issues*, *40*(6), 499–521.
Bryman, A. (2016). *Social research methods*. Oxford: Oxford university press.
Chatziefstathiou, D. (2012). Olympic education and beyond: Olympism and value legacies from the Olympic and Paralympic Games. *Educational Review*, *64*(3), 385–400.
Chen, S., & Henry, I. (2019). Schools' engagement with the Get Set London 2012 Olympic education programme: Empirical insights from schools in a non-hosting region. *European Physical Education Review*, *25*(1), 254–272.
Coalter, F. (2010). The politics of sport-for-development: Limited focus programmes and broad gauge problems? *International Review for the Sociology of Sport*, *45*(3), 295–314.
Coburn, A., & McCafferty, P. (2016). The real Olympic Games: Sponsorship, schools and the Olympics – the case of Coca-Cola. *Taboo: The Journal of Culture and Education*, *15*(1), 23–40.
Department for Culture, Media and Sport. (2008). *Before, during and after the Games: Legacy action plan*. London: The Stationary Office Limited.
Department of Culture, Media and Sport. (2010). *London 2012 Olympic and Paralympic Games Annual Report*. London: The Stationary Office Limited.
Friedman, A. L., & Miles, S. (2002). Developing stakeholder theory. *Journal of Management Studies*, *39*(1), 1–21.

Get Set. (2018). Home Page. Retrieved from https://www.getset.co.uk/

Girginov, V. (2013). *Handbook of the London 2012 Olympic and Paralympic Games. Volume One: Making the Games.* London: Routledge.

Girginov, V. (2016). Has the London 2012 Olympic Inspire programme inspired a generation? A realist view. *European Physical Education Review, 22*(4), 490–505.

Griggs, G., & Ward, G. (2013). The London 2012 legacy for primary physical education: Policy by the way? *Sociological Research Online, 18*(3), 1–7.

The Guardian. (2010). Teachers stunned after Michael Gove scraps "sport for all" funding. Retrieved from https://www.theguardian.com/education/2010/nov/20/schools-sports-funding-cuts-gove.

The Guardian. (2013). Lord Coe: I'm quitting to make sure Olympic legacy is delivered. Retrieved from https://www.theguardian.com/sport/2013/jul/19/lord-coe-quits-ambassador-olympic-legacy

Houlihan, B. (2016). Sport policy making. In A. Bairner, J. Kelly, & J. W. Lee (Eds.), *Routledge Handbook of sport and Politics* (pp. 16–27). London: Routledge.

Houlihan, B., & Green, M. (2006). The changing status of school sport and physical education: Explaining policy change. *Sport, Education and Society, 11*(1), 73–92.

House of Commons Education Committee. (2013a). *Appendix: School sport following London 2012: No more political football: Government Response to the committee's third report of Session 2013-14.* London: The Stationary Office Limitedhttps://publications.parliament.uk/pa/cm201314/cmselect/cmeduc/723/723.pdf

House of Commons Education Committee. (2013b). *Volume 1: School sport following London 2012: No more political football.* London: The Stationary Office Limitedhttps://publications.parliament.uk/pa/cm201314/cmselect/cmeduc/164/164.pdf

House of Commons Education Committee. (2013c). *Volume II: School sport following London 2012: No more political football.* London: The Stationary Office Limitedhttps://publications.parliament.uk/pa/cm201314/cmselect/cmeduc/164/16402.htm

House of Commons Education Committee. (2013d). *Volume III: School sport following London 2012: No more political football.* London: The Stationary Office Limitedhttps://publications.parliament.uk/pa/cm201314/cmselect/cmeduc/164/16402.htm

IOC. (2013a). *Olympic Charter.* Retrieved from https://stillmed.olympic.org/Documents/olympic_charter_en.pdf

IOC. (2013b). Factsheet London 2012 Facts and Figures. Retrieved from /https://stillmed.olympic.org/media/Document%20Library/OlympicOrg/IOC/Olympic_Games/Olympic_Legacy/London_2012/Legacy/EN_London_2012_Facts_and_Figures.pdf

Jensen, M. C. (2010). Value maximization, stakeholder theory, and the corporate objective function. *Journal of Applied Corporate Finance, 22*(1), 32–42.

Jung, H., Pope, S., & Kirk, D. (2016). Policy for physical education and school sport in England, 2003–2010: Vested interests and dominant discourses. *Physical Education and Sport Pedagogy, 21*(5), 501–516.

Kerr, S. (2018). The London 2012 Paralympic Games. In I. Brittain & A. Beacom (Eds.), *The Palgrave Handbook of Paralympic studies* (pp. 481–505). London: Palgrave Macmillan.

Kohe, G. Z. (2017). London 2012 (Re) calling: Youth memories and Olympic 'legacy' ether in the hinterland. *International Review for the Sociology of Sport, 52*(1), 24–44.

Kohe, G. Z., & Bowen-Jones, W. (2016). Rhetoric and realities of London 2012 Olympic education and participation 'legacies': Voices from the core and periphery. *Sport, Education and Society, 21*(8), 1213–1229.

Kohe, G. Z, & Chatziefstathiou, D. (2017). Olympic Education in the United Kingdom: Rethinking London 2012, Learning 'Legacies' and their Pedagogical potential. In *Olympic Education: An International Review* (pp. 60–72). Abingdon: Routledge.

Kohe, G. Z., & Collison, H. (2019). *Sport, education, Corporatisation: Spaces of connection, contestation and creativity.* Oxon: Routledge.

Lee, M. (2006). *The race for the 2012 Olympics: The inside story of how London won the bid.* New York: Random House.

Lenskyj, H. J. (2012). Olympic education and Olympism: Still colonizing children's minds. *Educational Review, 64*(3), 265–274.

Leopkey, B., & Parent, M. M. (2015). Stakeholder perspectives regarding the governance of legacy at the Olympic Games. *Annals of Leisure Research, 18*(4), 528–548.

Lindsey, I. (2010). Governance of lottery sport programmes: National direction of local partnerships in the new opportunities for PE and sport programme. *Managing Leisure, 15*(3), 198–213.

Lindsey, I. (2018). Analysing policy change and continuity: physical education and school sport policy in England since 2010. *Sport, Education and Society.* Advance online publication. doi:10.1080/13573322.2018.1547274

LOCOG. (2012). *Learning legacy: Lessons learned from planning and staging the London 2012 Games.* London: Author.

Macdonald, K. (2008). Using documents. In N. Gilbert (Ed.), *Researching social life* (pp. 285–303). London: Sage.

Mackintosh, C. (2014). Dismantling the school sport partnership infrastructure: Findings from a survey of physical education and school sport practitioners. *Education 3-13, 42*(4), 432–449.

Parent, M. M. (2008). Evolution and issue patterns for major-sport-event organizing committees and their stakeholders. *Journal of Sport Management, 22*(2), 135–164.

Phillpots, L. (2013). An analysis of the policy process for physical education and school sport: The rise and demise of school sport partnerships. *International Journal of Sport Policy and Politics, 5*(2), 193–211.

Rhodes, R. A. W. (2000). *Debating governance*. Oxford: Oxford University Press.

Telegraph. (2010). *Michael Gove forced into about-turn over scrapping School Sports Partnerships after outrage over cuts*. Retrieved from https://www.telegraph.co.uk/sport/othersports/schoolsports/8215108/Michael-Gove-forcedinto-about-turn-over-scrapping-School-Sports-Partnerships-after-outrage-over-cuts.html.

Tomlinson, A. (2014). Olympic legacies: Recurrent rhetoric and harsh realities. *Contemporary Social Science, 9*(2), 137–158.

UK Government. (2010). *Letter to the Youth Sport Trust*. Retrieved from https://www.gov.uk/government/publications/refocusing-sport-in-schools-to-build-a-lasting-legacy-of-the-2012-games

van Dijk, T. (1996). Discourse, power and access. In C. Caldas-Coulthard & M. Coulthard (Eds.), *Texts and practices:readings in critical discourse analysis.* (pp. 84–104). London: Routledge.

Viollet, B., Minikin, B., Scelles, N., & Ferrand, A. (2016). Perceptions of key stakeholders regarding national federation sport policy: The case of the French rugby union. *Managing Sport and Leisure, 21*(5), 319–337.

Whigham, S., & Bairner, A. (2018). Analysing sport policy and politics: The promises and challenges of synthesising methodological approaches. *International Journal of Sport Policy and Politics, 10*(4), 721–740.

Yin, R. K. (2003). *Case study research: Design and methods*. Thousand Oaks, CA: Sage.

Understanding the management challenges associated with the implementation of the physically active teaching and learning (PATL) pedagogy: a case study of three Isle of Wight primary schools

Oscar Mwaanga, Henry Dorling, Samantha Prince and Matthew Fleet

ABSTRACT
Enabled partly by government policies by the Department for Culture Media and Sport, some schools are beginning to shift towards promoting a physical activity culture which complements the traditional PE and school sports provision. For many, this entails using physical activity as a modality to promote academic performance. Physically Active Teaching and Learning (PATL) is one approach which has been adopted by schools on the Isle of Wight (UK) as part of a holistic island-wide intervention aimed at increasing pupil's educational attainment, health and wellbeing. To gain an in-depth understanding of PATL and examine the management implications of its implementation, this paper draws on qualitative data collected from three primary schools on the Isle of Wight. Overall, the paper supports PATL pedagogies as a holistic and joined-up policy response, however, critical conversations are crucial for unravelling and unlocking collaborative solutions when discussing physical activity in schools.

Introduction

The last decade has seen an exponential increase in the number of school-based interventions utilizing the relationship between physical activity and academic performance. Examples of such programmes include Maths of the Day, BBC super-movers, Premier League Primary Stars and EduMove (UK), Active Smarter Kids (Norway), Take 10! and Physical Activity Across the Curriculum and Energizer! (USA). In the UK, such interventions have been collectively called Physically Active Teaching and Learning (PATL), Physically Active Learning (PAL) or Physically Active Education. These methodologies innovatively utilize physical activity to promote academic performance, health and psychosocial wellbeing (Kibbe et al., 2011; Tomporowski, Lambourne, & Okumura, 2011). Delk, Springer, Kelder, and Grayless (2014), Babey, Wu, and Cohen (2014) have contended that such programmes are feasible, cost-effective, sustainable and scalable and are consistently shown to have an increase on physical activity levels when part of school-wide initiatives (Erwin, Abel, Beighle, & Beets, 2011; Holt, Bartee, & Heelan, 2013).

Overall, there is a good political will to consider interventions such as PATL in the midst of global concerns of physical *inactivity* that have become culturally imbedded and normalized.

This has resulted in a high prevalence of lifestyle-related non-communicable diseases and an unsustainable economic burden on national health services. It is probable that school leaders who are under constant pressure to get more children to achieve high grades in core curriculum subjects such as maths and science will consider interventions that promise to reduce sedentary curriculum learning while increasing academic performance. However, the perception held by some teachers is that physical education and sport is competing with other curriculum subjects such as maths, English and science for curriculum time, where physical education lessons are often replaced with revision lessons during examination periods. Hence, it is expected that school leaders will require proof of the potential effect of PATL on academic performance before schools adopt such approaches (Grieco, Jowers, Errisuriz, & Bartholomew, 2016; Ward et al., 2006). The increase in PATL interventions has also attracted research that aims to examine the positive relationship between physical activity and increased academic outcomes (Donnelly et al., 2016). Within the UK context and globally, the current policy climate has favoured such interventions and research. For example, the WHO advocates the increase in physical activity (not only sport and exercise) and embedding physical activity into public institutions. However, despite the increase in the number of programmes and interventions which combine physical activity with academic subjects, there has been a lack of research which examines the efficacy and implications of such programmes in the school environment.

The overall purpose of this paper is to understand how teachers negotiate and manage the delivery of PATL within the complex dynamics of the school environment. The primary objective is to investigate the management issues associated with the implementation of PATL programmes. In trying to understand how it is managed, it is imperative to ascertain the perceptions of PATL pedagogy. The primary data in the study was collected from teachers across three primary schools on the Isle of Wight who have implemented the PATL pedagogy as part of an Island-wide programme.

Overview of the relationship between physical activity and education

There is increasing evidence relating to the possible link between physical activity and academic performance. This includes executive function, cognitive processes, including memory, attention span and reasoning, all of which are necessary for goal-directed cognition and improved behaviour (Best, 2010; Chaddock, Hillman, Buck, & Cohen, 2011; Donnelly et al., 2016; Tomporowski et al., 2011). The evidence on the effectiveness of physical activity to develop cognition and academic achievement is favourable but also tentative (Donnelly et al., 2016; Erickson, Hillman, & Kramer, 2015; Gomez-Pinilla & Hillman, 2013; Sibley & Etnier, 2003). The work of Donnelly et al. (2016) helps to provide some clarity from the available science and through a comprehensive systematic review of peer-reviewed journals, predominately from the United Kingdom. While much of the research presented supports the view that physical activity benefits children's cognitive functioning, limited evidence is available concerning the effects of physical activity on learning (Donnelly et al., 2016). The evidence presented by Donnelly et al. (2016) indicates that whilst there are encouraging links between physical activity, fitness, cognition and academic achievement, the research is not consistent in its findings and the effects of various areas of physical activity on cognition need to be investigated further. Nevertheless, the literature does not suggest that any increase in physical activity *negatively* affects academic achievement or cognition and goes so far as to state that physical activity is essential for growth, development and general health.

There has been an expeditious increase in practitioners looking for further evidence highlighting the claimed benefits of physical activity and its influence on young learners. Physical activity advocates have long called for this necessary increase in physical activity in schools, suggesting that any time spent taking part in physical activity would benefit health and may even contribute to academic performance. This has resulted in a rise in the number of new organizations and programmes who are striving to promote physical activity and make a positive impact. Using the evidence that is currently available it is possible to determine that physical activity does have a positive influence on cognition, brain structure and function; however, more research is required to establish the mechanisms, long-term effects and to translate these laboratory outcomes to a school setting.

The PATL pedagogical approach

PATL is an active learning approach that aims to use movement and physical activity to enhance academic performance in core curriculum topics, such as maths, English, PSHE and science, while promoting health and psychosocial wellbeing (Kibbe et al., 2011; Mwaanga & Prince, 2014). In PATL, a wide range of enjoyable and engaging physical activities and games are presented at varying intensities demanding learners to complete kinesthetic tasks with the aim of triggering thinking and reflection. We postulate in this paper that a close examination of the concepts, assumptions, beliefs and rationales, may distinguish PATL from traditional teaching approaches in core subjects, physical education (PE) and sport in schools. While it is outside the scope of the current analysis to delve into a detailed justification of PATL as a different paradigm, it is crucial that some unique features of a PATL pedagogical approach are highlighted only to provide further context for the findings of this paper. Here we briefly present the three core arguments which help extricate the PATL approach within UK schools.

First, we suggest that PATL is unique in terms of its formative philosophical worldview. Traditional Western education is firmly based on the philosophical view of dualism which views the mind and body as separate, and arguably that the mind is superior to the body. This can be seen through the siloing of the UK primary curriculum areas and the obsession with an academic exam focused system. Dualism is encapsulated in the popularized proposition by René Descartes; "Cogito, ergo sum" which translates into English as "I think, therefore I am". Conversely, PATL is based on the notion of monalism, which takes the view of metaphysics which refers to reality as a unified whole where all existing things can be ascribed to or described by a single concept or system. Thus, the mind and body are one system. Keeping with the monalistic view of "I think therefore I am" is rearticulated to "I move therefore I am" to centralize the role and importance of movement within the holistic perspective of children's development. One clear implication of dualism is the prevalent practice that prioritizes and privileges the so called "cognitive" subjects (e.g. maths, English and science) at the expense of PE and the arts. PATL responds with movement driven education whose intended outcomes are equally cognitive, emotional and corporal.

Second, notwithstanding the multiple definitions of active learning, there is a consensus that active learning is positioned as an instructional method which promotes participation and engagement of students in the learning processes (Bonwell & Eison, 1991; Layne & Lake, 2014). This contrasts with traditional teaching approaches which tend to centralize the teacher as the dispenser of knowledge and students as the passive recipients. PATL can be viewed as an extension of the active learning methodology whose emphasis lies in the use of different types and intensities of fun physical activities to promote engagement and participation in the learning process. The collaborative approach to peer learning could be promoted as a deeper sense making process can be achieved through this notion of a decentred pedagogical approach. Petty (2009) refers to the constructivist approach to learning which the PATL method falls into. The addition of physical activity helps to stimulate this learning process and adds the element of fun and variety of challenge. Government policy has played a defining role throughout the years in this area. In 2000 "A Sporting Future for all" was published by the Labour Government. This policy, although "sport" focused, was part of Labour's modernization plans and sat within the wider social development policy agenda, position sport as a way to address issues within education, amongst other things. Game Plan (2002) was the follow-up policy that took one of the fist "crosscutting" approaches to policy creation, endeavouring to bring together sport, physical activity and recognized social issues, with a view to putting sport at the heart of wider socio-political agendas and addressing broader inequalitites within society. More recently the shift towards focusing on using physical activity to address such issues is reiterated in the latest government sport policy. The Department for Culture Media and Sport advocates the broader social, psychological, physical, community and economic benefits sport and physical activity can produce for individuals and groups (HM Government, 2015). The new policy marks a shift from previous policies which have focussed on the role of sport and the promotion of the London 2012 Games Legacy (see Department for Culture Media and Sport, 2012).

Based on the PATL paradigm, it is contended that physical activity should be embedded holistically in children's lives. With students sitting between four to five hours a day, the school is an ideal setting for increasing physical activity levels of children and reducing the amount of time spent being sedentary (Chaput et al., 2013). Traditional approaches to address physical activity, health and wellbeing have involved increasing the number of PE lessons and adding before school, lunchtime and after-school sports clubs. Although the methods can be embedded within these environments, PATL's main focus is on penetrating core curriculum lessons delivered during the school day by adding elements of physical activity. This involves embedding physical activity in the teaching of subjects such as maths, English and science, directly addressing the issues of sedentary during the teaching of subjects during the school day. Evidently, if PATL is to be delivered and embedded during the school day and combined with other subjects, an appropriate question is, how is PATL pragmatically embedded and managed within classrooms?

PATL methodology and the Isle of Wight context

There are two interrelated operational models through which PATL is delivered on the Isle of Wight. Thus, an understanding of these operational models and how they sit within the wider context of the Isle of Wight is cardinal to achieving the purpose of this paper. PATL delivery on the Isle of Wight is not a stand-alone intervention at selected schools but an integral part of an island-wide partnership called the Partnership for Education, Attainment and Children's Health (PEACH). PEACH is a "whole-school" framework that aims to support the development of the "whole-child" within and through Isle of Wight primary schools. PEACH is the partnership and co-production of key Isle of Wight education and health stakeholders including the Executive Headteacher Group, Public Health and EduMove Ltd (EduMove is a UK based social enterprise). It builds on the Healthy Schools Award whose funding ceased in early 2010 leaving behind a vacuum for coordinated and systematic approaches to addressing cross-cutting issues within education and health for children and young people. In line with the previous "National Healthy Schools Award", PEACH focuses on three domains: (a) personal, social, health and economic education, (b) emotional wellbeing and mental health, (c) physical activity and healthy eating.

The first conceptual model that frames both PEACH and EduMove interventions via PATL is the Social Ecological Model as shown in Figure 1 (adapted from the Centre for Disease Control, 2017). The Social Ecological Model has been adopted in similar studies to examine "whole-child" approaches to educational attainment (see Lewallen, Hunt, Potts-Datema, Zaza, & Giles, 2015), health promotion and public policy (see Golden, McLeroy, Green, Earp, & Lieberman, 2015) and more recently "whole-community" approaches to health promotion (see Wold & Mittelmark, 2018). For this research, it is useful because it considers the complex interplay between individual, relationship, community and societal factors to achieve desired behavioural change.

The rings in the Social Ecological Model categorize factors at play within each level and illustrate how factors at one level influence factors at another level. Besides helping to clarify these factors, the model also suggests that to effect behaviour change (e.g. learning, social and health related outcomes) it is necessary to act across multiple levels of the model at the same time. For example, it acknowledges the role of proximal (e.g. individual and interpersonal) and more distal (e.g. school physical environment, demographic factors, school policy) determinants of learning and health behaviour change as necessary to achieve sustained positive change in the development of the whole-child.

The justification of PEACH and the holistic island-wide approach takes into account the commonality between some schools as well as their diversity. In terms of commonality, the problems faced by most schools are reflected in their below-par performance when compared to national standards on key academic and health-related measurements. For example, in the Department of Education National curriculum assessments report (2017, the Key Stage 2 achievement of expected objectives in maths, reading and writing was lower than the rest of England, with a large gap between disadvantaged and affluent pupils. Furthermore, 43% of Isle of Wight primary school pupils are failing tougher SATs tests and teachers are fearing children will be branded as failures which will have an adverse effect on their wellbeing (Association for School and College Leaders, 2016) and self-esteem. In terms of physical activity, the Isle of Wight School Survey (2015) showed that locally less than one in five Year 6 (primary school) pupils are physically active (meeting 30 min per day), and by Year 10 (secondary school) this significantly decreases to less than one in ten. In keeping with the PEACH ethos, Isle of Wight schools with poor SATs results are advised to consider PATL programmes that tackle improvement in this area.

The second operational model deals with what happens within the school and relates to the organizational level of the Social Ecological Model. EduMove Ltd is a social enterprise that provides schools with resources aimed at empowering teachers to take ownership of PATL in their school (EduMove Limited, 2017; www.edumove.co.uk). Encouraging schools to take control over how they implement PATL is crucial because contextual dynamics will vary from one school to the next. Moreover, the appreciation and competence in delivering PATL will also vary between and within schools. According to the PEACH framework, these programmes are coordinated and championed by the school's sport specialist or PE teacher who form part of a core PATL team with representation from each year group. Currently, this operational model is being applied loosely at three Isle of Wight primary schools. These schools receive PATL training and online resources to support their delivery whilst also being mentored by EduMove Ltd staff. However, it very easy to get blinded by the plausibility of each of these approaches and downplay the fact that well-intended models can fail at the implementation level. Thus, this paper examines how various vested interest groups within schools negotiate and manage the delivery of PATL to achieve the PEACH targets.

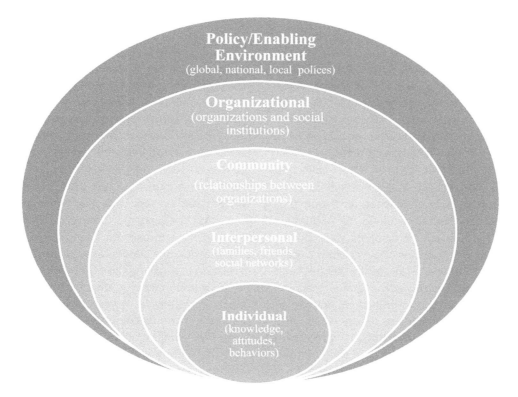

Figure 1. The social ecological model.

Research design

Evaluations linked to physical activity in children have most commonly relied on quantitative methods evaluating the magnitude of change and have typically not contributed to an understanding of why changes occur or how this impact has affected people or environments. The methodology adopted here to gather initial exploratory data was realist evaluation, an emerging methodology in the field of management. A realist evaluation is a form of theory-driven evaluation that looks to the idea of a configuration of context plus mechanism which equals outcome (C + M = O) and looks to unearth what works for whom under what circumstances and why (Pawson & Tilley, 1997). It aims to get to the heart of why things work or do not work and create a programme theory which is tested via a variety of methods. The methodology can compare whether a programme works differently in different localities (and if so, how and why) or for different population groups (Westhorp, 2014). Initial candidate theories (Jagosh et al., 2015) can then be tested, refined and developed via qualitative methods such as interviews with the vested interest groups to ascertain what they deem to be of importance, in use or applicable, i.e. to see if they hold true.

The theoretical drivers in realist evaluation allow an understanding of hidden mechanisms (confidence, engagement, motivation, enjoyment as examples) leading to particular outcomes which in a school environment and within a management context can be particularly powerful and influential. These theories are generated from a variety of domains; a researcher's or practitioner's experiences, existing literature, relevant data generated from previous research or from situational or needs analyses conducted within or in conjunction with the target population or community. The methods are then used to test and refine these initial theories utilizing the notion of retroduction to unearth the mechanisms at play. We argue therefore that realist evaluation, as a form of theory-driven evaluation, has the potential to understand what is working or not for whom, under what circumstances and why within the discourse of PATL and the associated pedagogical areas.

The primary method of data collection involved conducting realist interviews with seven primary school teachers and one programme coordinator working for EduMove ($n = 8$). The research participants were purposively sampled based on their existing experiences of EduMove within their school, and that they had utilized some active teaching and learning methods within their practice to date. Realist interviews are theory driven and focus on testing the programme theories with the input of the interviewee. The style of interview employed utilized the teacher-learner cycle (Manzano, 2016). Here, the interviewer presents and "teaches" the theories under test to the interviewee who then refutes or confirms their existence and the ways in which they manifest themselves. They then assume the position of the teacher and "teach" the interviewer about the theories from their perspective. This includes varying aspects of stakeholder involvement, the impact and overall influence of the mechanisms under discussion and how that interaction leads to the given outcomes. This means that the interviewer and interviewee play much more active roles in the process allowing a deeper understanding of what is working or not, why and how. This will happen through capturing the participants' stories because those related experiences of the programme illuminate the various processes and manifold outcomes (Patton, 2003). realist evaluation is unique in that it embraces subjectivity and lends itself to the idea of capturing effectively the richness and depth of data. It moves on from "tell me your story" to "what is it about your story that has made a difference, based on this given programme theory". The data were analysed using a coding method which cross-referenced the given programme theories and refined them based on interpretative interviewee responses.

Observations of EduMove lessons ($n = 11$) were also undertaken to test and refine the theories. The indicative criteria were decided upon based on existing research studies which had focused on pupil engagement levels via a behavioural interventions checklist. This checklist was concentrated on task behaviour which included examining the length of time on each type of task and the approximate intensity level of the activity. Additional fieldnotes were also gathered in relation to anything the observer felt were relevant or important, e.g. unintended outcomes, one to one interaction, peer to peer engagement or coaching and teaching styles employed. Tentative CMO configurations were then offered as were the subsequent thematic refinements and results as summarized below.

Findings

The empirical data bears out an interesting picture around the technocratic management within a primary school and the more specific and relevant management linked with a teacher's capacity to deliver PATL. Three key themes emerged from the analysis and are discussed in turn.

Head teacher influence and teacher (dis)empowerment

Within the primary school environment, the centrality of the teacher in the educational process of a child is undeniable. Therefore, the teachers' individual perception of empowerment or disempowerment to deliver innovative learning approaches are cardinal. However, the data exposes some fragility of teachers' empowerment relative to the school's culture, authority systems and curriculum restrictions. To a large extent, the data indicates that the senior leadership team (SLT) and, in many cases, the Headteacher themselves may be a source of this disempowerment. Teacher interview comments to underpin this are as follows:

> I get in trouble sometimes (with the Head) … I've had myself hauled over the coals because it's not been documented in their books. (Teacher 1)
>
> We teach to the test, nobody (SLT) is interested in anything other than teaching to the test. (Teacher 3)
>
> I said to SLT here (to introduce PATL methods) … but it's very hard … it's inertia. (Teacher 7)

The perspectives here point to the SLT as the cause of the teacher's disempowerment to implement PATL or other innovative pedagogical approaches. In the primary school context, SLTs are often made up of the Headteacher, Deputy Headteacher(s), Department Heads and the School Business Manager. However, a school policy analysis would quickly reveal that the SLT themselves are not the genesis of this policy stance. Rather, the SLT are the messengers who pass on the pressure from other influential policy drivers such as the Department of Education (via Ofsted) and school governors. The Social Ecological Model is useful for acknowledging that the position taken by an agent within the school context is always linked to factors operating beyond the individual. The teachers' perceptions and feelings of disempowerment must be understood within the cycle of overbearing policy that reproduces a rigid testing culture. By applying the Social Ecological Model as a loose policy analysis framework within the context of the Isle of Wight and PEACH, one is able to reveal other vested interests in pupil's health and learning. For example, Ofsted, governors, SLT, class teachers, parents and pupils can all be considered as having vested interests. Arguably, for teachers to adopt PATL and other innovative teaching approaches within PEACH, a collaborative approach in planning, delivery and research must be consolidated.

Recording evidence of learning

This pressure to succeed and to demonstrate an ability to "teach to test" means that the autonomy of a teacher to choose their own style and methods, which may include physically active methods, is diminished and in some cases totally eradicated. There is a further pressure to record evidence of learning and achievement which ultimately ends up being in the more traditional ways, i.e. in books and written.

> it was very much an emphasis on recording because probably from my personal thing I thought I needed for them to show me, show (the Headteacher), show everyone else what they had done. (Teacher 2)
>
> some schools do want a certain structure of learning, some having that recorded in their books. (Teacher 4)

In a similar vein, some teachers connected the recording of evidence to accountability in the role of a teacher.

> There's so much scrutiny on the grades that therefore possibly there might be a little bit more accountability for classroom teachers when that grade is scrutinised. (Teacher 5)
>
> teachers tend to play a bit more safe and tend to do what perhaps they're supposed to do and what they're encouraged to do and therefore because there's a different level of accountability, they don't have the flexibility. (Teacher 7)

The relentless requirement for evidence dominates within the primary school which halts creative development and the capacity of a teacher to make the decision to promote active strategies that have been shown to positively influence cognitive processes, on-task behaviours and as a result increase academic attainment levels. The pressure of a test dominated culture leads to a disrupted and disempowering environment where no one is actually to blame. Control is potentially taken away and decided outside the school which leads to disempowerment. This confirms the disempowering situation that leads to teachers not feeling confident in their abilities and their profession. This is further exacerbated by teacher training which focuses on teaching and pedagogy and *not* testing performance and evaluation. Relating back to the Social Ecological Model, it is evident that there is a detachment between the discussions at the policy level regarding testing and performance and at the individual level on pupils and teachers. Policy making is so removed from practice that it forms unrealistic targets to mediate this. For example, cultural restrictions at the community and interpersonal level will also affect individuals' health and education. Arguably, given the pressure on schools to achieve both health and educational outcomes, PATL could provide an alternative approach which empowers teachers to meet assessment targets *and* enables them to enjoy their teaching and "teach to teach" rather than "teach to test".

In this vein, there might be scope for PATL to be considered as a redeeming pedagogy where teachers can regain their control and empowerment over teaching and testing. For example, testing erodes the hedonic or happy moments in their teaching, yet when pupils enjoy learning through PATL pedagogies, the happy moments can be brought back. There is strong evidence in the literature which argue that physical activity leads to increased levels of endorphins in the brain, which act as internal psychoactive agents yielding a positive euphoric feeling. Within the context of PATL and learning, two further hypotheses are drawn from this. Firstly, the body's euphoric feeling leads to pupils experiencing a positive and energizing outlook to the learning experience (Hillman, Erickson, & Kramer, 2008). Secondly, a joyful PATL atmosphere encourages behaviours that further the supply of endorphins in pupils that make them more apt to learn how to successfully solve problems that may be perceived difficult. PATL is supported by principals of experiential education which is a philosophy of education that describes the process that occurs between a teacher and a pupil which infuses direct experience with the learning environment and content (Itin, 1999). For instance, kinesthetic learning or tactile learning hypothesis contends that PATL provides opportunities for students who learn best by using whole-body movement to process new and difficult information or learning with and through physical activities, rather than listening to or watching a lecture (Favre, 2009).

The teacher and classroom management

The classroom and its management are one of the many ingredients that need to be addressed and managed to create successful PATL integration. This also involves examining the interaction with pupils and how the styles of teaching and learning are affected. The data suggest that teachers perceive the classroom environment in two ways; first, those teachers perceive a lack of control, and second, some teachers do experience optimism and express the potential for control in the space.

Knowledge and understanding of certain methods of PATL for teachers are at best underdeveloped and, more often lost in the dense test-driven cultural expectations. There seems to be an element of worry around pupil behaviour and its unpredictable nature in the context of increased classroom movement and as such the lack of ability to engage with set learning outcomes.

> Obviously, in terms of 31 children in here all at once, doing that is very difficult. (Teacher 1)

Many of the teacher comments are linked to concern around classroom management linked to outcomes as well as having clear safety concerns around pupils who could be deemed out of control. Teacher interview comments to underpin this are as follows;

> In terms of safety obviously, there are times when I think, "Be careful!." (Teacher 4)

I would suggest everyone would go back into the classroom and sit down then do their writing in a controlled, calm environment. (Teacher 5)

if you do then take the children out of a controlled, safe, contained environment and you put them into a much bigger space, I think some teachers are a little bit put off by that sense of space and they don't quite manage their children in the same way. (Teacher 6)

There also seemed to be some consensus in the data around why they are perceived to have a lack of control stemming from Initial Teacher Training (ITT) experiences;

… they (NQT's) are just being brainwashed really into one way of teaching. (Teacher 2)

Lack of training, lack of time to do the job properly …. (Teacher 3)

The influence of the SLT also holds weight here in the sense that teachers seemed anxious about how to defend their use of physically active methods if pressed by a member of the SLT related to how are they meeting the curriculum objectives. For example, in more than one case SLT demanded a sample of pupil work to assess the content of written evidence for meeting curriculum objectives, and openly challenged the use of more active teaching methods as not producing the "correct" type of evidence. This creates an issue around confidence in the teacher and their capacity to develop an understanding of effectiveness which leads to a lack of classroom integration and a poor perception of PATL and its implementation strategies. Moreover, there is a clear link with school operational management in that SLT can directly influence the confidence of a teacher to implement more PATL methods within their classroom through an outcome driven curriculum and constricted and convoluted policies. Elements of the Social Ecological Model can again be applied here; the organizational influence weighs heavily on the practice of the teachers ultimately leading to restricted pedagogical approaches, which in turn affects their relationships with the pupils, prioritizing the need for testing and recording of evidence, once again pointing towards this lack of empowerment which then manifests itself as poor classroom management.

However, there were some teachers that viewed the space more positively when using PATL showing that there are some glimmers of potential if PATL was made more easily accessible and deliverable via the classroom management structure;

I don't think there's a right way or a wrong way of doing it. I think it's knowing the class that you're with, knowing the children, their learning styles, how they work together, so I think that's really important. (Teacher 2)

There's some children that get really conscious by that and there are some children that thrive by that. So, it's finding something that's fun for all of them which is difficult. It is really difficult. (Teacher 3)

A large part of this centres around the management of the teacher. This involves the pupil relationship and expectations between the two parties as well as the influence of SLT and related teacher autonomy.

I'm trying to think of lots of inventive ways for children to use the space …. (Teacher 5)

It makes the classroom a more interesting place to be. (Teacher 6)

there's so much of the curriculum that you can teach in an active way. (Teacher 7)

Pupil engagement and management within the classroom then becomes a highly influential factor with the use of interventionist strategies to attempt to unlock and alleviate some of the sedentary and oppressive nature of the classroom. Failure to perceive the classroom as a space which has potential to integrate physical activity could lead to a lack of opportunity for teachers to engage with PATL methods if they perceive physical activity as something which only happens outdoors or in the school hall. In this vein, a "whole-school" approach to the management of PATL becomes more difficult because it is compartmentalized into existing structures such as PE rather than being embedded holistically across the school.

In line with the secondary aim of this paper, perspectives provided by the current EduMove programme coordinator were useful in elucidating how EduMove programmes encapsulated some of the previously mentioned features of the PATL pedagogy. He contended that the EduMove M.E.E.L (Move Enjoy, Engage, Learn) criteria are key to understand how EduMove delivers the PATL pedagogy. Thus, to achieve the learning outcomes of any PATL lessons, children must enjoy engaging in tasks delivered via a fun movement activity;

> Overall, we want to make sure that all PATL programmes meet our M.E.E.L (Move, Enjoy, Engage, Learn) criteria. The MEEL underpins the PEACH work on the Isle of Wight as we deliver on the physical activity domain. (EduMove Coordinator)

Additionally, the EduMove coordinator emphasized EduMove interventions were able to be delivered inside the classroom in keeping PATL pedagogy. In this vein, he brought to light the EduMove classroom-based interventions;

> children are often seated for over 5 hours a day in the classroom. This lowers their metabolism and increases their chances of poor health in the long term. Lower metabolism also means poor blood flow to the brain which I believe lowers their concentration. We have three interventions to address this. Firstly, to do fun exercises every 25 minutes of sitting. secondly, using our MoveClass app where we integrate revision with exercise. lastly, we have a portal with lesson plans for low intensity and limited movement PATL activities. (EduMove Coordinator)

The EduMove Coordinator's narrative also responds to some of the challenges regarding the compartmentalization of physical activity in the school week. The coordinator asserts that PATL integration in schools doesn't only refer to high-intensity physical activity, but also refers to low-intensity physical activity which might involve pupils standing and walking around the classroom. Emphasizing lower intensity movements may also enhance the sustainability of such changes because there is greater flexibility for integrating short activities that don't require pupils to change into "PE kits".

Likewise, this programme has PATL features which are supported by some emerging evidence in a recent seminal review by Donnelly et al. (2016) who suggested that physically active lessons generally result in improvements in academic achievement, whereas attempts to increase activity in PE do not. However, Donnelly et al. (2016) advocate for more robust research due to multiple methodological shortcomings and inconsistencies among studies which support the efficacy of physically active lessons.

Conclusion and practical implications

In accordance with the overall purpose of this paper, which is to examine how teachers negotiate and manage the delivery of PATL pedagogy within the PEACH context, two paramount conclusions are worth underscoring. Consistent with emerging academic evidence (e.g. Donnelly et al., 2016) and as attested by the EduMove coordinator, PATL as pedagogy has significant potential and scope particularly when framed and "ring fenced" within the PEACH policy and ethos. However, within the complex dynamic of the school, the implementation of PATL and other innovative pedagogies face numerous management challenges that frustrate the implementation of PATL and lead to feelings of disempowerment and anxiety among teachers.

First and foremost, teachers seem to suggest that "teaching to test" is policed by the SLT and is what steers the curriculum and learning culture in their schools. Expectedly, there is a general dislike for both the "teaching to test" culture and the way the SLT emphasizes it in their school. This generated feelings and perceptions of disempowerment and anxiety among teachers which affected the impetus to implement PATL and other innovative pedagogies which are known to benefit the learning and health of the child. Within the complex dynamic of the school, teachers' perceptions of control (i.e. empowerment), positive mental wellbeing and confidence are cardinal in the delivery of an effective curriculum. Interpreting this dynamic context from the lenses of the Social Ecological Model reveals that, in addition to the SLT, there are a wide range of vested interests in pupils' health and education, for example, Ofsted, governors, parents the Department of Health and private sector provides. Thus, the perception that headteachers are the *source* of the testing culture in schools is incorrect because headteachers experience pressure from external stakeholders such as school governors and Ofsted. Instead, we must explore collaborative management and teaching approaches that ensure achievement of Ofsted targets, which are used to judge performance of the SLT, while developing "whole-child" learning and health needs. These needs are more complex than solely academic performance measures because they are long-term in impact and beyond the scope of Ofsted. The revelation of other policy entrepreneurs within the school dynamic shift the blame of failure from the teachers alone to include other agents within school context. Acknowledging the presence and role of other agents, as identified in Table 1, must help reshape the school policy landscape. For PEACH on the Isle of Wight, partners must consider clear roles and responsibilities of all stakeholders and vested interests when designing whole-child approaches.

Clearly, recommendations must focus on tackling the rigid testing culture and the empowerment of teachers to implement PATL. First, the work to promote PATL must facilitate rich conversation among PEACH stakeholders. These conversations should be targeted at unravelling the root causes of the testing culture and teachers' disempowerment to implement PATL. This can be achieved by incorporating praxis social analysis (also called action research) in all PEACH and PATL training and awareness programmes to encourage in-depth and critical discussions about "whole-child" approaches. Second, PATL training must prioritize empowering teachers to implement PATL in schools. Empowering mechanisms may include the support and mentorship of teachers which allow for the organic development of skills, confidence and attitudes to

Table 1. A description of social ecological model levels applied to PATL.

Level	Description
Individual	Characteristics of the agents (pupils and teachers) within a school context that influence or enable health and educational behaviours and preferences, including knowledge, attitudes, behaviour, self-efficacy, developmental history, gender, age, religious identity, racial/ethnic identity, sexual orientation, economic status, financial resources, values, goals, expectations, literacy, stigma and others.
Interpersonal	Formal (and informal) social networks and social support systems within or sides the school that can influence or enable the agents' (pupils and teachers) to acquire or sustain preferred health and/or learning behaviours including family, friends, peers, religious networks, customs or traditions.
Community	Relationships among Isle of Wight organizations, institutions, and informational networks within defined boundaries, including the built environment (e.g. parks), village associations, community leaders, businesses, and transportation. A good example is the Partnership for Education, Attainment and Children's Health (PEACH).
Organizational	Schools' authority structures (rules and regulations and expectations as stipulated by inspectorate, e.g. Ofsted) for operations that affect how, or how well, teachers teach and assess and also how children learn and meet expected criteria in health (Chief Medical Officer guidelines) and educational (Ofsted) and empowerment of teachers to teach.
Policy/Enabling environment	Local (Isle of Wight), national and global laws and policies can be enabling or disenabling (e.g. new WHO policies on physical activity and health, whole-child approaches, PE and Sport Premium and Ofsted inspections and PEACH on the Isle of Wight).

develop their own realistic approaches for integrating PATL. In this research, teachers alluded to lower levels of physical activity intensity within classrooms which can be simpler to introduce and sustain. When teachers are empowered to take control over deciding how PATL is delivered and how often it is embedded, the impact of overall management of physical activity across the curriculum and the whole school can be positively addressed.

The case study of PEACH indicates the powerful effect of such an outlook which can be highly influential in positively affecting the management structure and, in turn, the introduction and monitoring of these physical activity opportunities within a holistic joined-up policy response. This paper indicates the need to create realistic and targeted policy responses regarding the nature and acceptance of PATL methods. Organizations such as EduMove Ltd, Maths of the Day, Premier League Primary Stars and Premier School Sport Coaching are aligning themselves with this shift which is reflected in the products and programmes being offered to address academic and health outcomes. A more collaborative, empowering and less technocratic management style are advocated but they will only result if Ofsted targets are incorporated and achieved via PATL. Thus, the authors support the PEACH ethos and agenda which advocates for a collaborative management approach that focuses on the empowerment of teachers and managers to deliver PATL.

Disclosure statement

The authors certify that they have affiliations with the two named organizations. However, the content is solely the responsibility of the authors and does not necessarily represent the official views of the EduMove Limited and Solent University.

Funding

This research reported in this publication was supported by EduMove Limited as one outcome of a knowledge and transfer partnership between EduMove Limited and Solent University.

ORCID

Henry Dorling http://orcid.org/0000-0003-1524-5820

References

Association for School and College Leaders. (2016). Retrieved February 2018, from https://www.ascl.org.uk/download.FB925165-E0CD-4148-A305D9BB5F1C6ED4.html

Babey, S. H., Wu, S., & Cohen, D. A. (2014). How can schools help youth increase physical activity? An economic analysis comparing school-based programs. *Preventive Medicine, 69*, S55–S60.

Best, J. R. (2010). Effects of physical activity on children's executive function: Contributions of experimental research on aerobic exercise. *Developmental Review, 30*(4), 331–351.

Bonwell, C. C., & Eison, J. A. (1991). *Active learning: Creating excitement in the classroom (1991 ASHE-ERIC Higher Education Reports)*. Washington, DC: ERIC Clearinghouse on Higher Education, The George Washington University.

Centre for Disease Control and Prevention. (2017, December 8). *The social ecological model: A framework for prevention*. Retrieved from http://www.cdc.gov/violenceprevention/overview/socialecologicalmodel.html

Chaddock, L., Hillman, C. H., Buck, S. M., & Cohen, N. J. (2011). Aerobic fitness and executive control of relational memory in preadolescent children. *Medical Science Sports Exercise, 43*(2), 344–349.

Chaput, J. P., Saunders, T. J., Mathieu, MÈ, Henderson, M., Tremblay, M. S., O'loughlin, J., & Tremblay, A. (2013). Combined associations between moderate to vigorous physical activity and sedentary behaviour with cardiometabolic risk factors in children. *Applied Physiology, Nutrition, and Metabolism, 38*(5), 477–483.

Delk, J., Springer, A., Kelder, S., & Grayless, M. (2014). Promoting teacher adoption of physical activity breaks in the classroom: Findings of the Central Texas CATCH middle school project. *Journal of School Health, 84*(11), 722–730.

Department for Culture Media and Sport. (2012). *Creating a sporting habit for life: A new youth sport strategy*. London: HMSO. Retrieved June 2018, from Government Services and Information: https://www.gov.uk/government/uploads/system/uploads/attachment_data/file/78318/creating_a_sporting_habit_for_life.pdf

Department of Education National curriculum assessments report. (2017). Retrieved May 2018, from https://assets.publishing.service.gov.uk/government/uploads/system/uploads/attachment_data/file/667372/SFR69_2017_text.pdf

Donnelly, J. E., Hillman, C. H., Castelli, D., Etnier, J. L., Lee, S., Tomporowski, P., ... Szabo-Reed, A. N. (2016). Physical activity, fitness, cognitive function, and academic achievement in children: A systematic review. *Medicine and Science in Sports and Exercise*, 48(6), 1197–1222.

EduMove Limited. (2017). *Isle of Wight research, monitoring and evaluation guide*. Southampton: Author.

Erickson, K. I., Hillman, C. H., & Kramer, A. F. (2015). Physical activity, brain, and cognition, current Opinion. *Behavioral Sciences*, 4, 27–32.

Erwin, H. E., Abel, M. G., Beighle, A., & Beets, M. W. (2011). Promoting children's health through physically active math classes: A pilot study. *Health Promotion Practice*, 12(2), 244–251.

Favre, L. R. (2009). Kinesthetic instructional strategies: Moving at-risk learners to higher levels. *Insights on Learning Disabilities*, 6(1), 29–35.

Golden, S. D., McLeroy, K. R., Green, L. W., Earp, J. A. L., & Lieberman, L. D. (2015). Upending the social ecological model to guide health promotion efforts toward policy and environmental change. *Health Education and Behaviour*, 42(1S), 8S–14S.

Gomez-Pinilla, F., & Hillman, C. (2013). The influence of exercise on cognitive abilities. *Comprehensive Physiology*, 3(1), 403–428.

Grieco, L. A., Jowers, E. M., Errisuriz, V. L., & Bartholomew, J. B. (2016). Physically active vs. sedentary academic lessons: A dose response study for elementary student time on task. *Preventive Medicine*, 89, 98–103.

Hillman, C. H., Erickson, K. I., & Kramer, A. F. (2008). Be smart, exercise your heart: Exercise effects on brain and cognition. *Nature Reviews Neuroscience*, 9(1), 58–65.

HM Government. (2015). *Sporting future: A new strategy for an active nation*. Retrieved June 2018, from https://www.gov.uk/government/uploads/system/uploads/attachment_data/file/486622/Sporting_Future_ACCESSIBLE.pdf

Holt, E., Bartee, T., & Heelan, K. (2013). Evaluation of a policy to integrate physical activity into the school day. *Journal of Physical Activity and Health*, 10(4), 480–487.

Isle of Wight School Survey. (2015). Retrieved from https://www.iwight.com/azservices/documents/2552-Children-and-young-peoples-survey-2015-final.pdf

Itin, C. M. (1999). Reasserting the philosophy of experiential education as a vehicle for change in the 21st century. *The Journal of Experiential Education*, 22(2), 91–98.

Jagosh, J., Bush, P. L., Salsberg, J., Macaulay, A. C., Greenhalgh, T., Wong, G., ... Pluye, P. (2015). A realist evaluation of community-based participatory research: Partnership synergy, trust building and related ripple effects. *BMC Public Health*, 15(1), 725.

Kibbe, D. L., Hackett, J., Hurley, M., et al. (2011). Ten years of Take 10!®: Integrating physical activity with academic concepts in elementary school classrooms. *Preventive Medicine*, 52, S43–S50.

Layne, P. C., & Lake, P. (Eds.) (2014). Global innovation of teaching and learning in higher education: Transgressing boundaries. *Methods in Molecular Biology*, 11, 3–4.

Lewallen, T. C., Hunt, H., Potts-Datema, W., Zaza, S., & Giles, W. (2015). The whole school, whole community, whole child model: A new approach for improving educational attainment and healthy development for students. *Journal of School Health*, 85(11), 729–739.

Manzano, A. (2016). The craft of interviewing in realist evaluation. *Evaluation*, 1–19. doi:10.1177/1356389016638615

Mwaanga, O., & Prince, S. (2014). *EduMove Maths toolkit for key stage 1*. Southampton: EduMove Limited.

Patton, M. (2003). Qualitative evaluation checklist. *Evaluation Checklists Project*. Retrieved from https://wmich.edu/evaluation/checklists

Pawson, R., & Tilley, N. (1997). *Realistic evaluation*. London: Sage.

Petty, G. (2009). *Evidence based teaching* (2nd ed.). Cheltenham: Nelson Thornes.

Sibley, B. A., & Etnier, J. (2003). The relationship between physical activity and cognition in children: A meta-analysis. *Pediatric Exercise Science*, 15(3), 243–256.

Tomporowski, P. D., Lambourne, K., & Okumura, M. S. (2011). Physical activity interventions and children's mental function: An introduction and overview. *Preventive Medicine*, 52, S3–S9.

Ward, D. S., Saunders, R., Felton, G. M., Williams, E., Epping, J. N., & Pate, R. R. (2006). Implementation of a school environment intervention to increase physical activity in high school girls. *Health Education Research*, 21(6), 896–910.

Westhorp, G. (2014). *Realist impact evaluation – An introduction*. London: A Methods Lab Publication, Overseas Development Institute.

Wold, B., & Mittelmark, M. B. (2018). Health-promotion research over three decades: The social-ecological model and challenges in implementation of interventions. *Scandinavian Journal of Public Health*, 46, 20–26.

Environmental sustainability and sport management education: bridging the gaps

Jeffrey Graham, Sylvia Trendafilova and Vassilios Ziakas

ABSTRACT
Although sport management higher education has recognized the need to include environmental sustainability in curricula, little is known about the scope and content of environmental sustainability curricula. This study conducted an inventory of environmental sustainability courses offered in sport management programs. A questionnaire was distributed to 553 faculty members from North American higher education institutions. Additionally, a panel of experts were interviewed about the benefits, drawbacks and challenges of including sustainability in a sport management curriculum. Findings reveal that very few programs currently have stand-alone courses dedicated to environmental sustainability in sport. There are significant barriers to adopting environmental sustainability in sport as a stand-alone course and as a module, which certainly makes developing stand-alone coursework a long-term process. However, these challenges have not stopped many programs from incorporating these topics into their programs of study in other creative ways. The paper suggests ways to overcome barriers and integrate environmental and sport management education.

Introduction

Sport organizations have recently started to pay considerable attention to environmental sustainability as part of their response to industry trends and policies of making the sport sector more sustainable (Trendafilova, Babiak, & Heinze, 2013). Correspondingly, sport management higher education, being a key stakeholder of the sport sector that prepares upcoming specialists to ideally develop sport in a sustainable manner, has recognized the need to include environmental sustainability in curricula (Pfahl, 2015). This can enable future professionals to develop skills and be equipped with the tools to manage the environmental impacts of sport. However, little is known about environmental sustainability curricula in sport management and how topics of sustainability can best be integrated into the standard coursework.

Therefore, the purpose of this study was to conduct an inventory of current environmental sustainability courses offered in sport management programs. Additionally, we sought the input of a panel of faculty who are experts in the area of environmental sustainability in the sport context to give insight into these programmatic trends. The paper first reviews the literature on the resonance of environmental sustainability for the sport sector and the underlying issues, gaps and perspectives in sport management education. The methods employed in the study are explained followed by the presentation of results and a discussion of key findings.

Resonance of environmental sustainability in the sport context

The sport industry has recently witnessed a shift in which organizations have begun to place considerable importance on becoming more environmentally conscientious at the collegiate, professional and international levels (Babiak & Trendafilova, 2011; Casper, Pfahl, & McSherry, 2012; Greenhalgh, LeCrom, & Dwyer, 2015; Trendafilova et al., 2013). For example, there have been numerous on-campus efforts in collegiate sports such as the development of recycling programs and increased attention given to the issue at campus recreation and associated sporting events (Casper, Pfahl, & McCullough, 2014; Pfahl, 2015). Similarly, at the professional level, major sport leagues in North America are collaborating with the National Resources Defense Council (NRDC) in order to implement systems, structures and specific programs to engage in greening initiatives (Trendafilova & Babiak, 2013). Furthermore, at the international level, Australia has a number of leaders in environmental building and design practices within the sport sector. Many of the efforts were inspired by the 2000 Sydney Olympics, and since then, the Sydney Olympic Park Authority (SOPA) have expanded the design and use practices to all those residing within its community (Trendafilova, McCullough, et al., 2014). These examples demonstrate how important sustainability has become in the sport context. Accordingly, environmental initiatives within the sport industry are taken as part of community outreach that encourages sport personnel to give back to the local community (Carroll & Shabana, 2010; Pfahl, 2015). This underlines essentially a movement away from exploiting the environment to one of being responsible and valuing the protection of the natural environment (Glicken & Fairbrother, 2000).

However, environmental sustainability is not adopted with the same pace and determination along different sport sectors and domains. For example, as Mallen, Adams, Stevens, and Thompson (2010) observe, environmental sustainability is slowly gaining credibility and becoming a priority at sport facilities in North America, although these facilities may lack the financial investment to support quick and impactful advancements in sustainability initiatives. Similarly, Trendafilova, Kellison, and Spearman (2014) examined the environmental practices of small-scale sport facilities and concluded that multiple challenges prevent sport facility managers from adopting environmentally sustainable initiatives such as lack of education, the age of the facility, limited funding, and insufficient human power. In this regard, deficiencies in the adoption and application of environmental initiatives in the sport industry illustrate that there is a need for a broader framework to encompass the integration of environmental sustainability into different sport industry sectors and contexts. Moreover, Mallen et al. (2010) reviewed the sport management literature and discovered the paucity of research regarding environmental sustainability. They pointed out multiple gaps including challenges, barriers, best practices, competencies and education.

Environmental sustainability and sport management education

A foundation for the development of a comprehensive understanding of environmental sustainability across the sport industry is education. In particular, the natural environment provides opportunities for experiential learning, as it touches all aspects of organizational operations in both strategic and operational ways (Pfahl, 2015). The inclusion of the natural environment within various components of a sport management curriculum ultimately develops a student's theoretical and applied understanding of what managing a sport organization involves (Pfahl, 2015). Consequently, a number of scholars have expressed the need for students to be educated on the topic of sustainability. This call cuts across the sport management, tourism and recreation sectors (Casper & Pfahl, 2012; Hales & Jennings, 2017).

On a broader level, a growing recognition has emerged that environmental sustainability should be embedded into higher education aimed at changing students' thinking and behavior regarding the environment (Mitchell & Walinga, 2017; Thomas, 2009). Hales and Jennings (2017) suggest that even though progress in education for sustainable development has been limited, there has been some improvement in sustainable practices in higher education in terms of government-led incentives, socio-economic expectations of education, partnership platforms, student leadership and experiential practice in the curriculum. However, these changes have not been sustained in universities (Tilbury, 2011). That is, most higher education programs do not have a critical dimension to the extent that the major socio-economic and environmental problems are pedagogically addressed in order to produce more reflexive practitioners (Hales & Jennings, 2017). As Thomas (2009) found, higher education should develop student problem-solving skills and the ability of students to assess environmental impacts, initiate and manage environmental change, identify the important attributes of the environment, and acquire knowledge regarding sustainable development while encouraging them to adopt values conducive to environment.

In this respect, Hales and Jennings (2017) maintain that learner-centered, critical and transformative approaches are important in facilitating the development of more complex ways of thinking about sustainability. Similarly, it has been suggested that there is an urgent need to educate students through comparative analysis that is creative, effective, and acceptable to the transformative principles of sustainable development (Liu, Horng, Chou, & Yung-Chuan Huang, 2017). Along these lines, Hales and Jennings (2017) argue that transformational learning constitutes a key pedagogical approach suited to sustainability in the classroom as it facilitates the adaptive capacity of individuals and groups to uncertainty. As such, they emphasize that the need for more attention to sustainability education needs to be imbued with a conscious focus on offering a transformative educational experience that enables students to develop the capacity for solutions to complex problems.

Within sport management education, environmental sustainability remains tentative and dispersed across different courses and subjects. Yet, its importance has been highlighted in order for becoming a distinct part of sport management higher education programs. This argument lies at the reasoning that the sport management curriculum is a pre-hire anticipatory socialization stage in which students are preparing themselves for personal and career challenges within the sport industry (Pfahl, 2015). As such, their experience affects developing environmental perceptions and understanding of environmental issues, as well as their inclination to take action (Casper & Pfahl, 2012). This brings to the fore the potential of sport management education to shape future actions in the sport industry (Pfahl, 2015). Incorporating the environment into sport management education can shape assumptions, encourage innovative strategies and options that drive the advancement of environmental sustainability (Mallen et al., 2010). The challenge then is how environmental sustainability can be effectively incorporated into the sport management curriculum.

Mallen et al. (2010), guiding sport management educators in embedding environmental sustainability throughout the curriculum, put forward three central themes. First, a shift in thinking is needed to foster a vision of advances to managing effectively the business–nature interface by changing the ways of thinking about doing business (Sharma, Pablo, & Vredenburg, 1999). Second, developing responsiveness about the environment is important for shaping managerial and operational performance strategies. Third, determining the appropriate environmental impact of sport could alter the direction of sport for environmental responsibility. This type of change in thinking may require a transformative learning experience (Mezirow, 2003, 2009). Transformative learning is when problematic frames of reference, such as fixed mindsets, sets of assumptions or expectations, are challenged and encouraged to become more inclusive, discriminating, open, reflective and emotionally able to change (Mezirow, 2009). Pfahl (2015) argues for a shift from focusing on single aspects of environmental initiatives, such as disposal waste, recycling or renewable energy systems, to a holistic approach and balanced understanding of environmental issues in the sport context in order to enable students see what actions are needed. This argument is based on the idea that such a broad approach should seek to connect intellect, application, philosophy and emotion into an immersive set of applied experiences that result in the necessary transformative learning experience (Mezirow, 2003, 2009; Pfahl, 2015).

Consequently, a holistic perspective on environmental sustainability within sport management education can be grounded in transformational learning. From this perspective, it is pivotal to enable the adaptive capacity of students for working and living in an uncertain world where the challenges and potential solutions are directed by the contextual demands of the lived experience of the students. This can help develop more complex thinking about sustainability, thereby facilitating critically aware, reflexive, autonomous learners (Hales & Jennings, 2017). On this basis, a fundamental premise to transformational change needed to address the complex problems of sustainability is the development of concepts that change the way students think and act (Hales & Jennings, 2017). In this vein, the nexus of relationships and issues between sport and the natural environment can be more effectively revealed, examined and understood by students.

Methods

The data collection process incorporated a survey and interviews. Prior to any data collection, an IRB approval was acquired. Initially, a questionnaire was distributed to 552 faculty in North American higher education institutions, which offered a sport management degree (either undergraduate or graduate). These institutions were identified through the North American Society for Sport Management affiliated program page. The questionnaire was circulated online via publicly available faculty email addresses, which were collected manually using institutional directories. The survey contained 28 questions, which were developed based on the review of literature and in consultation with an expert in the area of environmental sustainability in sport. Of the 28 questions in the survey, 6 were open-ended and solicited a response from the participant. Two follow-up invitations to participate in the survey were sent out over the span of three weeks. At the conclusion of data collection, 123 respondents had completed the questionnaire, providing for a response rate of 22.28%. The moderately low response rate limits the generalizability for the study as those programs that did not respond to the survey request may be systematically different from those that did respond to the survey. Even so, the responses do provide insight into the current practices of programs of a number of different universities offering sport management instruction.

In addition to the survey, a panel of experts in the area of environmental sustainability in sport were invited to participate in an interview about coursework in sport management, and more specifically environmental sustainability. For the purposes of this study, experts were identified as university faculty members who are currently highly engaged in research involving environmental sustainability in sport, and whose work has historically been most cited within academia in regard to the focal topic. The panel consisted of six individuals, two of which are associated with institutions outside the United States. The interview protocol contained five main questions, including the following:

- In your experience, do you feel there is a significant and important relationship between sport organizations and environmental sustainability?
- For students entering and starting a career in sport management, why might learning about environmental sustainability be important? What disciplines within sport management have the strongest connection with environmental sustainability? (e.g. facilities, marketing, event management, etc.?)
- How might instructors approach building a stand-alone environmental sustainability course dedicated to sport management?
- How might an instructor dedicate a module within a course to environmental sustainability? Would such a module be useful?
- Should environmental sustainability become one of the pillars of sport management education?

Follow-up questions provided for more in-depth information. The interviews lasted about 30 minutes and were conducted individually with each participant. The goal of these interviews was to gain insight into the importance, benefits and challenges of including environmental sustainability in the sport management curriculum.

The quantitative data were analyzed with descriptive statistics to find trends and patterns in the responses. For the qualitative panel interviews, data were categorized with a deductive coding in which the investigators looked specifically for the benefits, drawbacks, and challenges the participants addressed. The research team reviewed and analyzed both data sets (i.e. the qualitative and quantitative data) independently. Results from the survey as well as the expert panel interviews are listed in the following section.

Results

Survey results

Results from the survey are summarized in Table 1. These figures represent the descriptive data for whether a full course or specific module was offered and at what level (undergraduate or graduate), when the course/module was offered, what prevents a course/module from being offered and if the program has plans for offering a course/module in the future. For stand-alone courses, it is instructive to note

Table 1. Descriptive statistics for programs offering environmental sustainability in sport.

Item	Stand-alone course n	Stand-alone course %	Module within parent course n	Module within parent course %
Content offered				
Yes	10	8.94	84	71.19
No	112	91.06	34	28.82
Class level				
Undergraduate	1	10	28	35
Graduate	4	40	16	20
Both undergraduate and graduate	5	50	36	45
Timing of offering				
Every semester	1	10	32	40.00
Once per academic year	5	50	45	56.25
Every other academic year	4	40	3	3.75
What prevents it from being offered				
Lack of student interest	9	8.49	1	3.31
Lack of faculty interest	25	23.58	14	43.75
Lack of resources	32	30.19	6	18.75
Lack of admin support	2	1.89	1	3.13
Other not listed	38	35.85	10	31.25
Plans to offer course in future				
Definitely yes	0	0.00	1	3.13
Probably yes	10	9.35	3	9.38
Might or might not	23	21.50	10	31.25
Probably not	57	53.27	13	40.63
Definitely not	17	15.89	5	15.63

that in every case in which a stand-alone course in environmental sustainability in sport was offered, it was instructed by a faculty member with expertise in this area. Overall, 8.94% of respondents reported offering a stand-alone course, and 71.19% offered some content related to environmental sustainability in sport as a module within a parent course.

The parent courses for the environmental sustainability in sport modules varied. Some respondents reported that this content was taught in sport marketing (8.70%) and financial aspects of sport (2.90%). Other respondents reported the module being taught in special topics courses (5.80%) or issues and trends in sport courses (10.14%). The majority of modules were found in sport and event management (21.74%) and sport facility management (35.51%). In addition, 15.22% of respondents reported that this content was covered in another course that was not listed among the options (15.22%). In the comment box provided in the survey, the respondents listed courses including introduction to sport management, sport management foundations, sport and tourism, sport and society, sport policy, global perspectives in sport, ethics in sport, sport governance, sponsorship in sport and strategic management in sport.

Respondents were also asked to provide brief feedback about the benefits and challenges of offering this material as a stand-alone course and/or as a module. In addition, if respondents noted that they did not offer a course in environmental sustainability in sport, they were prompted to comment on the factors that prevented them from offering the content as a module and/or as a stand-alone course. In general, respondents who discussed the benefits of offering environmental sustainability as a stand-alone course or as a module mentioned increased levels of understanding, awareness, and importance about the relationship between sport and the environment. In addition, some reported that offering environmental sustainability material as a module within a different course allowed them to see their primary content (e.g. marketing) through a new and valuable lens. Some of the challenges brought up in the comments focused on the lack of interest by students, underdeveloped materials to draw from and not having enough time to fit the material in during a semester. Some respondents also mentioned how students in certain regions are unfamiliar with the concept of environmental sustainability in general, which makes introducing topics and discussing the content somewhat of a challenge. For those respondents who did not offer coursework in environmental sustainability, the lack of time, faculty members, general expertise, accreditation requirements, research and general development in the field all were major factors preventing programs from offering environmental sustainability in sport as a stand-alone or module within a different course. Table 2 provides a summary of this feedback with representative quotes.

Interview results

Results from the interviews with experts revolve around three key issues: (1) the role and importance of sustainability in the context of sport, (2) challenges associated with implementing coursework in sustainability and (3) the future of environmental sustainability in the sport management curriculum. These three issues are discussed in more detail in the following subsections.

Role and importance of teaching sustainability in sport

Each of the panel experts discussed the role and importance of sustainability in the realm of sport and consequently the importance of educating students on the topic. As participants indicated, the relationship between sport organizations and the environment is reciprocal. In other words, sport impacts the natural environment and at the same time the natural environment impacts sport. For example, one

Table 2. Benefits and challenges of offering environmental sustainability in sport content.

Themes	Stand-alone course	Module within parent course
Benefits of offering the course/module	"They have certainly gained a much better understanding of the concept of sustainability and how it relates to sport. My hope is that they will use that information in their future decision making." "It is important to teach emerging topics like environmental sustainability to student to embrace future trends in the industry."	"Students are aware of the importance of environmental sustainability in sport tourism" "Generates awareness of the impact sustainability has on the operation of facilities and events." "Yes, it is a great opportunity for students to approach marketing from a different perspective."
Challenges of offering the course/module	"Not all students believe this is important when paired against revenue generation or keeping stakeholders (coaches) happy." "Students are not brought up with the concept of sustainability in this region so it is a bit of a challenge to open them up to the concept in the first place"	"The text used in the course only briefly discusses environmental sustainability." "The students don't seem interested" "Finding the expertise to teach apart from simple concepts." "Lack of time during semester long course."
Obstacles preventing offering course/module	"Lack of available faculty" "Limited academic class space" "Not evaluated as important as a separate course" "Not part of COSMA" "Sports focus is still new"	"Lack of research" "Lack of expertise in this area" "We only offer a few sport management courses and the courses are already packed with crucial content"

participant pointed out, "There needs to be a response that echoes the call from the United Nations to integrate sustainability development goals into the sport industry." Another respondent connected the importance of environmental sustainability in sport with the need to teach this content in higher education:

> There needs to be a paradigm shift in our professional preparation of sport management students to understand the simplicity to consider more environmentally sustainable decisions across organizations. This can include and primarily apply to facility and event operations. However, there are more considerations that should be factored into sport management education including strategy, marketing, sponsorship, and law.

One of the panel respondents noted that a detailed background in the exact science of environmental sustainability may not be necessary to teach the course or convey the importance of it, saying:

> Every student, no matter his or her particular career goals, needs to understand his or her environmental impact when working in sport ... becoming an environmental scientists or expert in green chemistry is not what is needed. Mindfulness of issues is a starting point. Mindfulness leading to application or practice in ways that minimize environmental issues to the greatest extent possible is the goal.

Another respondent connected the idea of the importance of learning about environmental sustainability in sport with ways this will help students be more competitive in the job market, by stating the following:

> Learning about sustainability is important for students interested in sport management careers, especially those related to events, venues, and operations. It is important, because it represents a "new" skill and one that older venue managers may be less inclined to pursue due to a lack of familiarity of best current practices.

In summary, experts in the field of environmental sustainability in sport independently agreed not only that the topic is important, but also that students should at least be exposed and become aware of the connection between sport and the environment. For example, a participant shared:

> I think that every sport management student should have an understanding of the importance of environmental sustainability, an understanding of the impact that environmental protection plays within sport (and

sport operations), and the understanding of how to implement environmental sustainability (internally and externally) as future sport managers.

This comment clearly emphasizes the purpose of educating students in the area of environmental sustainability in the sport industry as understanding the role of environmental protection within sport and how to implement it. This leads to the next issue of implementing coursework on the topic.

Challenges associated with implementing coursework in sustainability

The second issue the panel experts discussed related to the challenges associated with implementing courses/modules specifically focused on sustainability in sport. Participants agreed that the lack of faculty expertise in the area of sustainability within the department could be a challenge in offering a stand-alone course. For example, one participant indicated: "I would see this being hard for those who have a base knowledge and interest in the subject." However, experts suggested that a module in nearly every sport management course can be implemented. For example, one of the participants pointed out: "Environmental sustainability should be integrated into every component of sport management education as it is not a stand-alone topic." Specifically, in a marketing class, a discussion can take place revolving around campaigns that are designed to change other behaviors like recycling more or taking public transit to games, and a finance class can discuss the payback period for facility upgrades as well as cost savings due to adoption of more environmentally responsible practices.

Another important component related to course design was the idea that coursework should provide for some hands-on experience. One of the panelists recommended that: "It would be hard to keep the focus of students without an integrative experiential learning experience." Additionally, a suggestion was made to use case studies as a way of introducing sustainability issues in various courses. Lastly, an interesting challenge related to coursework in environmental sustainability was the lack of published materials as one panel expert summed it up:

> Environmental sustainability should be an aspect that is incorporated into classes, but this will not happen until materials are readily made available to instructors through texts, modules, case studies, etc. If there are these materials then it is more likely that environmental sustainability becomes more prevalent in our sport management education.

Although several challenges were identified, the overall vibe was that environmental sustainability would soon find its place as another pillar of sport management education.

Future of environmental sustainability in sport management curriculum

There was no doubt about the importance of environmental sustainability becoming one of the pillars of sport management education as it encompasses all areas of sport management (e.g. facility, events, marketing, law, ethics, finance). The consent among the panel experts was that by addressing the negative environmental impact of sport, the field of sport management has the potential to make a cultural shift for the next generation. For example, one participant pointed out:

> The high profile of sport means that it has had, historically, no choice but to be a platform for social issues to manifest themselves (e.g., race, gender, economics, politics, now environment). This important social standing and contract should be embraced and not feared.

Similarly, another participant shared:

> Sport managers must account for environmental concerns as much as they do financial issues or personal well-being. It is an organizational DNA element and not just a community/CRS initiative designed for goodwill.

When asked whether environmental sustainability should become one of the pillars of sport management education, participants shared:

> Absolutely – sport must do their part to safeguard the natural environment for use today and in the future of sport. The communication capabilities of sport make it a terrific vehicle to aid in developing solutions to the environmental issues.
>
> Sport is a key influential voice in the discussion and learning about environmental issues, especially when applied to educational settings (e.g., schools).

It is encouraging to see that experts in the area of sustainability not only see the power of sport as a vehicle for social change and a platform for environmental education, but to feel the optimism in their voice that environmental sustainability would become a new pillar in the sport management curriculum.

Discussion

The above results suggest that indeed environmental sustainability, especially in the context of sport management, is still a developing field of instruction. Very few programs currently have stand-alone courses dedicated to environmental sustainability in sport, and feedback from the questionnaire also indicates that there are also very few programs looking to add a dedicated environmental sustainability in sport course. There are significant barriers to adopting environmental sustainability in sport as a stand-alone course and as a module (e.g. acquiring materials, building expertise, finding examples, making programmatic space, etc.), which certainly makes developing stand-alone coursework a long-term process. However, these challenges have not stopped many programs from incorporating these topics into their programs of study in other creative ways.

As indicated by the interview participants, and supported by results from the survey, in cases in which resources are not available for a stand-alone course in environmental sustainability, it would be logical and natural to incorporate sustainability topics into already existing courses (e.g. sport event management, sport facility, financial aspects of sport, sport marketing, legal aspects of sport, strategic management of sport organizations, etc.). What is important to note here is that such integration would provide for a tangible, practical, application-based and hands-on type of approach to environmental sustainability knowledge. For example, instructors in facility management may approach a module covering environmental sustainability by asking students to research trends and practices currently being utilized by recreation, collegiate and professional sport organizations. Alternatively, instructors in a sport and event management course might ask students to engage in a case study in which they evaluate the positive and negative efforts regarding environmental sustainability at a local sporting event. This approach to application and hands-on learning would help students to engage in the topic in a way that would allow them to become aware of best practices in the industry.

Although the application of this type of knowledge is critical, approaching environmental sustainability from a different angle may also be beneficial to students. That is, instructors might engage students by asking questions about the duty of care and the responsibility to the natural environment that all stakeholders (e.g. athletic departments, fans, participants, employees, event organizers, etc.) involved in the delivery and consumption of sport have. Courses such as ethics in sport, sociology of sport, sport and social issues, global perspectives in sport or sport policy may be particularly suited for this type of instruction and discussion. For example, an instructor in a global perspective of sport course might require students to research the harmful environmental effects of mega-sporting events, especially those taking place in underdeveloped regions, and discuss the consequences of these actions. Or, an instructor in sport policy might have students study the focal events leading up to the International Olympic Committee adopting environmentalism as the third pillar of Olympism. By challenging students to think about environmental sustainability at a higher level in this way, future industry practitioners will be better prepared to understand the complex and multidimensional nature that dealing with environmental sustainability in sport requires.

The data from the quantitative portion of the study highlighted the concern from some faculty about not being an expert in the field of environmental sustainability. However, a detailed background in the exact science of environmental sustainability may not be necessary to teach material related to environmental sustainability or convey the importance of the topic. In general, by adopting an integrative approach and incorporating environmental sustainability as a module into every component of sport management education, instructors could eliminate many of the barriers preventing programs from offering the content as a stand-alone course, such as the need to have the specific content expertise in the area. Instructors can leverage outside experts to visit the class as guest speakers to deliver this content. Such guest lectures could be delivered by faculty from areas of expertise in natural resources management, ecotourism, environmental impact assessment or even practitioners in the field. In other words, involving units on campus that are active in the area of sustainability would treat campus as a learning laboratory with athletics being the focal point and provide a great opportunity for students to learn about sustainability from different points of view.

Overall, there are multiple opportunities for instructing students in sport management programs about the need for and importance of environmental sustainability. Ultimately, it falls on the faculty in sport management programs to instruct and educate students on the ways in which they can deliver high-quality sporting experiences, while also caring for the environment. By creatively working to overcome the current challenges preventing many programs from providing instruction on environmental sustainability in sport, students will be better prepared to enter the industry as they start their careers, and more knowledgeable as their careers progress and they transition into the individuals who will be leading the industry into the future.

Conclusion

This study addressed the pressing need to bridge the underlying gaps between environmental sustainability and sport management education if it is to re-shape the future of the sport sector. While the status of environmental sustainability within sport management higher education curricula remains secondary, the sport industry is becoming progressively interested and active in environmental sustainability. Subsequently, sport management programs, given the resource constraints, need to find creative ways to integrate topics of environment protection and stewardship in their offering. Incorporating discussions of environmental sustainability into the curriculum can challenge students to think of non-traditional ways of delivering sport while caring for the environment. Even programs with limited faculty, resources or expertise in the area of environmental sustainability can still weave this topic into existing coursework.

Drawing upon the findings of this study, future research may focus on examining the coursework components and teaching/learning strategies that can optimize the integration of sport management and environmental education. Such an inquiry needs to develop a holistic framework that encompasses a balanced understanding of environmental issues in the sport context while designing transformative learning experiences for students. Accordingly, a holistic perspective on environmental sustainability within sport management education can be based on transformational learning and change aimed at nurturing the adaptive capacity of students for developing more complex thinking about sustainability. From this perspective, the intricate relationship between sustainability and environmental impacts of sport can be addressed by changing the affective, cognitive and behavioral frame of students' attitudes towards "what is needed" for building a sustainable sporting future.

Disclosure statement

No potential conflict of interest was reported by the authors.

References

Babiak, K., & Trendafilova, S. (2011). CSR and environmental responsibility: Motives and pressures to adopt green management practices. *Corporate Social Responsibility and Environmental Management*, 18, 11–24.

Carroll, A. B., & Shabana, K. M. (2010). The business case for corporate social responsibility: A review of concepts, research and practice. *International Journal of Management Reviews*, 12, 85–105.

Casper, J. M., & Pfahl, M. E. (2012). Environmental behavior frameworks of sport and recreation undergraduate students. *Sport Management Educational Journal*, 6, 8–20.

Casper, J. M., Pfahl, M. E., & McCullough, B. (2014). Intercollegiate sport and the environment: Examining fan engagement based on athletics department sustainability efforts. *Journal of Issues in Intercollegiate Athletics*, 7, 65–91.

Casper, J., Pfahl, M., & McSherry, M. (2012). Athletics department awareness and action regarding the environment: A chapter of NCAA athletics department sustainability practices. *Journal of Sport Management*, 26, 11–29.

Glicken, J., & Fairbrother, A. (2000). Environment and social values. *Human and Ecological Risk Assessment*, 4, 779–786.

Greenhalgh, G., LeCrom, C. W., & Dwyer, B. (2015). Going green? The behavioral impact of a sport and the environment course. *Journal of Contemporary Athletics*, 9(1), 49–59.

Hales, R., & Jennings, G. (2017). Transformation for sustainability: The role of complexity in tourism students' understanding of sustainable tourism. *Journal of Hospitality, Leisure, Sport & Tourism Education*, 21, 185–194. doi:10.1016/j.jhlste.2017.08.001

Liu, C.-H., Horng, J.-S., Chou, S.-F., & Yung-Chuan Huang, Y.-C. (2017). Analysis of tourism and hospitality sustainability education with co-competition creativity course planning. *Journal of Hospitality, Leisure, Sport & Tourism Education*, 21, 88–100. doi:10.1016/j.jhlste.2017.08.008

Mallen, C., Adams, L., Stevens, J., & Thompson, L. (2010). Environmental sustainability in sport facility management: A Delphi study. *European Sport Management Quarterly*, 10(3), 367–389.

Mezirow, J. (2003). Transformative learning as discourse. *Journal of Transformative Education*, 1(1), 58–63.

Mezirow, J. (2009). An overview on transformative learning. In K. Illeris (Ed.), *Contemporary theories of learning* (pp. 90–105). New York, NY: Routledge.

Mitchell, I. K., & Walinga, J. (2017). The creative imperative: The role of creativity, creative problem solving and insight as key drivers for sustainability. *Journal of Cleaner Production*, 140, 1872–1884.

Pfahl, M. E. (2015). Teaching sport management and the natural environment. In J. M. Casper & M. E. Pfahl (Eds.), *Sport management and the natural environment: Theory and practice* (pp. 29–37). Abingdon: Routledge.

Sharma, S., Pablo, A., & Vredenburg, H. (1999). Corporate environmental responsiveness strategies: The importance of issue interpretation and organizational context. *The Journal of Applied Behavioral Science*, 35, 87–108.

Thomas, I. (2009). Critical thinking, transformative learning, sustainable education, and problem-based learning in universities. *Journal of Transformative Education*, 7(3), 245–264.

Tilbury, D. (2011). Higher education for sustainability: A global overview of commitment and progress. In GUNI (Ed.), *Higher education in the world 4. Higher education's commitment to sustainability: From understanding to action* (pp. 18–28). Barcelona: GUNI.

Trendafilova, S., & Babiak, K. (2013). Understanding strategic corporate environmental responsibility in professional sport. *International Journal of Sport Management and Marketing*, 13(1–2), 1–26.

Trendafilova, S., Babiak, K., & Heinze, K. (2013). Corporate social responsibility and environmental sustainability: Why professional sport is greening the playing field. *Sport Management Review, 16*(3), 298–313.

Trendafilova, S., Kellison, T. B., & Spearman, L. (2014). Environmental sustainability in sport facilities in East Tennessee. *Journal of Facility Planning, Design and Management, 2*(1), 1–11.

Trendafilova, S., McCullough, B., Pfahl, M., Nguyen, S. N., Casper, J., & Picariello, M. (2014). Environmental sustainability in sport: Current state and future trends. *Global Journal on Advances Pure and Applied Sciences, 3*, 9–14.

Index

Note: **Bold** page numbers refer to tables and *italic* page numbers refer to figures.

ACT, Inc. 97; "Work Readiness Standards and Benchmarks" report 97
Active Forests 74, 76
active labour market programmes (ALMP) 97
Active Labour Markets (ALM) 96
active learning 156
Active People Survey (2005–2015) 63
Active Smarter Kids (Norway) 154
Adams, L. 169
agency costs 10, 16, 18
agency theory 10, 19
Agha, N. 140, 147
The Alliance 65–6, 73
apprenticeships 98
Association for School and College Leaders 149
associative democracy 24, 27, 35
Australian Bureau of Meteorology 46
Australian Government Department of Environment 46
autonomy 26, 71, 91, 97, 101–2, 107–9

Babey, S. H. 154
Bairner, A. 144–5
Bambra, C. 96–7
Barker, J. 107
Basic Psychological Needs (BPN) 101, 104
Basic Psychological Needs theory (BPNT) 97, 101, 109
Baumeister, R. F. 101
BBC "Get Inspired" clip 127–8
BBC super-movers programme 154
Beck, U. 70–1
Berkhout, F. 39, 45, **52**, 53–4
'Big Society' 24
Binder, D. 138, 146, 148
Blair, Tony 138
BMX: building legacy for 133–4; legacy projects, methods used in evaluation of **121**; reaching the "hard to reach" with 131–2
BMX programme legacy evaluation: methods and challenges of 119–23; process and procedures in 121–2; stakeholder in-depth interviews 122–3
BMX World SuperCross event, Manchester 115–34; coaches perspective 130–1; communities and sport development impacts 117–34; event legacies and non-mega events 117–34; from event to engagement 127–31; impacts of BMX event-based programme with PRU based young people 127–31; learning about legacy, leverage and impacts from BMX projects 132–4; legacy plans and 118–19; mechanisms, contexts and outcomes 131–2; methods and challenges of BMX programme legacy evaluation 119–23; overview 115–17; process outcomes and consequences 131–2; programme staff and coaches'/volunteers' perspectives of the impact of Street BMX on regular BMX sessions 125–7; reaching "hard to reach" with BMX 131–2; Street BMX programme impacts and mechanisms 123–5; working with more challenging groups 130–1; young participants perspectives on BMX experience 128–30
Boersma, S. N. 106
bonding costs 10
Boyatzis, R. E. 104
British Mountaineering Council 62
British Olympic Association 142, 149–50
British Paralympic Association 142, 149–50
Brookes, S. 117
Broyer, G. 63
Brudney, J. L. 10
Bruening, J. E. 99
Bryman, A. 144
Burnham, Andy 115

Caers, R. 10
Cairns, Linda 146
Cameron, David 1
capital: human 97, 99; psychological 97; social 97, 101–2

Carer's Allowance (CA) 97
Carmichael, F. 115
Central Council of Physical Recreation 66
Centre for Social Justice 100
Chalip, L. 8, 117
charity 65, 84; religious 86; in Swedish social policy 84; value-based 90
charity organisations 83
Chartered Institute for the Management of Sport and Physical Activity 28
Chatziefstathiou, D. 143, 146
Chen, S. 138, 141
CIMSPA survey 28
classroom management: PATL and 162–4; poor 163; teacher and 162–4
climate change: impacts of 39–41; as management issue for sport stadia 41–4; MASS organizations and adaptation to 52–4; organizational perceptions of 46; organizational uncertainty about public policy for 47
climate-dependant agriculture 42
climate-dependant sport 40–1
climate-dependant tourism 42
climate-dependent assets 40, 42
climate-dependent industries 42
CLOA 23
Closed Loop Recycling system 49
Coakley, J. 99
Coalter, F. 99–100
Coburn, A. 143, 148
Coca Cola 143
Coe, Lord Sebastian 137–8, 143–4
Cohen, D. A. 154
Collins, M. 99, 117
commercialisation 143
Commonwealth Games (CWG) 118
communities and sport development impacts 117–34
community action organisation (CAO) 28, **29**
community groups 23, 24, 37, 75, 83, 119, 123
community sport organizations (CSOs) 11
competence: defined 101; in gaining new skills 101; PATL and 158; as psychological need 105–6
Compulsory Competitive Tendering (CCT) 24
corporate social responsibility (CSR) 84
corporate sponsorships 7
costs, trusts ability to reduce 29–31
Cotrufo, R. J. 99
County Sport Partnerships (CSPs) 65
Crabtree, B. F. 104
Creating a Sporting Habit for Life (DCMS) 74
Crocker, P. R. 101
Crum, B. 70

Davis, J. H. 10
deCharms, R. 101

Deci, E. L. 101
Delk, J. 154
democratic deficit 36
Department for Education (UK) 141, 145, 147
Department of Culture, Media and Sport (DCMS) 65, 73, 75, 115
Department of the Environment Forestry and Rural Affairs (DEFRA) 66
Descartes, René 156
Dey, P. 25
Diaper, Mike 146
Disability Premium 97
disadvantaged communities: leverage of sport events for legacy in 115–34
Donaldson, L. 10
Donnelly, J. E. 155, 164
"double bottom line" 25
Doyle, Jackie Brock 146, 148
dualism 156
Dunning, E. 72

Eastland Leisure Trust (ELT) 116
education: physical activity and 155–6; sport management 168–78
EduMove Ltd 157–8; classroom-based interventions 164; lessons 160
EduMove M.E.E.L (Move Enjoy, Engage, Learn) criteria 164
Edwards, Jonathan 146–7
Elias, N. 72
elite club CSR representative 85
ELT BMX Supercross legacy programmes 119
employment subsidies 98
energy-intensive industries 40
environmental sustainability: benefits and challenges of offering environmental sustainability in sport content **174**; challenges associated with implementing coursework in 175; curricula 168; descriptive statistics for programs offering **172**; future in sport management curriculum 175–6; resonance of, in sport context 169; role and importance of teaching sustainability in sport 173–5; and sport management education 168–78
Euro-centrism 143
European Commission 44
European Outdoor Group (EOG) State of Trade report 61
event-based Development programme 119
event legacies and non-mega events 117–34
Executive Headteacher Group 157
"extreme weather events" 42

Facebook 123
factory owner 85, 91

Fairley, S. 140
feebased programing 7
Fenwick, J. 27
Festival of Social Science event 28
first modernity 70–1
Forestry Commission 65, 74
foundation executive 85, 87–8
foundation manager 85, 89
Freeman, H. E. 132
Friedman, A. L. 139
Fuller, R. D. 99
Fusch, P. I. 103

Game Plan policy 157
Gazley, B. 10
gender discrimination 143
George Abbot School 146
Get Set programme 137–51
GHG mitigation 41, 53
Gibbon, J. 27
Gibson, H. 140
Gilchrist, P. 117
Give us a Chance (GUAC) (consortium of social landlords) 100
Glasgow Housing Association project 96–110; autonomy 107–9; literature review 97–102; relatedness 106–7; role of the Housing Association 109; workreadiness/competence 105–6
goodwill: motives of 89–90; political potential of 90–2; position of 87–9
Gove, Michael 141–2
governmental rationality 83, 86–7
Grayless, M. 154
Green, M. 141, 147
greenhouse gas (GHG) emissions 39–40, 40–2, 47–52, 55
Grix, J. 115
Gunnell, K. E. 101

Hales, R. 170
Hardey, M. 70
Hartmann, D. 99
Haudenhuyse, R. 99, 117
Heere, B. 98
Hefetz, A. 10
Henry, I. 138, 141
"high-salience" industries 42
Hills, S. 98
Hodgkinson, I. R. 26, 35
Holland, J. 71
Holloway, I. 71, 72
Houlihan, B. 99, 141, 147
House of Commons Education Committee inquiry 139, 144
Housing Association Charitable Trust 110
Hoye, R. 101
Huberman, A. M. 104
Huberman, M. 104
Huberman, M. A. 104
human capital 97, 99
Hutchinson, R. 8
"hybrid strategy" typology 26

Incapacity Benefit or Severe Disablement Allowance (IB/SDA) 97
Income Support for lone parents (IS-LP) 97
Inspire Mark scheme 148
Instagram 123
International Olympic Committee (IOC) 137–8, 140, 142–50, 177
International Paralympic Committee (IPC) 138, 142–50
Isle of Wight School Survey 158

Jeanes, R. 96, 116
Jennings, G. 170
Jensen, M. C. 10, 140, 148, 151
Jobseeker's Allowance (JSA) 97
Jowell, Dame Tessa 147
Jung, H. 141, 146

Kaydo, C. 71
Kelder, S. 154
Kellison, T. B. 169
Kelly, L. 99
Kirk, D. 141
Korpela, K. 69
Krabbenborg, M. A. M. 106
Krauss, W. 46
Kwauk, C. 99

"landfill gas" 49
large leisure trusts 23–7, 36; small sport trusts and 34–5
learning: about legacy, leverage and impacts from BMX projects 132–4; recording evidence of 161–2
Leary, M. R. 101
legacy plans and SuperCross World Cup 118–19
leisure trusts: large 23–7, 36; small 27–8; trusts ability to reduce costs 29–31
Lenskyj, H. J. 148
Leopkey, B. 139, 141, 147
Levermore, R. 99
Levitas, R. 98, 100
Linder, S. 8
Lindsey, I. 99, 140, 141, 147
Lipsey, M. W. 132
Little League Baseball 7
local community needs: enterprise and innovation in response to 31–4
Localism Act (2012) 24
Logic model for PRU-based BMX programme *120*

London 2012: bidding and hosting cost of 139; educational legacy programmes 142; Get Set programme 137–51; politicisation of school sport during 138; public and political discourses surrounding 137

London 2012 education-based legacy programmes: missed opportunity 147–9; overview 137–9; stakeholder relations in 137–51; theoretical standpoint 139–40; UK policy and education space 140–4

London 2012 Olympic and Paralympic Games *see* London 2012

London Organising Committee of the Olympic and Paralympic Games (LOCOG) 137–50

McCafferty, P. 143, 148
Macdonald, K. 144
McGannon, K. R. 104
Mack, D. E. 101
McKee, K. 100
Magee, J. 96
major Australian sport stadia (MASS) 41, 44; climate change issues for **50**
Mallen, C. 169, 170
managerial agency 49
market-based corporations 83
Marmot, M. 97
MASS organizations 41; and adaptation to climate change 52–4; climate change issues for **50**; energy issues and **47**, 47–8; media reportage and 49–50; medium-sized enterprises (SME) and 44; overview of **45**; public policy for climate change and 47; responses by **52**; three categories of 44–6; waste issues and **47**, 48–9; water issues and 47, **47**
Maths of the Day programme 154, 166
Meckling, W. H. 10
Mendenhall, Michael 64
metaphysics 156
Midol, Nancy 63
Miles, M. B. 104
Miles, S. 139
"Millennium Drought" 43, 47
Miller, W. L. 104
monalism 156
monitoring costs 10
The Mountain Training Association 62
movement cultures 69

National Cycling Centre (NCC), Manchester 4, 116, 118–27, 130–3
national governing bodies (NGBs) 63, 64, 65–6, 73–6
National Greenhouse and Energy Reporting (NGER) Act 48
"National Healthy Schools Award" 157

National Parks 65, 74
National Resources Defense Council (NRDC) 169
The National Trust 65, 74
Natural England 64, 65; "Outdoors for All" programme 66
"nature deficit disorder" 68
"need thwarting" 101
neo-philanthropic governmental rationality 86
neo-philanthropy 86
Ness, L. R. 103
Nettleton, S. 70
New Deal polices 98
New Public Management (NPM) 7, 9
Nichols, G. 3
Nicholson, M. 101
non-governmental organisations 83
non-profit sport development organisations 3
North American Society for Sport Management 171

O'Connor, J. 116
Office of National Statistics 96
Ofsted 161, 165–6
Olympism 137–8, 142–3, 146–7, 177
organizational perceptions of climate change 46
organizational uncertainty: about public policy for climate change 47
outdoor exercisers 69
Outdoor Industries Association (OIA) 66; report 61–2
outdoor recreation 65; craving for self-realisation 70–1; rediscovery of the body 72–3; restorative nature of 67–9; shift in UK movement culture towards second modernity 69–70; trend towards individualisation 71–2
outdoor recreation participation: background UK policy context 64–7; as opportunity for sport development in UK 61–76; overview 61–4; theoretical explanation of shift towards outdoor recreation 67–73

Parent, M. M. 139, 141, 145, 147
Partnership for Education, Attainment and Children's Health (PEACH) 157–8, 161, 164–6
Pawson, R. 119
Peale, Derek 147
peer learning 156
Penney, D. 116
Pension Credit 97
Percy, V. E. 99
Petty, G. 156
Pfahl, M. E. 171
philanthropy: in Swedish social policy 84; through sports-based interventions in Sweden 82–94

Physical Activity Across the Curriculum and Energizer! (USA) 154
physical activity and education 155–6
Physical Activity Teaching and Learning (PATL): as active learning approach 156; classroom management and 162–4; delivery of 155; description of social ecological model levels applied to **165**; effect on academic performance 155; head teacher influence and teacher (dis)empowerment 160–1; Isle of Wight (UK) and 5, 157–9; management challenges in implementation of 154–66; notion of monalism and 156; PATL methodology and the Isle of Wight context 157–9; recording evidence of learning 161–2; relationship between physical activity and education 155–6; teacher and classroom management 162–4
'Physical Education, School Sport and Club Links' (PESSCL) strategy 142
Physically Active Education 154; see also Physically Active Learning (PAL); Physically Active Teaching and Learning (PATL)
Physically Active Learning (PAL) 154; see also Physically Active Education; Physically Active Teaching and Learning (PATL)
Physically Active Teaching and Learning (PATL) 154; see also Physically Active Education; Physically Active Learning (PAL)
Pitstops programme 102
Pope, S. 141
Pop Warner Football 7
Premier League Primary Stars 154, 166
Premier School Sport Coaching 166
PRU-based BMX programme: Logic model for 120; methods used in realistic evaluation of **121**
psychological capital 97
psychological need thwarting 101
public employment services 97
Public Health England: *Everybody Active, Every Day* report 66
public–private partnerships (PPPs) 8–9; collaboration 14–15; control 15–16; formation 12–14; goal achievement 17; goal alignment 13–14; management 14–16; outcomes 16–17; utility maximization 12–13, 16–17; in youth sport 9
public–private partnerships in youth sport 7–20; discussion and implications 18–19; literature review 8–9; methods 11–12; overview 7–8; results 12–17; theoretical framework 9–11
public services: third sector delivery of 24–5

quasi-non-governmental organisation (QUANGO) 64

Reconomics: The Economic Impact of Outdoor Recreation in the UK – The Evidence (Comley & Mackintosh) 64–6
recording evidence of learning 161–2
Reed, Andy 147
Reid, G. 25–7, 34–7
relatedness 106–7
religious charity 86
residual losses 10
restorative nature of outdoor recreation 67–9
Rhodes, R. A. W. 139–41
Rossi, P. H. 132
Ryan, R. M. 101

"School of Hard Knocks" (sports-based Intervention) 108
School of Hard Knocks Charity 102
Schoorman, D. 10
Schulenkorf, N. 100
second modernity 70
selective sampling 44
senior leadership team (SLT) 160–1, 163–5
Sherry, E. 98–9
Shipway, R. 71
Siegrist, J. 97
Simmons, R. 25–7, 34–7
small leisure trusts 27–8
small sport trusts: large trusts and 34–5
small to medium-sized enterprises (SME): European Commission definition of 44
Smith, B. 104
Snowsport England 62
social capital 97, 101–2
social ecological model 158, *159*; description of levels applied to PATL **165**
social entrepreneurs 25, 82–4
social entrepreneurship 25
social media 123
social rights 84, 86, 93
social solidarity 84
Solid Waste Disposal Sites (SWDS) 49
Spaaij, R. 96, 98–9, 116
Spearman, L. 169
sport and physical activity: issues, challenges and trajectories 1–3; overview of contributions 3–5; present tensions, future avenues 5–6; purpose and scope 1
Sport and Recreation Alliance (SRA) 64, 65, 74
Sport England 62, 75; Active People surveys 118; Toward an Active Nation strategy 65
sport federations 83
Sport-for-Development and Peace movement 2
Sporting Future 65
sport management curriculum: future of environmental sustainability in 175–6

sport management education: environmental sustainability and 168–78
sports: events, leverage of, for legacy in disadvantaged communities 115–34; importance of teaching sustainability in 173–5; role of teaching sustainability in 173–5
sports-based interventions: empirical material 84–5; motives of goodwill 89–90; overview 82–5; philanthropy in Swedish social policy 84; political potential of goodwill 90–2; position of goodwill 87–9; in Sweden 82–94; theoretical and methodological framework 85–7
sports employability programmes 107
sports gear CSR representative 85
sport stadia: climate change as a management issue for 41–4; data collection and analysis 45; energy issues 47–8; limited vulnerability and significant resilience 46–7; managerial agency 49; organizational perceptions of climate change 46; organizational uncertainty about public policy for climate change 47; sampling 44–5; waste issues 48–9; water issues 47
Springer, A. 154
Stevens, J. 169
stewardship theory 10
Steyaert, C. 25
Street BMX 119; attendances at sessions by gender *128*; impacts and transitions 123–5; mechanisms in 123; methods used in realistic evaluation of **121**; perspectives of youth workers 123–5; programme staff and coaches'/volunteers' perspectives of impact on regular BMX sessions 125–7; progression in, and achievement of legacy objectives 126–7; "reach" of the project into local communities 127
Street BMX initial logic model *120*
structural worklessness 97
Sweden: philanthropy through sports-based interventions in 82–94
Sydney Olympic Park Authority (SOPA) 169
Sydney Olympics 169

Take 10! (USA) 154
teacher and classroom management 162–4
Theeboom, M. 99
theoretical sampling 44
Thomas, I. 170
Thompson, L. 169
Thomson, R. 71
Tilley, N. 115, 119
Timpone, R. J. 101, 106
Tough Guy challenge 64

Tough Mudder series 64
trusts ability to reduce costs 29–31
"Try for Change" programme 102

UK Sport Development Network (UKSDN) 2017 conference 1
United Kingdom (UK): craving for self-realisation 70–1; Department for Education 141, 145, 147; ESRC 28; *Game Plan strategy for sport* 65; outdoor recreation participation 61–76; rediscovery of the body 72–3; sport development in 61–76; *A sporting future; A new strategy for an active nation* 1–2; theoretical explanation of shift towards outdoor recreation 67–73; trend towards individualisation 71–2
United Nations 174

value-based charity 90
Van den Broeck, A. 101
van der Veld, W. M. 106
van Dijk, T. 144–5
Vansteenkiste, M. 101
Villadsen, K. 84, 86–7
Viollet, B. 140
Vollebergh, W. A. M. 106
voluntary leisure trusts: drivers to and benefits of sport facility provision by 24–8
volunteer-led sport facilities: changes taken place in 35–6; comparison of small sport trusts, to large trusts 34–5; drivers to and benefits of sport facility provision by voluntary leisure trusts 24–8; enterprise and innovation in response to local community needs 31–4; overview 23–4; research approach 28–9
von Storch, H. 46

Walt Disney 64
Ward, G. 141
Warner, M. E. 10
welfare, defined 84
"Welfare to Work" programmes 97, 98
Western societies 70
Wheaton, B. 72, 117
Whigham, S. 144–5
WHO 155
Wiggan, J. 117
Wilson, P. M. 101
Wolf, J. R. L. M. 106
Wolfenden Report 117
worklessness 96–7; defined 97; policy responses to 96; structural 97
workreadiness: andcompetence 105–6; defined 97; developing 96–110; role of the Housing Association 109

work readiness skills 105
"Work Readiness Standards and Benchmarks" report 97
Wu, S. 154

X Games 64

Yin, R. K. 45, 144
youth sport: PPPs in 9; public-private partnerships in 7–20
Youth Sport Trust 141, 142

Zumbo, B. D. 101

Milton Keynes UK
Ingram Content Group UK Ltd.
UKHW010017230824
447265UK00008B/49